Children of the Dragonfly

Children of the Dragonfly

NATIVE AMERICAN VOICES
ON CHILD CUSTODY AND EDUCATION

Edited by Robert Bensen

THE UNIVERSITY OF ARIZONA PRESS   TUCSON

A portion of the royalties from
this book will be donated to agencies
that serve Native American children.

The University of Arizona Press
© 2001 The Arizona Board of Regents
First Printing
All rights reserved

06   05   04   03   02   01   6   5   4   3   2   1

Library of Congress Cataloging-in-Publication Data
Children of the dragonfly : Native American voices on child custody and education /
edited by Robert Bensen.
p. cm.
Includes bibliographical references.
ISBN 0-8165-2012-7 (cloth : alk. paper)
ISBN 0-8165-2013-5 (pbk. : alk. paper)
1. Indians of North America—Cultural assimilation. 2. Interracial adoption—North
America. 3. Indians of North America—Education. 4. Child welfare—North America.
5. Indians of North America—Ethnic identity. I. Bensen, Robert, 1947–
E98.C89 C55 2001
305.897—dc21   00-011169

British Library Cataloguing-in-Publication Data
A catalogue record for this book is available from the British Library.

Publication of this book is made possible in part by the proceeds of a permanent
endowment created with the assistance of a Challenge Grant from the National
Endowment for the Humanities, a federal agency.

The man looked at the children and saw that all but one were Cherokee. He saw a very light blond child, and he asked, "Are all these children yours?"

"Yes," said the mother because she cared for the little blond girl.

Maybe because he knew only a bit of the language and maybe because he didn't want to offend the mother or maybe because he was just tired, the man did not question further. He marked an F by each of the children's names, meaning that they were full-blood Cherokee.

The little girl grew up and married a Cherokee, and all of their children except one looked like their Cherokee father, but there was one little blond child.

In the Cherokee village in each generation there have been children who are officially Cherokee but they look like their Great-great-great Grandmother Goldilocks.

—Mary Ulmer Chiltoskey, "Goldilocks Thereafter"

Contents

Foreword

All the elders I know tell me things happen for a reason. This book has happened for a reason, which Bob Bensen describes eloquently in his preface. Their daughter came to them—and by her, in a good way, the three of them came into new selves, and a sense of American history, that seem to me more true than before. The Bensens had the good sense and were given the grace to talk with Indian elders and learn about what was going on as the Dragonfly story has unfolded for all of us.

This book does a great service to American citizens generally: it lets us see American history better. Without the Dragonfly story, it is all too easy for us to see that history as (on the one hand) a sci-fi movie like *Alien* or (on the other) a fairy tale like "Hansel and Gretel." The Dragonfly story—the actual Zuni story, which has become the heart of this book, sending life into the body of the book around it—shows us a beautiful way for people struck by disaster to make their history good. By making this clear, the book lifts us up and encourages us to believe that human courage and ingenuity may keep alive our finest human values, though at great cost and with painful losses.

So these remarks won't be taken as Pollyanna's, let me unfold some-what the two bitter analogies just mentioned: the *Alien* and "Hansel and Gretel" versions of American history as (for Indians) disaster. The goal of Europeans has always been to gain absolute possession of North,

Central, and South America. To achieve that goal, they have worked, and still are trying by all possible means, to exterminate the native populations in these parts of the earth, whether by simple killing or by complex conversion. The means have always included military ones, but for weapons of mass destruction, germs, Bibles, and whiskey bottles have been more effective than bullets. Warriors, women, and children can be killed with bullets, but killing hearts and minds is better done with words. As with the reptilian critters in *Alien,* once the "seminal" books get in through mouth or ear, they begin converting what is there to a version of the Alien, which presently emerges as a raging "American Only," determined to repeat the process.

That image may be too extreme for readers, so let me change it to one less "alien" but still true to the facts. The folk tale of "Hansel and Gretel" is probably as well known as the movie *Alien.* When Hansel and Gretel's mother dies, their father remarries, and the stepmother begins planning (for what we may call "economic" reasons) to get rid of the children. She succeeds in getting them lost in the forest, where they come upon a marvelous house made of candy and cake, but in which an old witch lives. The witch takes them in with apparent love and kindness and encourages them to eat the candy and cake—but it turns out that she is a cannibal, and what she wants is to fatten up Hansel so she can roast and eat him, and she enslaves Gretel to help in this. But Gretel is too smart. It is the witch who ends up roasted, the wicked stepmother who is vanquished, the children who are reunited with the good parent in the end.

It is a fairy tale ending, and in ordinary life not a common one. I know there are many good stepmothers, and there can be fairy godmothers as well as wicked witches, but we are talking here about American history and, in general, that history is the story of getting rid of Indian children, one way or another, because their inheritance—this part of the earth—is wanted, "needed," by the stepparents or foster parents. The "Hansel and Gretel" story in American history ends with the children in the oven, and the stepmother in full possession of their inheritance. (For an interesting variant of the story, see Sherman Alexie's *Indian Killer.*)

It is painful to talk this way. The kindness, the love, the generosity of a great many non-Indians is as clear and apparent as can be. Nearly always, it is from one viewpoint an act of generous humanity to make possible a "good life" for an Indian child who is in a "dysfunctional family" and in poverty, far from the "amenities" and the "opportunities" available to children in families living in plenty and comfort. I must therefore ask the logical question: Why not devote as much effort and allocate as much money to making it possible for the children to live well AS Indian children? Why not see that the Indian nations have a land base, and sovereignty, and a language, in which to live freely and well as Indian people?

It is possible to re-imagine, around an Indian family, a clan, many clans, a village and band, many bands. There would be songs, cere-monies that speak and give thanks for their place on this earth and in this universe, in Indian languages—to go with, not against, songs and ceremonies in the English language, with its intense special understand-ing of the American place in this universe. Much conversation is given, during every election, to ways in which our "inner cities" or our "rural poor" might find a better way for themselves, and be helped by those others who have more than enough for themselves. Why could there not be a place for many small nations within this great one, all the differ-ences celebrated among humans as they are among trees, flowers, birds? Why should an apple be educated into an orange and be told that unless it changes, it is a failure?

Easier to re-imagine such things than to achieve them. But consider one small and interesting fact: In the Europe that is the mother, sister, brother of the United States, there ARE small nations existing and flour-ishing. Why could there not be Indian nations within the boundaries of the United States comparable to Andorra, San Marino, Liechtenstein, even Monaco? There is a Switzerland, a Wales, a Scotland, if we look to older examples still, and the range is from "completely independent" small countries to "domestic dependent" ones. Monaco lives by its ca-sinos; Andorra by sheep and tobacco and its special tax arrangements for car dealerships and the like; Liechtenstein by its banks; San Marino to some extent by its tourists. Why not an Oglala nation, a Ponca nation, an Osage nation, using one or more of those ways to provide for their dual citizens? Why not put a small nation around Indian families and see whether in that small nation the families and individuals could regain some of the health they once had?

It is a possibility that frightens otherwise sensible people. I have seen, in British newspapers, the term "tribalizing" used as though it explained what happened in Bosnia and Kosovo and Rwanda. The journalists appeared to think that falling into tribal rivalries is how World Wars begin: yeah, sure. Germany and England and France were small tribal nations, their empires not really part of the reasons they began, in 1914, the "tribal" wars that continue everywhere today. Real nations never fight; they have sophisticated diplomats, intelligent leaders, armies no one would dare challenge. Only small nations are a real threat to world peace.

And, of course, so long as there are Indian children still being born and raised as Indian, the threat must be dealt with. I hope reading this book will not only clarify the results of such thinking, but show some good ways to survive and create better history. I am grateful to Bob Bensen and to the many speakers and writers in this book for giving us their words, and to the University of Arizona for printing them.

—Carter Revard

Preface

When the county social worker wrote, months after our daughter came to us, that she was "Mohician" (sic), Mary Lynn and I realized that the child possessed an even greater difference from us than we had tacitly assumed. We wondered what we should do, if anything. We were sure only that she was not Mohician.

Our friends' adoptive daughter had just been assigned to research her ancestry, which she knew to be at least partly German. Surely our daughter was entitled to reliable information about her ancestry, by birthright as well as New York State social service law, and not to have to submit to what Mary Lynn called "second-class status" because she was adopted. On the advice of Arlinda Locklear and Bertram Hirsch on the Indian Child Welfare Act of 1978, we began a process of research, education, and litigation that identified her Native American and European ancestry from both birth parents, who were pleased at our interest.

The need asserted itself to raise her awareness of her ancestry. I, at least, little thought how much she would be teaching us.

"I may be only half Indian, but my heart is whole Indian. And it is my heart I listen to!" our first-grader shouted from the highest platform on the school's play set to an empty field. What gets into the child, I wonder. Before she was old enough to do it herself, she had me write down certain dreams. Sometimes she draws them. One of the authors of this book said that he doesn't think there are special spirits flying around just for Indian people. A Lakota friend said, "Of course not. They're for everyone. We just pay attention."

We're paying attention. Everything about a child, especially what comes from within, is cause for wonder. We have taken seriously the assurances that, as we were told, "She has been given to you. The Creator wanted her to be yours. She may learn more about who she is, about who her people are, about what she's supposed to do."

Knowing her ancestry heightened our sense of the privilege and responsibility of caring for someone who is both ours and not ours—as any child, adoptive or biological, truly is. Brad Bonaparte (Mohawk) tells a story about a child of two worlds, whose father is a Thunder-being and whose human mother is allowed to return with him to her parents on earth, with the stern warning to let no harm come to him. One day he runs out to play in a tremendous storm with his Thunder-cousins, disobeying his grandmother and utterly ruining the new clothes she had just laboriously, lovingly made. As she raises her hand to strike him, she forgets his nature, and a bolt of lightning through the roof returns the child to his home in the sky.

To think of adoption in the terms of "taking custody" of a "surrendered" child is forbidding, given the thunderous historical echoes of that language.

I'd been invited to a healing ceremony in North Carolina two days before it was to take place. After several Internet conversations, and with Mary Lynn's blessing and a sacrificial airline ticket, I found myself in one of the chairs at the *lowanpe* ("they sing") ceremony. A medicine man, a pipe carrier, singers, the five of us to be doctored, and friends and relations were in the outbuilding's large room that had been swathed and sealed in black through the afternoon. Now it was late in the rain-drenched night out in the mountains, dark as the first dark before first light, as the dark in which the fetal eye grows. In such a dark anything can come to be.

For us the people sang songs of calling forth, of praise, petition, and prayer. For us the prayers and homilies and humor. Songs that made the way for bear. The cry and breath of eagle. Touch of spider. Doctoring. Sending back.

We suffered from conditions the doctors could do little for: Lyme disease, multiple sclerosis, spinal degeneration, heart-valve problems. One of the last to know his tribal language was losing his memory. *Mister* Ghost Horse, as our daughter calls him, was telling each of us in the chairs what would be done for our maladies. "Bob B. Bob," he said. "That's what I always call you." It's true. He does. "You have a good heart. The spirit sees that good, good heart and wants to help you." I can live with that. "Bob, you have a wonderful daughter." Yes, that I can see in the dark.

"That wonderful daughter of yours. You're going to learn a lot of things from her. She's what we call *lakol.* The *Lakota* are the People. She's *lakol,* one of the Red People. You, you must never doubt her dreams. Never. Her dreams tell her who she is. The one who visits her will help her decide a lot of things, maybe save her some heartbreak along the way. One day she's going to be a great person. She's going to be a very great person."

In his pause, I listened for any motion, any stirring, any breath at all out there in the dark. Everyone was perfectly still. There was no sound of rain. No wind. Nothing but the waiting for what was to come.

"And you're going to be right there with her. Now, you have some *wasichu* disease, what we call a *toka,* an enemy. Spirit's going to help you with that. It's not going away all at once, but your daughter is part of the knowing and the healing that's going to take place."

Outside the rain poured over the thirsty spring mountains, over the trout pond above us, over the shacks along the steep, rutted road, over the cars scattered across the way, over the tar paper roof that sealed in the dark of this world and the others. But these words poured over me like water over live red rocks, each sentence another dipper full of words, their breath misting my understanding, which had begun to grow.

One of the many things I have learned from having our daughter is the need for this book, which begins with the need to give something in return for the great gift she is and to learn from the people who helped put it into words.

This book gathers, for the first time, the literature of Native American childhood from both sides of the US-Canadian border. It expands the subject from the industrial boarding school to education over four centuries, to the Sixties Scoop and the child welfare crisis, to the impact on children of enrollment and allotment and discouragement of Indian identity, to traditional child-rearing practices and the recent campaign against childbearing through involuntary sterilization.

The literature in part documents the struggle for cultural survival and in part conducts the struggle and makes survival possible.

The literature of Native American childhood includes traditional stories of childhood and child-rearing, testimony, autobiography, fiction, nonfiction, poetry, and dream song. And for this anthology to comprehend and redefine the history that gave rise to the literature, it includes the history of governmental authority over children, their custody and upbringing, as a function of Indian policy and law.

The official side of the story is readily available, but I found little by or about the children from the "gray market" that occurred in the United States before the Indian Child and Welfare Act of 1978 (ICWA) or from the Sixties Scoop in Canada. Those who responded to my invitation to tell their stories are presented here. I wanted to contribute to the growth of literature but was surprised and pleased to hear from a number of authors that, as one put it, "The most healing part of the process was the discovery that I wasn't alone, that there were others like me. Your book will reveal that to others as well."

Another writer looked at the contents and exclaimed that it should be in every social worker's library in the country. The book is also a source for writers and scholars, who will find the accounts here ground for work needing to be done. I also hope it will encourage the many who considered writing for this volume, but who found it not possible: the vet who rediscovered longhouse life in a Vietnamese hut, the professor who shied away, the Oklahoman who believes Orion's belt is a dragonfly, the Manitoba woman with the federal case, the Montana Blackfeet official with cold feet, the North Carolina writer who wants a book to herself, the St. Louis adoptive mother, the Native woman whose sister was murdered by an adoptive son and who was seeking his release, the Chicago woman and all those who "have no knowledge of their past, don't even know what tribe they are from or if they have any family out there somewhere," the Shoshone switchboard operator, the Cheyenne cook, the Lewis and Clark University PhD, the lawyer, judge, doctor, journalist, poet, song maker, flute maker, silversmith, and others. I hope that those with stories they cannot find it within themselves to tell will follow those who have.

Acknowledgments

This book is truly "a poem by a lot of people, including you," a contributor said, and many have shaped that poem with words and work and help of many kinds. I offer my first thanks to the steadfast friends of this project: poet and essayist Carter Revard; Richard Haan, professor of history at Hartwick College; and William A. Starna, professor of anthropology at SUNY–Oneonta. Warm thanks also to attorneys Peter Hill, Arlinda Locklear, and Bertram Hirsch for their generosity and expertise; to Janice Brenner and the Otsego County Social Services staff; to colleagues and administrators Thomas C. Beattie, Susan Gotsch, Kim Noling, John Pontius, Margaret Schramm, Marilyn Wesley, and Emily Wilson-Orzechowski for friendship and support; to Marie Fouche, Lee Francis and the WordCraft Circle, Beverley McKiver, Jordan Dill and the First Nations/Wounded Knee group, and the NativeLit–L group for bringing this project to people. Thanks for valuable information to Vine Deloria, Kim Blaeser, Nadine Jennings, Rae Peppers, Velva-Lu Spencer, and Anne Barnard. Thanks to Barbara Landis, Carlisle Indian School Research Specialist for the Cumberland County Historical Society, for her insights into Marianna Burgess and *Stiya*. Thanks to Hartwick College faculty and staff, including Marilyn Dunn, Dawn Baker, Edward Sargent, Jr., Regan Brumagen, Susan Stevens, and archivist Shelley Wallace at the Stevens-German library; John Willis, Louise Netreba, and Kali Lord for computer services; Jan Stankiewicz, faculty secretary; Sandy (Claire) Huntington, professor of religion; and George Abrams, museum director. Thanks to Buck, Vicki, and Paul Ghost Horse for their kindness and love. My gratitude goes to the late Hon. Robert Nydam for his courage and support, as well as to the late Hon. George Kepner.

Early on, Kathleen Avery Frascatore's able research and editorial assistance strengthened this book, as did Daniel J. Shapley's interest and editorial help at a later stage. Acquiring editor Patti Hartmann's vision and enthusiasm for this project were invaluable at many crucial points. Heather Hopkins of Arizona Editors not only corrected and sharpened the text, she showed me more ways the book could affect parenting decisions than I had imagined. The late historian Winifred B. Wandersee's encouragement and friendship meant a great deal to me, as does her legacy of the Scholar-in-Residence appointment that bears her name. Financial help came from the Hartwick College Board of Trustees, and from the National Endowment for the Humanities and the Newberry Library through travel and seminar funds for several summers of work.

Most of all I thank Mary Lynn for the faith and love that gave me the strength to persevere, and for her ideas and advice. She, Annalee (for whom this book was conceived), and I acknowledge all our relations, those who went before us and those with us—especially her grandmothers Leona and Anna Bernice, her grandfathers Elmer and John, her aunts Karen and Jean and their families, and the family that grows with Annalee, especially Phil and Honey, Courtney, Caitlyn and Benjamin, and Midge and Charlotte.

Children of the Dragonfly

Introduction

It is said that history is written by the conquerors, literature by the survivors. In the forms of autobiography and essay, fiction and poetry, testimony and interview, the many voices in *Children of the Dragonfly* tell the collective story of struggle and survival in the area where all cultures are most vulnerable: childhood.

In widespread Native American cultural traditions, children are consistently figured as those who hold the future, their protection as the greatest imperative, and their loss as the greatest of losses. The childhood of Native people has been the site of a long and vital struggle between the Native nations on the one hand, and the United States and Canada on the other. Native childhood has been subject to US and Canadian policies of assimilation—first, through education, and more recently, through health and child welfare services. Both federal systems reduced Native nations from original sovereignty to the legal status of dependent children, then assumed parental rights over the children themselves. That is one version of North American history.

Yet from those who face such assertions of power, quite another discourse emerges from counter-assertion: a multivocal, endless re-creation of integrity and identity. The stories in *Children of the Dragonfly* enact a complex process of survival, adaptation, and renewal, one that is painful and powerful and poignantly humorous, as swift and unstoppable as Dragonfly in flight, as persistent as the thrum of its wing beat.

Children of the Dragonfly

In the Zuni story "The Origin of the Dragonfly and of the Corn-Priests," Dragonfly flies between the present world and the spirit world, carrying the prayers of a hungry boy and girl to the Corn Sisters (Cushing 55–124). He is a very old spirit in the body of a new toy, the children's creation and their helper, their means of restoring the way of life that had been taken from them. Yet what was restored and recovered was changed in the process, and the children, as the story goes, lead them all.

The children's people offended the Corn Sisters, wasting rich harvests by turning the crops into weapons for a food-fight. The spirit sisters bring a famine that drives the people to another village, where they work in servitude for food. In their haste and selfishness, the people leave the two children behind in the abandoned village.

To amuse his sister and console her loneliness, the boy makes a toy insect out of corn leaves. The girl in desperation asks the creature to fly away and bring them corn. The boy's love and the girl's prayer bring a powerful spirit to be embodied in the creature. He carries their story to the Corn Sisters, who remember them with fresh stores of food and a field full of corn. The people return to find the children, their pueblo and way of life abundantly restored, and the children selected to lead them in a new devotion to the source of their lives and sustenance, the Corn Sisters. The children, through Dragonfly, bring the spirit and present world together again in growth and harmony.

Children of the Dragonfly takes this story as the pattern for the lives recounted in the collection. Through the storyteller's faithfulness, the writer's devotion, and the poet's playful invention come very old ways of being in new forms of identity. The desire for connection is sometimes most powerfully expressed after its severance, and the search thereafter becomes the source of art and expression. Dragonfly may well live in the writing itself.

"It was when we began to create with this new language that we named it ours, made it usefully tough and beautiful," writes Joy Harjo in *Reinventing the Enemy's Language;* "We've transformed these enemy languages" (22–24). The transformation of English into an Indian language is "pretty scary sometimes," according to Simon J. Ortiz in his introduction to *Speaking for the Generations: Native Writers on Writing,* "because it means letting one's mind go willfully [. . .] into the Western cultural and intellectual context" (xvi). Ortiz puts misgivings aside because of the great many topics that need to be addressed, and he implies that what language the writer speaks is secondary to the concepts and relationships of which the writer speaks and what the writer says, from which comes, Ortiz says, his own "Native voice" (xviii). The individual Native writing her personal story, according to Gloria Bird, can help "decolonize" Native America (29). Autobiography (as distinct from the traditional oral communal storytelling) can be testimony to the individual's "processing of the complexities of inheritance [. . .] in the aftermath of colonization" (Ortiz 29). The writer's "hardest work is tracing back through generations the aspects of colonization that have directly affected our lives, to identify those instances in which we have internalized what we are taught about ourselves in schools and in history books all our invisible lives [. . .]" (30).

Children of the Dragonfly gathers written autobiography, oral testimony, and storytelling, as well as fiction and poetry, from Native people on both sides of the U.S.–Canadian border, for whom childhood has been conflicted by the larger struggle for cultural survival. The writers in this book will tell their stories within that struggle, but first let us trace through history colonial aspects of Indian education and child welfare, and other areas of Indian policy as they affected Indian childhood.

Children of Nature, Children of the State

But you, who are wise, must know that different nations have different conceptions of things; and you will therefore not take it amiss, if our ideas of this kind of education happen not to be the same with yours. We have had some experience of it; several of our young people were formerly brought up at the colleges of the northern provinces; they were instructed in all your sciences; but when they came back to us [. . .] they were totally good for nothing. (qtd. in Franklin 10: 387)

In 1784 Benjamin Franklin may have concurred with this assessment of colonial education by the Iroquois leader Canassatego, who spoke to commissioners from Virginia at Lancaster, Pennsylvania, in 1744

(Barker 47). On behalf of the sachems who refused the Virginians' offer to educate twelve young Iroquois men at the College of William and Mary, he offered instead to host twelve sons of Virginia's gentlemen, promising to "take great care of their education, and instruct them in all we know, and make Men of them" (qtd. in Franklin 10: 386–87). As a revolutionary with a sense of humor, Franklin must have admired the Iroquois's satiric send-up of the Virginians' arrogance and ignorance.

Within twenty years of Franklin's writing, however, a competing conception of Indian-white difference would gain ascendancy in the young republic, one which asserted parental authority over the Native nations: "*Children.* [. . .] the great Chief of the Seventeen great nations of America has become your only father," wrote William Clark and Meriwether Lewis to the Otoe in 1804, addressing them as "children" eighteen times, e.g.: "*Children.—*Do these things which your great father advises and be happy" (qtd. in Carroll 16). Thomas Jefferson's seaboard America looked west at a continent-wide "Indian problem" it sought to reduce by reducing Indians to children. Jefferson held contradictory views of Indians, using their physical, intellectual, linguistic, social, and political equality with whites as evidence against the environmental degeneracy theory that was popular in Europe, but calling them "children" when perceiving them as impediments to expansion (Grinde 197, 208).

Such opportunistic parentalism "required children to have no independence or life of their own," according to Michael Paul Rogin in his study of the Jackson-era subjugation of American Indians (10). Since Columbus, Europe had conceived of indigenous people as having childlike qualities (Todorov 34–40), but the United States and Canada transformed them from children of nature to children of the state, and gradually assumed parental authority over them in matters of territory, commerce, and religion. The metaphor of Indians as children was soon placed at the center of the legal definition of Indian status, when Chief Justice John Marshall wrote that tribes "are a people in a state of pupilage. Their relation to the United States resembles that of a ward to his guardian" (The Cherokee Nation *v.* The State of Georgia, 1831, qtd. in Norgren 101). Marshall's figure of speech justified subjugation and relocation of the Cherokee and others. Describing the Cherokee removal in his 1838 report, Secretary of War Joel R. Poinsett asserted that "Humanity, no less than sound policy, dictated this course toward these children of the forest" (qtd. in Rogin 247).

In Canada, the original partnership between Crown, Indian nations, and colonies was expressed in the Royal Proclamation of 1763 as a nation-to-nation relationship that protected Indian sovereignty (Canada, *Report* 1.9.2). The next century of frustrated legislative efforts to civilize and assimilate Indian people led Canada to create a framework of political, social and cultural jurisdiction through the Indian Act (1876) that has persisted to the present. The Interior Department's report for 1876, written under the same theory as the Indian Act, repeats Marshall's language from forty years before, revealing that Canadian Indian law "rests on the principle, that the aborigines are to be kept in the condition of tutelage and treated as wards or children of the state" (qtd. in Canada, *Report* 1.9.8).

And if Indians are reduced to children, then their parental role is debased, and their children will be raised by some agency of the parent-state. The metaphor of custodial parentalism presaged the development of Indian education and child welfare as instruments within the larger effort to eradicate Indian culture. The effect of other efforts, such as the end of government-to-government treaty-making in the United States in 1871 and in Canada in 1876, and the US General Allotment Act of 1887, was to further erode Indian sovereignty and disrupt the passing of Native ways from parents to children, interrupting family, clan, and other relations (Priest 96; Canada, *Report* 1.9.2). According to Robert Berkhofer, the 1870s saw US federal assumption of "full responsibility for native education" through actions that moved Indian tribes from "being domestic dependent nations [. . .] to being wards of the state." Such actions submitted their children to Captain Richard H. Pratt's military-like regimen at the Carlisle Indian Industrial School, where they were "treated [. . .] as utterly dependent wards in order to prepare them for American individualism" (*White Man's Indian* 171).

In Lewis's terms, the less the great father's adult Indian "children" followed his advice, the more he and his government believed that future accommodations for Native Americans depended on children. In his 1831 report, Secretary of War Lewis Cass wrote that "Our hopes must rest upon the rising generation," a hope that would be renewed each new generation, as each grown generation defeated that hope (qtd. in Prucha 141). The adult Indian, that "simple child of nature" whose mind was "dwarfed and shriveled," the Board of Indian Commissioners reported in 1880, was beginning to see the value of education for his children (qtd. in Iverson 20). In 1889, Commissioner of Indian Affairs Thomas Jefferson Morgan predicted that all Indian children would be in school within two or three years, but the number fell far short of his prediction. The 1892 Lake Mohonk Conference asserted that it was not "desirable to raise another generation of savages," and that "the government is justified, as a last resort, in using power to compel attendance" when "parents, without good reason, refuse to educate their children" (qtd. in Prucha 707).

Education

The history of Indian education is also the history of Indian resistance, as policy and practice developed at least as much in reaction to evasion, avoidance, and noncompliance as it did from the creation of new educational modes and means.

Assimilative European education began in the Americas in the 1540s, when Franciscan friars began "to take the children of the lords and chieftains and send them to live" in schools established in Mayan towns, according to Fr. Diego de Landa. Parents, he said, were "reluctant to give over their children," but eventually the children "made so much progress in the school and [. . .] catechism that it was a wonderful thing" (qtd. in Karttunen 91). De Landa inaugurated the main themes of education as cultural replacement, including the destruction of indigenous culture. Finding Mayan books in local libraries, he wrote, "we burned them all [. . .]" (qtd. in Karttunen 101).

The role of education in the colonial, commercial, and Christian projects was established early in British colonial policy. In 1619, the Virginia Colony's first legislature decreed that "eache towne, citty Borough, and particular plantation do obtaine unto themselves by just meanes a certain number of the natives Children to be educated by them in true Reeligion and civile course of life" (qtd. in Vaughan 69–70). The Indian college was not built because "parents refused to part with their children" (Vaughan 70).

A century later in 1711, Governor Spotswood of Virginia had little success in demanding two children from "the great men of each town" as hostages to guarantee the Indians' friendly disposition, with the intent of educating the children at a college in Brasserton. The college lasted until the Revolution, but with rarely more than eight or ten students. Parents saw little point in educating children to become servants in white households (Fletcher 76–77).

Fitful and misdirected early efforts to instruct Native people in Euro-American culture were carried on by churches, colonies, and eventually by the federal government, beginning with the Civilization Fund of $10,000 appropriated by Congress in 1819. The assimilative aims of education that radically changed Cherokee, Potawatomi, and other eastern peoples in the 1840s were advanced to the Plains after the Civil War. Indian education was approached with renewed urgency as prospects for a continent-wide country required a settled, English-speaking people who could participate in the economy as agricultural, industrial, and domestic laborers. To bring about that change in roughly one-third of a million people, to render them "civilized" and self-supporting people within the dominant system, "*education* must be regarded as [. . .] fundamental and indispensable," contended the Board of Indian Commissioners in 1875, recommending that a universal school system be provided by the federal government (qtd. in Prucha 688).

The boarding school movement began in Carlisle, Pennsylvania, in 1879, and within twenty years, twenty-four more schools opened across the country (Karttunen 57). Combined attendance at boarding and day schools grew from 4,976 in 1881 to 21,568 in 1900, with annual federal appropriations growing from $75,000 to $3,080,367 (in 1901) (Prucha 816). Pratt's idea of eliminating all traces of Indian identity through off-reservation boarding school education was supplanted in the mid-1880s by advocates of a more comprehensive and varied system, one that began with reservation primary schools and left more advanced studies to the Carlisle-style industrial school.

Education policy vacillated between on-reservation day schools, off-reservation industrial schools, and public schools. According to commissioner Cato Sells in 1914, when Indian and white students learn together in public schools, the Indians "appreciate the 'better ways' of the white man," which would lead to the "disintegration of the Indian reservations" and "elimination of the Indian as a distinct problem for the Federal or the State governments" (qtd. in Prucha 823). Ten years later, the 1923 Report of the Board of Indian Commissioners disfavored public schools and called separate Indian school systems the "most satisfactory" means of education (qtd. in Prucha 825). The 1928 Meriam Report and the 1931 report of the National Advisory Committee on Education criticized the inadequate facilities, health care, and staff, and the obsolete and centralized industrial curriculum of Indian schools that would "constitute a violation of child labor laws in most states" (Institute for Government Research 376). The Meriam Report recommended a formula that de-emphasized off-reservation schools (except for ninth grade and older students) in favor of building community-based day schools and eventually "mingling" Indian and white students in public schools (Institute for Government Research 415). The 1930s era of the Indian Reorganization Act saw the resurgence of day schools as community centers, the closing of twenty or more boarding schools, and the encouragement of curricula "utilizing Indian arts and crafts and Indian culture generally" (Prucha 797; Central Intelligence Agency House Committee on Indian Affairs Report, 1931, qtd. in Prucha 928). However, day-school staff and students were decimated during World War II and postwar demand for vocational training regenerated interest in boarding schools (Prucha 1062). In the 1950-60s Termination period, the federal government sought to withdraw from its Indian responsibilities, and reduced its support of on-reservation day schools in favor of contractual support of Indian enrollment in public schools (Prucha 1066).

The recent period of Indian self-determination, aided by Indian titles within the Civil Rights Act of 1968 and the Educational Amendments Act of 1978, resulted in a new Office of Indian Education in the Department of Health, Education and Welfare and a new National Advisory Council on Indian Education. Also important in assigning control of education to tribes and other Native groups in urban and rural settings were the Indian Education Act of 1972, and the Indian Self-Determination and Education Assistance Act of 1975 (Iverson 160–61).

As in the United States, education in Canada was to "elevate the Indian from his condition of savagery" and "make him a self-supporting member of the state, and eventually a citizen in good standing," according to Minister of Indian Affairs Frank Oliver in 1908 (qtd. in Canada, *Report* 1.10). Since the mid-nineteenth century, legal provisions for enfranchisement had strong inducements for education. Through the Gradual Civilization Act (Statues of Canada [SC] 1857), Indians who learned to read and write in French or English could be voluntarily enfranchised: that is, they could give up Indian status, gain ownership of fifty acres of reserve land, and be paid a share of treaty annuities. However, between 1857 and 1876, only one man volunteered to be enfranchised, and bands refused to fund schools whose agenda was assimilative (Canada, *Report* 1.9.5). The Indian Act (1876) made enfranchisement compulsory for those who obtained university education (Tobias 42–48).

Resistance of aboriginal people to these changes encouraged Canada to change from educating adults to educating children, who in the 1880s "were regarded as being the first generation which would become civilized and to whom the benefits of the Indian Act could be extended" (Tobias 48). In an 1879 report to the Canadian government, Nicholas Flood Davin recommended establishing a system of denominational industrial boarding schools that would follow the American model, a system that Canada inaugurated in 1884.

Canada's residential school system was one of the "past actions" for which the Canadian federal government declared its "profound regret" in January 1998 (Fernandez). In its *Statement of Reconciliation*, Canada acknowledged the role it played in developing and administering these schools, and stated that they "separated many children from their families and communities and prevented them from speaking their own languages and from learning about their heritage and cultures. In the worst cases, it left legacies of personal pain and distress that continue to reverberate in Aboriginal communities to this day." The government reserved its strongest apology for victims of physical and sexual abuse: "To those of you who suffered this tragedy at residential schools, we are deeply sorry." The demise of the residential school system after World War II, however, was not the end of efforts in either Canada or the United States to assimilate Indian children.

Indian Child Welfare

"Gradually, as education ceased to function as the institutional agent of colonization," Patrick Johnston wrote in 1983, "the child welfare system took its place" (24). Johnston's study *Native Children and the Child Welfare System* documented the disproportionate removal of Indian children by the child welfare system in Canada following 1951 revisions to the Indian Act. Indian child welfare services were poorly funded and

unevenly administered, leading H. B. Hawthorn and colleagues to con-
clude, in an early influential study in 1966, that "the situation varies
from unsatisfactory to appalling" (327). From 1955 to 1964, the number
of Native children in British Columbia's system rose from 29 to 1,446, or
from less than 1% to 34.2% of all children in care. That phenomenon,
repeated across Canada, has become known as the "Sixties Scoop,"
wherein social workers would "quite literally scoop children from reserves on the slightest pretext"—poverty, sanitation, housing standards,
nutrition—without regard for the effects on the child, family, or reserve.
Some reserves, according to Johnston, "lost almost a generation" (23).

The US counterpart to Canada's Sixties Scoop was, in Bertram
Hirsch's phrase, the "gray market" for Indian children, which developed
under the pressure on local welfare agencies to provide Indian children
for adoption (United States, *Indian Child Welfare Program*, 70). Such
pressure grew from the demand for adoptive children in the prosperous
post-World War II era, and from the agenda of the Bureau of Indian
Affairs (BIA). In 1958, even as renewed tribal self-determination brought
education under greater Indian control, the BIA began its Indian Adoption Project with the Child Welfare League of America, to promote the
adoption of Indian children by non-Indian families. In 1961 the BIA
funded care for 2,300 children during the process of removal, foster
placement, and eventual adoption (Prucha 1153).

As state welfare agencies joined the activity, the rate of separation of
Indian children from their families grew rapidly. Since removals were
routinely carried out without consultation with tribal authorities or
Indian communities, many groups felt powerless to resist them. The
Devils Lake Sioux Tribe of North Dakota in 1968 asked for the assistance of the Association on American Indian Affairs (AAIA), whose 1969
study was presented at the 1974 US Senate hearings concerning the
widespread removal of Indian children. The Oglala Sioux, Standing
Rock Sioux, Sisseton-Wahpeton Sioux, and three affiliated tribes of the
Fort Berthold reservation passed resolutions demanding that removals
and trans-racial placements end (Unger, cited in Mannes). The AAIA
surveyed the situation in 1969 and reported the results of its monitoring
in the *Indian Family Defense* newsletter.

Native protest and AAIA activity led to a 1974 hearing before the
Senate Subcommittee on Indian Affairs, where many Native mothers,

children, and officials testified that removal of children from birth families had become epidemic. "For decades Indian parents and their children have been at the mercy of arbitrary or abusive action of local, State, Federal, and private agency officials," said Sen. James Abourezk in his opening remarks, adding that "Unwarranted removal of children from their homes is common in Indian communities" (United States, *Indian Child Welfare Program* 1). In data presented at that hearing, up to thirty-five percent of all Indian children were living in non-Indian settings. Indian parents could expect their children to be removed from their homes at rates up to twenty-five times higher than children from non-Indian homes. In Minnesota, Indian children were placed in adoptive or foster homes at a rate twenty-two times higher than for all children. In South Dakota, Indian children comprised seven percent of the population, but were involved in forty percent of adoptions made by the Department of Public Welfare from 1968 to 1974. In Wisconsin, the risk of Indian children being separated from their parents was nearly sixteen hundred times greater than for non-Indian children (United States, *Indian Child Welfare Program* 4).

In 1976, the AAIA conducted a study for the American Indian Policy Review Committee on the increasingly disproportionate rate of foster care and increasing rate of placement in non-Indian homes. After the 1977 hearing of the Senate Select Committee on Indian Affairs on proposed legislation, the Indian Child Welfare Act of 1978 (ICWA) was passed into law. Major provisions of the ICWA establish procedures for placements and adoptions, assure tribal jurisdiction in custody proceedings, and assure tribal and parental authority in state court proceedings. The ICWA protects the rights of adoptive children to tribal enrollment. It also authorizes the interior secretary to fund tribal efforts to establish programs and services to prevent the breakup of Indian families (Prucha 1153–56). Moreover, the law provides an "effective underpinning" to tribes solving their own societal and familial problems, according to B. J. Jones, who writes that the ICWA "gives Indian tribes and families some breathing space while they go about the process of cultural rebirth."

The ICWA has been both abhorred and envied in Canada. Bradford Morse noted in 1984 that the reduced flow of American Indian children to non-Indian families "has led to an increasing demand for Canadian children of Indian ancestry to be adopted south of the border" (275). Yet the ICWA has been envied because of impediments to creating similar national legislation. With far less sovereignty than US tribes have, Canadian bands have no tribal court system, and the responsibility for Indian child welfare is a federal-provincial "jurisdictional nightmare" (Morse 274). While provinces administer child care and welfare services, the federal government has authority over Indians and their reserve lands, which lets "both levels of government absolve themselves and argue that the responsibility rests with the other" (Johnston 4). Further, under the complex system of registration created by the Indian Act (1876), federal and provincial authorities each hold the other responsible for off-reservation Indian and Métis populations (Johnston 4–7).

But because of these difficulties, Canada has taken a longer, more conceptual approach to analyzing child education and welfare in the whole pattern of relations between aboriginal people and the government. Canada has also studied the effects on children, families, and communities more extensively than has the United States, which, having made a law, has preferred to study the law, its language, and its operation, rather than the situation that made the law necessary.[1]

In 1984, Bradford Morse listed five results of colonialism as probable causes of the Sixties Scoop: the destruction of traditional economies, the disregard of traditional values by the social service system, the resulting surrender of their values by Indian people, the conflict between federal and provincial jurisdictions, and finally the "continuing manifestations of colonialism" in the apparent "connection between the decline of residential schools [. . .] and the rise of Indian child apprehensions" (259, 265–70). The results he calls "devastating": parents despair and give up, and their children, "lost between two cultures [. . .] endure foster and group homes until they end up in jail or as victims of suicide" (270).

Several parliamentary, provincial, and First Nations interest groups studied the problem. Justice Edwin C. Kimelman's 1985 inquiry found that the Manitoba system of adoption and placement had "gone awry," creating estrangement and violence in child care (qtd. in Canada, *Report* 3.2.1). Separate reports by the House of Commons Special Committee on Child Care (1987); the National Indian Brotherhood, Assembly of First Nations (1989); and the Native Council of Canada (1990) directed attention to the need for programs and standards that would provide holistic care, encourage strong identities in children, and preserve families, all in accord with Native cultural values and practices. In 1991, Helen McKenzie prepared a background paper for Parliament on day care as an aspect of broader child welfare practices. She concurred with the needs identified in earlier studies for Native designed and implemented policies and programs, adding that early childhood support is essential for remedying the economic situation and ensuring the cultural survival of the First Nations (25–26).

In 1996 and 1998, Canada took major steps in redirecting its relations with aboriginal peoples, first with the publication of the *Report of the Royal Commission on Aboriginal Peoples (*RCAP*)*, and then by responding to the report by instituting Gathering Strength—Canada's Aboriginal Action Plan—and by issuing a *Statement of Reconciliation*. Based on extensive hearings and studies, the RCAP report is an encyclopedic five-volume study of past injustices and the current situation. It makes recommendations intended to lead to the reparation, healing, and renewal of aboriginal people and communities. The report studies education and child welfare separately, but both are placed in the context of the whole history of federal, provincial, and aboriginal relations, with particular attention to intergenerational effects, community healing, and cultural differences in family structure, childhood concepts, and values (3.2.5). Gathering Strength, in response, "is a sustainable, long-term plan that is leading to stronger and more self-sufficient Aboriginal communities," and that is designed to benefit "particularly Aboriginal youth and children" (Canada, *Backgrounder*). The RCAP report and the government's 1998 language and actions on behalf of reconciliation have no counterpart in the United States.

As heartening as these documents are, and as ultimately successful as they may be, subsequent cases reveal the persistence of jurisdictional conflict, ingrained colonial attitudes in child welfare practice, and the narrow limits of self-governance.[2] Yet Canada has, and the United States has not, recognized that education and child welfare were instruments of colonial policy that contributed to the breakdown in social, family, and individual identity.

PART 1

Traditional Stories and Lives

The belief that children are a gift from the spirit world to renew this world has informed family life for generations of Native American peoples and inhabits the stories and languages of many nations. The Lakota word for child means "stands sacred," and embodies the importance of children in Lakota life, according to Severt Young Bear and R. D. Theisz ("To Say 'Child,' " 1994).

Early transcriptions of Native stories were often popular as children's stories, although the literature abounds with stories that teach and remind adults about children, how they should be raised, and who is responsible for them. Zitkala-Ša's "The Toad and the Boy" (1902) and Delia Oshogay's "Oshkikwe's Baby" (1977) address the theft of children, the depth of parental grief, and the imperative to seek their recovery. Michele Dean Stock's version of the Seneca legend "The Seven Dancers" tells the origin of the constellation that reminds Haudenosaunee parents of the Creator's desire that they be grateful for children, pay attention to them, and include them in ceremonies and activities. The Cherokee woman in Mary Ulmer Chiltoskey's story adopts Goldilocks in a traditional way after the girl escapes from the house of the three bears ("Goldilocks Thereafter"). Through the government official's ineptitude, Chiltoskey satirizes the white world's biased construction of racial identity based on blood quantum, while affirming a humane, inclusive tradition of caring for children.

Against the background of traditional stories, Marietta Brady portrays growing up Navajo in two works of fiction. "The Skirt" is a small girl's story of family generosity, remembrance, and strength that gives her a way of keeping her identity at boarding school. With the experimental "Higher Ground," Brady counters the romantic notion that all Indian children are taught by being told stories by firelight. The changes in narrative voice signify a succession of rebirths that Frida undergoes in enduring a hard lesson. The experience brings her into harmony with her mother, who learns new ways of showing her daughter how to live.

These tales reflect various Native perspectives about the value and place of children in their culture. They are the background for understanding the enormous struggles of those whose personal reflections appear in this anthology: Native people who were subject to cultural replacement through education and child welfare and other impositions in the United States and Canada.

To Say "Child"

SEVERT YOUNG BEAR AND R. D. THEISZ

Knowing the real meanings behind certain terms clarifies their importance.

The terms for man, woman and child are also revealing. *Wicasa* (man) is based on *wi* (sun), *can* (wood or staff) and *sa* (red). *Wi* is the highest form the Great Mystery can take; *can* refers to the staff a warrior can touch the enemy with; and *sa* (red) is the color of the sacred. In this way the spiritual Lakota warrior is defined. The word *winyan* (woman) is also made up of *wi* (sun) and then *inyan* (rock). A woman is the foundation of the home, so she combines the great power of the sun and the rock, the beginning of creation and the foundation. The word for child is also illuminating when we look at its parts. *Wakanyeja* is our Lakota word for child. It is made up of two parts, *wakanyan* (sacred) and *najin* (to stand); so for us a child stands sacred in this world, a special gift from the Creator.

The Toad and the Boy

ZITKALA-ŠA

The water-fowls were flying over the marshy lakes. It was now the hunting season. Indian men, with bows and arrows, were wading waist deep amid the wild rice. Near by, within their wigwams, the wives were roasting wild duck and making down pillows.

In the largest teepee sat a young mother wrapping red porcupine quills about the long fringes of a buckskin cushion. Beside her lay a black-eyed baby boy cooing and laughing. Reaching and kicking upward with his tiny hands and feet, he played with the dangling strings of his heavy beaded bonnet hanging empty on a tent pole above him.

At length the mother laid aside her red quills and white sinew-threads. The babe fell fast asleep. Leaning on one hand and softly whispering a little lullaby, she threw a light cover over her baby. It was almost time for the return of her husband.

Remembering there were no willow sticks for the fire, she quickly girdled her blanket tight about her waist, and with a short-handled ax slipped through her belt, she hurried away toward the wooded ravine. She was strong and swung an ax as skillfully as any man. Her loose buckskin dress was made for such freedom. Soon carrying easily a bundle of long willows on her back, with a loop of rope over both her shoulders, she came striding homeward.

Near the entrance way she stooped low, at once shifting the bundle to the right and with both hands lifting the noose from over her head. Having thus dropped the wood to the ground, she disappeared into her teepee. In a moment she came running out again, crying, "My son! My little son is gone!" Her keen eyes swept east and west and all around her. There was nowhere any sign of the child.

Running with clenched fists to the nearest teepees, she called: "Has any one seen my baby? He is gone! My little son is gone!"

"Hinnú! Hinnú!" exclaimed the women, rising to their feet and rushing out of their wigwams.

"We have not seen your child! What has happened?" queried the women.

With great tears in her eyes the mother told her story.

"We will search with you," they said to her as she started off.

They met the returning husbands, who turned about and joined in the hunt for the missing child. Along the shore of the lakes, among the high-grown reeds, they looked in vain. He was nowhere to be found. After many days and nights the search was given up. It was sad, indeed, to hear the mother wailing aloud for her little son.

It was growing late in the autumn. The birds were flying high toward the south. The teepees around the lakes were gone, save one lonely dwelling.

Till the winter snow covered the ground and ice covered the lakes, the wailing woman's voice was heard from that solitary wigwam. From some far distance was also the sound of the father's voice singing a sad song.

Thus ten summers and as many winters have come and gone since the strange disappearance of the little child. Every autumn with the hunters came the unhappy parents of the lost baby to search again for him.

Toward the latter part of the tenth season when, one by one, the teepees were folded and the families went away from the lake region, the mother walked again along the lake shore weeping. One evening, across the lake from where the crying woman stood, a pair of bright black eyes peered at her through the tall reeds and wild rice. A little wild boy stopped his play among the tall grasses. His long, loose hair hanging down his brown back and shoulders was carelessly tossed from his round face. He wore a loin cloth of woven sweet grass. Crouching low to the marshy ground, he listened to the wailing voice. As the voice grew hoarse and only sobs shook the slender figure of the woman, the eyes of the wild boy grew dim and wet.

At length, when the moaning ceased, he sprang to his feet and ran like a nymph with swift outstretched toes. He rushed into a small hut of reeds and grasses.

"Mother! Mother! Tell me what voice it was I heard which pleased my ears, but made my eyes grow wet!" said he, breathless.

"Han, my son," grunted a big, ugly toad. "It was the voice of a weeping woman you heard. My son, do not say you like it. Do not tell me it brought tears to your eyes. You have never heard me weep. I can please your ear and break your heart. Listen!" replied the great old toad.

Stepping outside, she stood by the entrance way. She was old and badly puffed out. She had reared a large family of little toads, but none of them had aroused her love, nor ever grieved her. She had heard the wailing human voice and marveled at the throat which produced the strange sound. Now, in her great desire to keep the stolen boy awhile longer, she ventured to cry as the Dakota woman does. In a gruff, coarse voice she broke forth:

"Hin-hin, doe-skin! Hin-hin, Ermine, Ermine! Hin-hin, red blanket, with white border!"

Not knowing that the syllables of a Dakota's cry are the names of loved ones gone, the ugly toad mother sought to please the boy's ear with the names of valuable articles. Having shrieked in a torturing voice and mouthed extravagant names, the old toad rolled her tearless eyes with great satisfaction. Hopping back into her dwelling, she asked:

"My son, did my voice bring tears to your eyes? Did my words bring gladness to your ears? Do you not like my wailing better?"

"No, no!" pouted the boy with some impatience. "I want to hear the woman's voice! Tell me, mother, why the human voice stirs all my feelings!"

The toad mother said within her breast, "The human child has heard and seen his real mother. I cannot keep him longer, I fear. Oh, no, I cannot give away the pretty creature I have taught to call me 'mother' all these many winters."

"Mother," went on the child voice, "tell me one thing. Tell me why my little brothers and sisters are all unlike me."

The big, ugly toad, looking at her pudgy children, said: "The eldest is always best."

This reply quieted the boy for a while. Very closely watched the old toad mother her stolen human son. When by chance he started off alone, she shoved out one of her own children after him, saying: "Do not come back without your big brother."

Thus the wild boy with the long, loose hair sits every day on a marshy island hid among the tall reeds. But he is not alone. Always at his feet hops a little toad brother. One day an Indian hunter, wading in the deep waters, spied the boy. He had heard of the baby stolen long ago.

"This is he!" murmured the hunter to himself as he ran to his wigwam. "I saw among the tall reeds a black-haired boy at play!" shouted he to the people.

At once the unhappy father and mother cried out, " 'Tis he, our boy!" Quickly he led them to the lake. Peeping through the wild rice, he pointed with unsteady finger toward the boy playing all unawares.

" 'Tis he! 'tis he!" cried the mother, for she knew him.

In silence the hunter stood aside, while the happy father and mother caressed their baby boy grown tall.

Oshkikwe's Baby

DELIA OSHOGAY

Matchikwewis and Oshkikwe were out picking cranberries and staying by themselves. One day Oshkikwe found a tiny pipe with a little face on it. The eyes were looking at her and would wink at her. She showed it to her older sister and said, "Look at this little pipe! I guess we're not really alone in the world. There must be somebody else in the world."

Matchikwewis said that they had once lived in a village and that their father had been the head man. When he died, she took Oshkikwe away, because she didn't want her to be abused by the people.

Matchikwewis knew that her sister was going to give birth to a child because of the pipe. One time, when they woke up, they saw a *tikinagan* (cradleboard) with wraps and everything set for a baby, including a little bow and arrow. Oshkikwe took sick and found a little boy and a little pup.

Matchikwewis took good care of her sister, and everything was going fine. One day Matchikwewis told her sister that she'd had a dream which told her not to leave the baby out of her sight for ten days but always stay with him, for otherwise an old witch would come for him. Once Oshkikwe just went outside to get a stick of wood, and when she came back she could see the swing moving. The pup used to guard the little cradleboard. While she went out, she heard the pup barking. When she got back, both the baby and the pup were gone. All that remained was a piece of the hindquarters of the witch which the dog must have bitten off and a little piece of the *tikinagan* which the pup must have got too.

As soon as she saw this, she said that she'd get ready to look for the child and the pup. She told her sister she'd be gone for ten days. The sister told her to work on her breasts, so they wouldn't run dry. She had been nursing the baby on one breast and the pup on the other. The sister also said that the further the witch went with the child, the bigger he'd get, and soon he'd become a man.

The mother started walking, and she crossed a deer trail. She kept on going and came to another trail: a man's tracks, deer tracks, and a dog's tracks. This was her son's tracks, because the witch had so much power that it didn't take the child long to grow up. Finally, Oshkikwe came to a wigwam. Outside of it, she saw a man who must have been her son already grown up.

The man went into the wigwam to tell his "mother" what he had seen. He told her that he had seen a young woman. But the witch said, "Don't you dare look at that woman, because she's just a dirty old witch. As soon as you look at her, you'll become ugly."

The young man said, "Well, I don't like to see her trying to build a wigwam of old birchbark and things. Why don't you give her some nice birchbark, so it won't rain on her?"

The witch didn't like to do it, but she had to. Whenever this old witch knew that there was a new-born boy, she'd kidnap him, and as soon as they got into her territory, the boy would grow up and go hunting and work for her, so she got all the profit out of it.

This man of Oshkikwe's got home early one afternoon, because he had to make arrows before it got dark. Just as he went by Oshkikwe's wigwam, she had her breasts open. The pup was hanging around Oshkikwe, because he remembered her.

While the young man was whittling his arrows, the first thing he knew Oshkikwe was sitting on a woodpile, showing her breasts to her son. He knew that there was something he couldn't remember, but he couldn't remember what it was. He suspected something, though. In his dream he made a wish that his "mother" would sleep soundly, so that he could go over and visit this young woman whom his "mother" called an old witch. So his "mother" slept soundly that night. He went to see the young woman, accompanied by the pup. When the pup got there, he went to nurse at the woman's left breast. Oshkikwe said to him, "You are my son, and here is the milk you lived on before this old witch got hold of you."

He couldn't remember, but she told him, and she brought a piece of his cradleboard made of cedar and shells, and also a piece of the old witch's hindquarters, and showed them to her son. He asked his mother how she managed to live and whether the old witch gave her anything to eat. Oshkikwe said, "When she gives me something, she brings only the livers and dirties them on the way." Then the man told his mother he'd go back with her, but not for a while. The minute he'd go back to her, he'd turn right into a baby. At the same time, though, he had to find out the real facts about who his mother was.

That night he pretended to be sick and started to moan. His "mother" asked him what was the matter, and he said he was dying and that the only thing that would save him would be the sight of his old cradle-board. The old lady went out and got a very old cradleboard, but he said that wasn't his. Then she got his real one, with the pretty shells, and he saw that part of it was missing, and he knew then that Oshkikwe was right, since she had the missing part. Then he started to moan again. His "mother" asked him what the matter was. He said he had to taste the milk he used to nurse on. She pulled out her own breast and squeezed out some old yellow stuff and gave it to him to taste. He thought it was funny that he'd ever grown up with such awful stuff for food. He had to find out one more thing. He said, "The only way I can live is if you pull up you skirts high and dance around a little." So she danced for him and lifted up her buckskin dress. He called out, "Higher, ma!" Then he knew that Oshkikwe was right. The old witch went to sleep after that.

The man went back to his mother and told her that he'd go hunting the next morning. He planned to kill a deer and hang it high up on a tree, and then come back and tell the old witch to go and bring it back because his feet were all blistered.

The next morning he came back and told the witch that he'd killed two deer, one near and one far. He told the witch to send Oshkikwe to go and get the more distant deer, and she should get the other one. They both set out, but instead of going on, Oshkikwe came right back.

The old witch had two children. The man banged them both on the head with a club and killed them. Then he stuck two sugar cookies in their mouths and made it look as though they were still alive.

Then he and his mother picked up one stake of the wigwam and went down into that hole a long ways. The man and the puppy got smaller and smaller. By the time the old witch got home, her boy was gone, and here were her two children with sugar cookies in their mouths. She yelled at the kids, because they were eating something she was saving for their brother; but when she got closer to them, she saw that they were dead.

Then she spoke aloud to her son: "Huh! What do you think? This world is too small for you to get away from me!" She found the hole they had gone down and followed them. By this time the man and the puppy had become very small. He told his mother to put him in the cradle-board which she'd brought along. The last thing he managed to tell his mother was that she should make a big mark with his arrow, and there the earth would split. She took the arrow and marked the ground just as the witch came along. Then the witch fell into the split, and that was the end of her. When Oshkikwe got home, she found her sister all dressed up and her hair oiled. She said that if Oshkikwe hadn't arrived that night, she would have gone after her the next day.

The Seven Dancers

MICHELE DEAN STOCK

Many years ago, when the Iroquois Nations still lived in longhouse villages, there came a time when the parents of the village's children forgot the Creator's instructions. They became too busy to answer the questions of their children or to guide them, and they neglected the children's needs. Children would ask their parents how things were to be done, or what things meant, or to seek answers to their questions, and the parents would say, "Don't bother me now! Can't you see I'm busy?" Or they'd say, "I can't help you now. Go and do your chores!"

Now this was not a good thing, because children are to learn from their parents, as the Creator gives the children as a precious gift to the people who walk on the earth. The children and the Creator were becoming more and more unhappy about what was happening, and a small group of boys began to form a friendship and a kind of club to meet and discuss their problems.

These eight boys would meet to talk in the late afternoon near the edge of the fields by the woods. Since their chores were done and the evening meal was not yet ready, these boys had time to meet, and they felt that no one would really care about them if they were not at home anyway. The boys soon formed their own special bond.

While the boys were talking one day, they began to hear strange and beautiful music coming from the woods. They stopped and listened, and excitedly agreed that they had never heard these songs before. They grew more curious about who was singing and longed to go into the woods and see. One boy reminded them that they were not allowed to wander into the woods without adults, and that it could be something evil drawing their attention. But the boys felt that no adults would come if they asked, and they had nothing to lose by going to see who was singing. So they crept into the woods following the sound of the drum, until they came to a clearing. There they saw a gentle boy, a little older than they were, singing and beating the water drum. When he finished the song, he looked up through the trees and asked the boys to come and join him. Even though the boys were hiding, he knew they were there, and the boys exchanged surprised glances, whispering to one another as to whether they should go or stay. The strange boy said in a gentle voice, "Don't be afraid. I want to be your friend. I know that you are troubled and that you need friendship. I'd like to be your friend and teach you this music, because I know it will lift your spirits."

The boys wanted to learn the songs very much, because it is a source of great honor to know many songs and it's fun to sing and share them with one's people. As the strange boy waited, they decided that, since their parents didn't seem to notice or care about their needs, they might as well befriend this kind boy and learn his songs. So they cautiously walked toward him and sat on some logs near the one he was sitting on. "Thank you for deciding to join me," he said. "I want to be a part of your group, if you'll let me, and we can sing together every day at this same time. I have many songs I'd like to teach you if you want." The boys said they would like that, and the boy pulled out a sack filled with new and well-made water drums and rattles and passed them around. As each boy took an instrument, they began to talk with the strange boy, and they grew more comfortable by the minute. The boy started to teach them a new song.

The time went by quickly and the strange boy had to remind them that they needed to get back for dinner. As the boys reluctantly gave back the instruments, the strange boy invited them back for the next day, and they eagerly accepted. So, as they ran back toward their long-houses, they talked excitedly about their adventure, their new song, and their new friend. They couldn't wait to tell their families and share the new song! But suddenly, one boy stopped the group and spoke.

"If we tell them, they'll scold us for going in the woods alone, and they won't let us see him again." The boys exchanged knowing glances. He said, "Let's keep this our secret for now, and later we can tell them and even bring him back to meet them!" All the boys agreed that this was the best choice and went to their respective longhouses.

The next day, the boys could hardly wait for the late afternoon, so they could meet their new friend and learn new songs. Again, as they did their daily chores, no attention or help came from their parents, and the boys were each shunned or brushed off when they needed help. But their plans for the day seemed to give them hope, and they went off to join the strange boy at the appointed time.

They learned a new set of songs, and they talked and laughed with their new friend. This soon became their daily routine, and the boys were becoming anxious to tell their parents about him and sing the new songs for the village. But first, the boy suggested that they might have a special feast, to make their friendship and bond stronger, to celebrate their happiness, and to sing their new songs in the woods. Since a feast is a special event, the boys were eager to do it, and it would be a great opportunity to practice their songs before they sang them for the village. So the strange boy said, "Let's all bring a little food to share. It doesn't have to be much, so maybe you could ask your parents for the leftover scraps from the evening meal to bring to our feast. I'll bring something too."

When the boys were home and finished their meals, each went to his parents to ask for the scraps and maybe some dried foods in storage. Each boy received the same response: "How can you ask such a thing! Why do you need to have a feast anyway! There is plenty of work to be done, and our food is important for our survival. We cannot spare even the scraps for something so silly! You know better than to ask such things! Now leave us alone and prepare for bed!"

The next day, the boys dejectedly performed their daily chores, and the day seemed to last forever, until the time finally came to go and meet their friend. As they slowly entered the clearing, their friend greeted them with firm and warm squeezes on their shoulders and invited them to sit down. "I know what has happened," he said gently, "and I am sorry. But don't worry. I've brought enough dried meat and berries for all of us, and we will still have our feast!" Though the boys were still sad, their spirits were lifted little by little by their new friend, who shared words of comfort as they ate their food. When the meal was finished, he made an announcement.

"I can tell you now why I'm here. I was sent by the Creator, because he saw how your parents were neglecting you and forgetting his instructions to them. I want to be your friend and for us to become our own new family, so you will always feel cared about and you will be happy and content forever. If you want this to happen, you will have to leave your own family and promise to come with me. I'll teach you new music and dances that will lift your spirits high, and your parents will learn of their wrongdoing through you." The boys, though confused, were happy to consider such an offer, because they had begun to feel that they no longer had families at home, and they wanted desperately for this to change. They finally agreed to join the strange boy, and the boy smiled and thanked them. He then said, "Now, once you make this decision, remember: there is no going back. We will be together forever and be each other's family. So think very hard before you return tomorrow, because I don't want to force you to do what you don't want to do. If you decide to take this step, join me a little later in the afternoon tomorrow. Wear your finest ceremony clothes and come to me in the woods again." The boys agreed and set out to return home for the last time.

As the boys walked back, they were troubled and had mixed feelings. They still loved their parents and they loved their new friend, but they didn't feel that their parents cared about them much anymore. So they all decided they would give their parents one more chance, and that they would try to tell them about their friend and that they were thinking of going away. So that evening and the next day, all of them tried to tell their parents what was about to happen, and in each case, the parents were less receptive than ever at hearing what they had to say. Hard as they tried, each boy met resistance from his parents, and none of the parents wanted to take the time to hear what the child had to say. The boys decided to leave that night.

After the day's chores were done and each boy was sure he'd be alone in the longhouse, each sneaked out his best clothes and wandered outside the stockade to the edge of the field to meet his friends. The boys changed clothes at the edge of the woods, leaving their everyday clothes behind on the ground as they went to meet their friend. They found him dressed in a magnificent outfit, and a drum and rattle were placed near each of their seats. The strange boy spoke. "I'm glad to see you all, and welcome you to your new family. You are very brave and special children who will long be remembered because of this night. Tonight, you will learn new songs and a dance you have never done before, and the music and dance will lift your spirits and carry them high. You will feel joy inside you and a release of your cares and sadness, and something very special will happen to you. But remember, you cannot go back to your former families, and you cannot look back if they call to you."

After a pause, he said, "Are you ready?" The boys excitedly agreed and lifted their instruments, and the boy began the song and the dance. As they learned, the sun set and evening set in. The music filled the boys with joy and peace of mind, and as they sang and danced, the song seemed to grow louder and a little faster.

The song soon grew loud enough for the villagers to hear, and they came out of the longhouses to see what was going on. One of the boys' mothers asked if anyone had seen her son. As they searched, others soon realized that their sons were also missing, and the village began to panic. Soon the song grew louder, and the people began to worry that their boys were somehow connected to this, as they were nowhere to be found. So the villagers followed the sound of the music and discovered the boys' clothes laying near the edge of the woods. Some screamed out in anguish, beginning to feel the guilt of their neglect as they realized their boys were gone. They began screaming the boys' names as they ran to the woods, where the music was coming from. The boys were dancing around a large fire, and as the song grew louder, the approaching parents witnessed a sight that frightened them. The boys had begun to rise off the ground as they sang and danced, as the song truly lifted their spirits and bodies higher and higher. The parents screamed their names louder to be heard over the loud music, but the boys kept rising farther and farther into the night sky. As the boys got higher, one by one they began to appear as twinkling stars in the sky. As the last boy was nearly out of sight, he looked back one last time, and as a result, became a shooting star.

The shooting star always reminds us of this story and the importance of remembering the Creator's instructions: that our children are a valuable resource and are the key to our future. When the cluster of the seven stars reaches its peak in the mid-winter sky, we hold our Mid-Winter (New Year's) Ceremony after the first new moon, and we prepare for the coming reawakening of Mother Earth. And we remember the Creator's instructions to be thankful for our children, to help teach them, and to attend to their needs.

Goldilocks Thereafter

MARY ULMER CHILTOSKEY

We all have heard the story of Goldilocks and the bears. We can learn from this story that stories don't end at the end of the telling; they go on and more story can be told.

If you remember, Goldilocks wandered into the home of the three bears (against her mother's wishes). In the house she tasted the hot porridge and the cold porridge and she ate up the baby bear's porridge. She sat in the hard chair and the soft chair and when she sat in the baby's chair, it broke! Now she knew to leave, but her curiosity led her upstairs to a high, hard bed and a soft bed, and on the baby's bed, she fell asleep. You remember that the bears came home and at the sight of three bears, she jumped out the window.

Now Goldilocks was scared to stay at the bears' house, and she was also scared to go home because she knew her mother had told her not to go to the woods. She didn't know what to do. She wandered farther into the woods and she became really, really lost. She looked for a way out and she found nothing that she recognized. She wandered and she ran and she got very scared.

After a while, she had to stop running and she didn't know what to do and she was very hungry. She looked through the woods and saw a bit of smoke. She had found only a few nuts and berries, and she thought she had better go toward that smoke, no matter what she found. She walked toward the smoke and began to smell food cooking. It was the best smell in the world and she was very hungry.

She noticed the sun was suddenly brighter. She was coming to the edge of the woods. Soon she was in an area of grass that seemed to be a campground. She saw some people and she saw a cookfire and she thought she'd just run get some food. But then she thought she had better use her good manners.

Carefully, she approached the people close enough to see that they didn't look like her. These people were very brown and they had long dark hair, not at all like her pink skin and her yellow hair. These were several Cherokee families camped out as they did every fall to gather nuts for the winter.

Goldilocks heard the people talking, but she didn't understand a bit of what they said. One lady gestured to her to come to her and Goldilocks understood her smile. The lady offered some food but it was not on a plate; it was on a piece of chestnut bark.

The golden haired girl ate the Cherokee food and stayed the night with the people. Later, she tried to find out from the people how to get to her home, but she did not understand their language and they did not understand her.

Eventually the little pink-skinned, golden-haired girl became a part of the Cherokee family. She learned their language and the stories that they told in the evenings. She never found her family, but she had found a new family.

One day in the early winter several years later, a white man came to the Cherokee village to count the people for the American government. He spoke only a little of the Cherokee language. He was walking from village to village, and it was getting on toward afternoon.

The man was a census taker who asked the mother questions about how many people were in the family. The mother knew a little English. She told him the answers to his questions so the government could know the names and ages of each one in the family. He asked how many were girls and how many were boys.

The man looked at the children and saw that all but one were Cherokee. He saw a very light blond child, and he asked, "Are all these children yours?"

"Yes," said the mother because she cared for the little blond girl.

Maybe because he knew only a bit of the language and maybe because he didn't want to offend the mother or maybe because he was just tired, the man did not question further. He marked an F by each of the children's names, meaning that they were full-blood Cherokee.

The little girl grew up and married a Cherokee, and all of their children except one looked like their Cherokee father, but there was one little blond child.

In the Cherokee village in each generation there have been children who are officially Cherokee but they look like their Great-great-great Grandmother Goldilocks.

Two Stories

MARIETTA BRADY

for Estelle Yazzi

The Skirt

Grandma lived on Owls Peak. For generations my clan family has lived there. Grandma had fourteen children, seven boys and seven girls, and they all lived in one hogan that Grandpa collaged with huge pieces of limestone, each about the size of a four-wheeler tire. He lined the stones with cement around a circle with an opening for a door. He spun a swirl of logs for a roof above the circular wall. An airtight stove in the center sat with a pile of freshly chopped logs. Along the walls, clockwise, were a wash pan, a cabinet, and several rolled beds that trailed halfway around the hogan. Each mattress had its own design. Whoever made the mattresses must have sewn them with a lot of anger and jealousy. Each of Grandma's children had a mattress, and anyone who tried to sleep on another's mattress either couldn't sleep or woke up very sore. Next to the mattresses were a bureau with huge dresser drawers, a long cabinet full of dishes and sewing utensils, and a long wooden table with steel chairs that had spongy seats that erupted all over the floor. Next was another cabinet that was really two cabinets, then a gleaming stove. The children loved to touch the smooth surface and watched it with awe when Grandpa took bread out of the oven or boiled stew so that the flames from the butane fire danced under the pot.

The door was a drape of one of Grandma's rugs. If one looked carefully, one could see that she wove in the rug the hair of each of her children and stories of visitors from far away. If one looked more carefully in a certain area, one would see that Grandma had overlooked a strand or two, and that she had washed away the dye with her tears. Everyone remembered that day.

Grandma's eldest son had come back for a short while that day. He had gone away and gotten married to a chubby lady with beautiful, long, jet-black hair. Grandma loved her son dearly, and when he went away she was sad because he never came to visit her. Except for just this once.

Grandma was sitting under the window that faced the south. The breeze was blowing calmly from the open window. I was behind her rug digging in the sand. She sat on the ground with a basket of woolen yarn that was rolled up into a ball. Along the wall hung loops of freshly dyed wool. I started to make a huge cloud of sandy dust inside the hogan. Grandma got up and saw while passing the door that everyone else was lazing around underneath the shack outside. She got a dipperful of water from the pail and started to sprinkle it over the floor, to calm the cloud of dust I had made. When the water hit the dry sand, it collected itself into a ball, then dampened the ground. The aroma of the earth filled the hogan.

The aroma woke Grandpa, who slept at the west end, and he said, "What a beautiful smell. For a moment I thought it was raining. I am going to finish Kaibob's moccasins."

Grandma agreed and sat back down at her rug, which was half finished. I went to Grandpa and watched him make my moccasins. "Can I have those huge silver buttons that have a buffalo on the back of them for my shoes?" I asked.

"Yes," he said. "That is what I am going to do. Here, lick this string for me." As he held the string up for me to lick, I looked at his hand. The veins were swollen and were rooted through his hand and arm. While he worked, I touched his veins and played with them. They were so soft and tender. I wished I had veins like that. I started to feel tired and fell asleep on Grandpa's leg. I dreamed that Uncle Sony came to visit us.

The sound of a vehicle woke me. Someone shouted, "My mother!"

Grandpa looked out the window and said, "Well, it seems like Sony remembered us," and then someone yelled, "Come out here!" I heard a bunch of shouts from the shack, some of which were Sony's name. Grandma got up and started to head for the door, but the door was blocked by Sony's shadow. I ran to hide behind Grandma's skirt.

Outside I heard a lot of commotion and shouts, "This is yours! This is mine!" Sony came inside and shook Grandma's hand and I shook his hand, and then he gave me a mint stick. He went over to Grandpa and shook his hand too. Sony said, "I am coming from a distance but I am not hungry." There was an uneasy silence in the hogan for a moment, but then he said, "I brought things for all of you." He slipped some money to Grandpa, who nodded in return. Then Sony got up and left and came back with a bundle in his hand. Grandma looked up at Sony, who said, "My mother, this is for you." He threw a colorful bundle down before her, threw it so that it made a rainbow in the air. It landed very gently and scattered itself in front of Grandma. Then Sony went out without saying anything else. He got in his truck and drove off.

Grandma picked up one of the skirts that was in the bundle and looked at it. It had a wide waist and was made of layered material. Between layers were sewn tiny hearts with black strands of hair. Each of the five skirts had tiny hearts sewn into the layers. Grandma put the skirts in one of the huge drawers in the bureau and sat back down at her rug.

I woke with the earth shaking underneath me. Grandma was pounding very hard on her rug and it started to build up a cloud of dust. Grandpa was outside somewhere. I went to Grandma and saw a cup full of water near her, which I picked up and sprinkled around the hogan to calm the dust. The water collected into heart shapes and then soaked into the ground. Where Grandpa had sat, I saw my finished moccasins. When I put them on, they were soft, just like the veins on his hand.

Grandma finished the rug that summer, with many more stories in it. She cut her skirts in half, because the waist was too wide, so she had ten skirts altogether. Little did I understand then how Grandma would console herself with her skirts when she came to realize the relationships between people, events, and things while she wove. And that I too would come to use her skirts to console myself.

I created a lot of dust for my mother and myself when I left home for boarding school. At school, my Grandpa wasn't around to remind me of the harmonious scent of moistened red sand, and it would be a long time before the new cycle began with rain clouds. Among my friends and I, it was not enough to console one another with tear drops.

During my second semester at school, while I was unpacking, I found two skirts that had belonged to Grandma. Although their color had faded, the hearts were still clearly visible with Uncle Sony's wife's hair. I was honored to have those skirts, but I didn't dare wear them at school. To wear something old-fashioned was not cool. I wore the skirts only at home. However, they were my sanity. The rich, everlasting scent of the skirt was a reminder of my childhood, when my Grandpa awoke to the aroma of fresh rainwater that Grandma sprinkled on the earthen floor of the hogan.

As my Grandma had, I too saw the relationships between events and people through time, and the reason why I had gone to boarding school, as my mother had.

Higher Ground

1

It was a quiet morning, right before the light hit the horizon in the east. By her own conviction, she woke up at that time. By the time she was done stretching and had just started to run, she began hearing the birds sing to the first break of dawn. The sound of her own heartbeat was gone.

She ran from the timeworn darkness into the emerging twilight-blue air. Overhead, a morning star flickered when the night started to change: The biding blue air started to move westward. Red hues began to synchronize with the lagging blue air behind. An effusion of violet purple absorbed the middle ground, systematically clutching the lower half of her body as she ran swiftly away.

2

At thirteen years of age and in the seventh grade, I was careless and lazy. I remember after asking my mother how to do something, she would reply, "What are you saying! You should be always observing everything I do or someone else does, just in case someone tells you to do it!" She would get more mad and loud every time I asked. But I would not listen.

I was sensitive, and it hurt that my mother refused to show me how to do things. I compared myself to the Indian children in those old Westerns that I liked to watch with my dad. In those movies, I always saw an Indian mother telling stories and singing Christian hymns to the child in her lap. She also showed her daughter how to prepare meals step by step, telling her stories in between the steps. I remember after my mother yelled at me, I would storm out of the house and wonder why she didn't act like the mothers in the movies.

Now, after nine years, I realize how stupid and naive I was, comparing myself to the Indians in those degrading old Westerns. I didn't know they were actors portraying themselves as Indians from a white perspective. I wouldn't have been as sensitive and frustrated with my mother.

One day, she did give in a little about telling me how to do something, but as usual I didn't pay attention. It was a quiet morning. I woke up around 6 a.m. and went for a run. Later, I got ready for school, cooked breakfast for my mother, and cleaned the kitchen and living room just in time to catch the bus.

After breakfast at school, there was usually a free half an hour before the first bell rang. As we walked up and down one of the two hallways in the combined junior high and high school, my friends and I were laughing and talking.

"Hey, Frida, your mom is looking for you," Tina said as she caught up with the rest of the girls.

"Really?" Frida asked with a confused look on her face just as her mother, Isabel, zipped around the corner in the front of them. Concerned about what had brought her mother unexpectedly, Frida walked up to her and asked, "What's wrong? How come you are here?" The girls left Frida and her mother to talk, but Isabel seized Frida by the shoulder, shoved her outside, and said, "We are going home."

3

Her mother's silence made the ride on the bumpy dirt road home seem to last longer than it should have. Frida sat flushed in the pick-up until at last her mother spoke in a deep, disagreeable voice. "This morning I went to feed the sheep and there were none." To Frida, that was all she had to say to prove that it was her fault. Her mother was right.

I was grinding my memory, thinking of what I had done, hoping to redeem myself from oblivion, when I faintly heard my mother say that I had forgotten to close the sheep's pen the night before. I wanted to tell her that it wasn't me, but I bit my tongue. The silence in the car was so like glass that, if I spoke, it would shatter and cut me.

I could not remember step by step what I had done the evening before. I was shivering. In the corner of my eye, I saw my mother's wax face. Her full-bodied curls did not bounce. Her eyelids did not blink. She wore a blood-colored silk blouse that enhanced the white powder on her face. With that and her indigo Wrangler jeans, she could have been a mannequin in a showcase for a Western Warehouse. For pedestrians who looked at her, time might stop. They wouldn't have been able to tell the difference between one minute and an hour. Their wrist-watches would no longer make sense.

After fifteen minutes that felt like an hour to the two people in the maroon and beige truck, Isabel reached the intersection that led to the house and stopped the truck. From there you could see Tse Alkaa' Bee Ak'idi. This mesa was built by rocks, "Tse," piling themselves upon one another, "Alkaa'," until a huge mound was formed, "Bee Ak'idi." If you walked backwards and upward from this intersection, you would fall like a rock to the cliff's bottom. If you walked down and forward, you would come to Frida's home and beyond that another house that fit snugly into a huge piles of rocks at the edge of yet another cliff.

"From here you should be able to see farther away. I am going to come by in the afternoon to pick you up. You should have found them by then," Isabel said, and then she peeled off to return to work and left Frida dazzled in the dust. Isabel watched her rearview mirror until Frida flickered in the dust and disappeared.

Isabel left Frida standing at the intersection with only one clue as to how she could find the sheep, but she didn't pay attention. Instead, she went straight home, changed her clothes, and drank some water.

4

The calm, quiet morning had turned into a dust storm by the time Frida had dressed. The wind blew one hundred miles per hour, creating a thick perplexing fog of red sand on the surface of the earth. She went out to look for the sheep.

That morning in the wind, I wandered into places I wouldn't other-wise have gone. I went around my house in a five-mile radius through small canyons and cliffs, excited about having an adventure until I realized I was repeating the same circle. I did not go beyond the perime-ter into the mounds of red sandy hills, layered one after another, stretch-ing from east to west.

It was tiresome and frustrating to climb the never-ending hills, but I plunged ahead against the wind. Because I could see only two feet in front of me, I ran madly. Whenever I ran out of breath, I would stand still and listen. I started hearing sounds of bleating sheep in the wind. The sound did not come from south, north, west or east, but from beneath the wind, above the wind, inside the wind, behind the bushes, behind me, beside me, above me, from the ground, in the air. I tried running after the sound, hoping to see a sheep. When I stopped, a chorus of sounds came from all directions, mocking me. I squinted for a glimpse of white wool. I thought I saw them several times, but they were only the white cottony flowers of the milkweed. The sheep were hiding from me, disguising themselves. I shook the milkweed, but nothing happened. My legs began to ache and my eyes stung. I knelt down and closed my eyes. I started to make sheep sounds. My throat was dry and thirsty. I crawled on the ground hoping to feel the echo of pounding sheep hooves.

Not being able to see or hear clearly, Frida was unaware of what she was doing. She got up and let the wind take her, and it carried her home.

She got out of her sandy clothes, shook them out and put them back on. She drank a dipperful of water and started looking for something to eat. When she found a box of macaroni and cheese, her mother's truck could be barely heard in the wind.

5

Isabel had only a half-an-hour break, but she left early. As she drove up to the house, she looked toward the corral hoping to see some sheep. She hurriedly ran to the house to keep the wind from ruining her hair. Pausing at the entrance of the kitchen, Isabel asked her daughter, "Did you find the sheep?"

"No."

She sighed. "What! What are you doing here? You should be out there looking for them," Isabel said as she looked for the dipper. Getting more irritated, she demanded, "Where is the dipper?"

"I was thirsty and hungry. After I'm done eating, I will go out again," Frida replied calmly, handing the dipper to her mother.

"What! By the time you finish eating, the sheep will be far away," Isabel said with a deep sigh.

The house, a narrow, white, two-bedroom mobile home, sat barely propped up on several cracked cement blocks and flat donut tires. As it swayed and rattled in the wind, Isabel's voice got louder and louder. She couldn't stand competing with the wind crashing into the old trailer and rippling the outer metal sheath. She was anticipating when the old trailer would fall apart and blow away. She thought of her husband, who was not there to help out. He would have found the sheep in no time.

My mother asked me if I had tried to track the sheep down. "No," I said. "I don't know how."

"Didn't you pay attention to your dad when he tracked down the sheep," she said as a statement rather than a question.

Isabel got up and walked toward the door. She could feel the wind coming in every crack in the house and leaving trails of sand. She had a vision of herself when she was a young girl at home. She saw herself standing on the edge of the mesa among the age-old bristlecone trees. The mesa was not like where she lived now. The mesa she grew up on was more like a butte, with high steep walls and a flat top. There, the wind never blew with so much sand. It was clear wind. She liked to face the breeze as it lifted her hair and her clothes. She felt like a flying eagle above the earth and imagined herself traveling between worlds.

Isabel looked at her daughter. She saw her pale, sandy hair, her clothes shaded with red sand, and her eyes bloodshot with balls of red sand in the corners. The last thing she said to her daughter was to ask their neighbors if they had seen the sheep. With a sigh, she left quietly.

6

That afternoon, the wind came in waves, retreating every so often, but still blowing huge waves of red sand. Since the wind was retreating, Frida was able to recover her vision and hearing.

This time I took with me a small bag with a water jug. I went up to the intersection where my mother had dropped me off. From there I waited for the wind to retreat. I could see where I had walked that morning, and I couldn't believe how much area I had covered. I went to my neighbors, Mr. Ramon and his wife Eya, and asked if they had seen my sheep. They lent me a horse they said was fast and strong. They thought they would see me riding off into the horizon, but I only got the horse to trot along. I did not know how to ride very well.

By the time I got to the south canyon, Mr. Ramon and Eya had already gone ahead of me in their white truck, and it was their tracks I saw leading toward my other neighbor, who lived eight miles away. From around a hill, I saw the white truck. Mr. Ramon spoke for Eya and said that she had tracked the sheep, and that they were penned up at my neighbor's house. I was very thankful. They took the horse and I walked home.

While Frida walked home, the wind diminished to a nice clear breeze. When she discovered the tracks at the canyon, she couldn't believe how many different tracks there were: sheep, dogs, cows, and horses. She looked at them all the way home. Some sheep tracks were very old because they were only dimples in the sand. She found a few recent tracks that tore up fresh moist sand.

7

I remembered seeing those sheep tracks for the first time underneath a full grown poplar tree. We had moved four years earlier to live with my father's family, and we used to sit under the old tree and cool off. One day, my aunt was visiting. She always looked at the ground when she talked about what she had done or heard or seen. She picked up a stick and was poking at the ground, doodling. She stopped talking and commented on how the marks in the dirt looked like a sheep had been dragging its leg. My mother replied, "You're right. One of the goats had an overgrown nail that probably hurts, so it doesn't use it anymore. I keep wanting to cut it but I haven't." It was my turn to interrupt, so I asked my aunt how she knew. After she showed me by drawing with her stick, I asked what a horse print looked like. My mom got down on her knees and showed me, and after that a cow, a dog, a deer, and a baby. I knelt down on the ground, my hands imitating my mother's hands.

8

She ran back sun-wise four times, each cycle adding a color to the sunrise in the east until the time-worn sun emitted a potent ray of light. The violet-purple effusion shied away, becoming shadows of the day.

PART 2

Boarding and Residential Schools

The assimilated boarding-school graduate is epitomized in *Stiya: or, a Carlisle Indian Girl at Home* (1891), a work of fiction that provided Carlisle graduates with model attitudes and behaviors for returning home as educated young people. The novel also reveals what Leslie Marmon Silko (Laguna) called the "white perspective of Pueblo people" and the author's "projected [. . .] fears and prejudices." At first disgusted with her parents and home and everything Indian (chapters 1 and 2), Stiya decides to change them (chapter 3). Her project meets with success, as her father gets a job with the new railroad that brings tourists and business to the Southwest (chapters 15 and 16).

Stiya's promise of "untold satisfaction and happiness" for Carlisle boarding-school graduates was not kept for Black Bear ("Who Am I?"). His account creates a different portrait of the graduate, of one who suffers extreme emotional, physical, and spiritual damage, and whose identity and life are determined by the efforts he or she makes to overcome that damage.[1]

The boarding-school experience is also a subject for Native American fiction writers and poets. E. Pauline Johnson ("As It Was in the Beginning," 1913) reveals the racial hypocrisy beneath the false promise of assimilative education. In her fictive boarding-school experience, Esther is treated well and with seeming affection. She is the pet project of Father

Paul, who promised her Cree father to make her a "noble woman" and to save her from hell. For fourteen years her education prepared her for noble womanhood in Fr. Paul's terms, but when she is ready to assume that status by marrying Laurence, Fr. Paul's protégé and nephew, she overhears him tell Laurence he cannot marry her, because one "never can tell what lurks in *a caged animal that has once been wild.*" Esther, Fr. Paul says, reminds him of a "*snake.*" The dichotomy of Western views of women and of the noble-ignoble Native informs Fr. Paul's view of Esther's potential for nobility and wildness, which in turn determines her concept of self and her future. Fr. Paul has created for her a hell worse than that from which he had promised to save her.

The importance of language in the replacement of Indian culture "cannot be overstated," according to the Royal Commission on Aboriginal Peoples: "The entire residential school project was balanced on the proposition that the gate to assimilation was unlocked only by the progressive destruction of Aboriginal languages" (Canada, *Report* 1.10.1). Yet in "Black Robes" (1996), her grandmother will not let the young Lee Maracle speak her own language. Her advice to the girl is to "Master their language, daughter; hidden within it is the way we are to live among them." From that directive the writer's work grows.

Some of the most horrific punishments were given for speaking tribal language, since language, after all, is the chief repository of culture and collective memory. The prisoner in Gordon D. Henry, Jr.'s "The Prisoner of Haiku" (1992) suffers brutal attempts to force his language from him, and as a result he is silenced. Education has taken his voice, but not the consciousness behind that voice, which escapes the confinement of muteness and finds expression through his hands and through his "artful crimes." Further silenced in prison, he learns to write the poetry of dream songs and haiku, which stream from him and carry him through to a strange yet fitting end, in which his own poetry serves as the defining source of meaning and understanding at last.

Luci Tapahonso's "The Snakeman" (1993) sketches the night world of a young girls' dormitory. The girls' imaginations—not the curriculum—enable them to piece together their own lore, beliefs, and family-imparted wisdom to handle their fears and loneliness. They are learning very well, confined at school, how to take good care of each other.

Joy Harjo's poem "The Woman Who Fell from the Sky" (1994) tells the story of Johnny and Lila, who went separate ways after boarding school but were reunited in the parking lot of a Safeway store, when Lila fell from the sky world into Johnny's arms. Johnny's luck had changed and Lila's destiny had come to pass, and the poem enacts what boarding school had not destroyed: the strength of survivorship in him, and in her, the capacity for the old stories to be relived.

From *Stiya: or, a Carlisle Indian Girl at Home*

EMBE (MARIANNA BURGESS)

Chapter 1: Disappointment

When I was told at Carlisle that I could go to my home in the West—a place I had not seen for five years—I was truly delighted; and all the time I was packing my trunk, and all the way while we, a merry party of forty Indian girls and boys, all going home, were laughing and having a good time, at every thought of home and mother and father and the friends I should find on my arrival, my heart gave a great thump of joy.

After five days and nights of travel, every mile of which I enjoyed, for we were so very comfortable in the cars, and we saw so many interesting things which then I could understand about, in the middle of one hot afternoon the train stopped at the station at which I was to get off, and I realized that I was at the end of my railroad journey.

My father and mother, who were at the station waiting for their daughter, rushed in my direction as soon as they saw me, and talking Indian as fast as they could tried to help me from the train.

My father took my valise, and my mother, seizing me by the arm, threw her head upon my shoulder and cried for joy.

Was I as glad to see them as I thought I would be?

I must confess that instead I was shocked and surprised at the sight that met my eyes.

"*My* father? *My* mother?" cried I desperately within. "No, never!" I thought, and I actually turned my back upon them.

I had forgotten that home Indians had such grimy faces.

I had forgotten that my mother's hair always looked as though it had never seen a comb.

I had forgotten that she wore such a short, queer-looking black bag for a dress, fastened over one shoulder only, and such buckskin wrappings for shoes and leggings.

"*My* mother?" I cried, this time aloud.

I could not help it, and at the same time I rushed frantically into the arms of my *school*-mother, who had taken me home, and I remembered then as I had never before how kind she had always been to us. I threw my arms around her neck and cried bitterly, and begged of her to let me get on the train again.

"I cannot go with that woman," I pleaded.

My school-mother, in a voice so tender I shall never forget, said, "My dear girl, you must stop crying. You must not feel in this way towards your own parents. This is your mother. She loves you. You will get used to her ways by and by. Come, now," she continued, trying to withdraw from my embrace, "be a woman! Make the best of these people, and go to your mother. Go, *now*, to your mother. Shake hands with her as a dutiful daughter should."

Almost broken hearted, I did as I was bid, for I knew nothing else than to obey my school-mother.

I also took my father's hand, and through my tears smiled as best I could; but he never shall know how I suffered with mortification and regret that he was such an Indian.

Somehow, I had my mind made up that my parents would be different, and it was hard for me to realize that they had been going backward while I had been going forward for five years.

By this time the locomotive bell began to ring, and my school-mother stepped aboard the train.

Soon she and the coach full of school companions I had left passed out of sight, and as I gazed after them, my eyes thoroughly blinded with tears, my heart felt heavy with sadness.

"Oh, my! Oh, my!" I sighed; "what have I come to?"

[. . .]

Chapter 2: My Home

The landing at the top of the ladder was the flat roof of the house underneath ours.

This roof had been covered with dirt, which had in time become thoroughly packed and almost as hard as flagging, so it really formed a stone-like balcony to our house.

There was no railing around it, and I don't see how the Indians manage to keep their babies from falling from the tops of these houses. There are many in the village just like ours, and in many there are more children than at our house.

There were only six of us children, every one of whom, except myself, died when quite small of the small-pox and diphtheria, and at the time of which I am writing I wished that I had gone with the rest.

[. . .]

My mother, after making the fire, took down a piece of meat from a line.

It was mutton, and had been cut very thin and hung up on the line to dry, as people in civilized countries hang their clothes on lines to dry.

The line was stretched across the room from side to side, and was full of meat.

Flies?

If I should say that a million flies flew from the meat when my mother shook the line you would think that I was not telling the truth, but there were certainly thousands upon thousands of them.

But, then, *that* was nothing.

My father and mother and the visiting Indian didn't care how many flies roosted upon the meat, so that they did not eat it up, and they didn't.

The piece that my mother tore was about as large as two dinner plates and as thin.

This she broke up into smaller pieces and pounded with a stone into quite fine threads, and then she put it into a stew pan and stewed it.

The stew, with tea and some Indian bread baked the day before, made up our supper.

Had I not watched the supper being prepared, had it been placed on a table instead of on the floor at our feet, I might have felt like eating.

I was hungry, but could not eat; and excusing myself with a headache went outside and stood on the balcony, stood there in the bright moonlight and pure clear air, and thought.

All was still as death.

There were no lights in any of the houses.

In the moonlight I could see human beings stretched on blankets on the tops of adjoining houses.

They thus come out in the cool air to sleep and escape the vermin inside of their filthy abodes.

I know not how long I stood there, thinking, thinking, oh, I cannot tell what, so much passed through my mind, and I was so desperately homesick for Carlisle; but I was awakened finally from my reverie by my father and the man with him coming from the room.

They did not seem to notice me, for which I was thankful, but descended the ladder and passed out of sight.

Then I went into the house, found my mother had pushed the dishes back in the corner with the general heap by the fire-place, and was placing blankets on the floor ready for the night.

The light in the room was poor, only that which the few burning sticks on the fire-place gave out.

The room was full of tobacco smoke, my father and the Indian with him having smoked several cigarettes after supper, and there were odors of meat and supper enough to stifle one, but there was only one window, which was rarely ever opened, and the door and the fire-place for ventilation.

My mother was a small woman and very quick in her movements, so she soon had the beds ready.

Mine, I could see, was given an extra blanket or two and a soft sheepskin.

It was made in the corner of the room farthest from my father's and mother's bed.

Chapter 3: Unsettled

My father soon returned. After smoking another cigarette, and talking a few minutes, he curled down in his nest for the night.

Neither my father nor mother minded the thick air, and were soon sound asleep.

How I did want a bath before going to bed, and as I wished, again the memory of the first night at Carlisle came to me. How they put me into a large bath-tub, combed my hair, and put me to bed between two clean white sheets. I did not appreciate the kind treatment then.

Then I was lonesome for this very place that now I was loathing with all my heart.

As I lay on the hard floor, for all the blankets they gave me and the sheepskin did not seem to make it soft,—as I lay there, not a wink of sleep coming to my tired eyes, I thought and discussed and planned thus:—

"Would that I had never been at school!

"Would I had never learned better ways. It makes it harder for me to endure this life now."

A moment after I heard myself saying, "I do not wish anything of the kind. I am glad I went away to school. I would not take the world for what I learned at dear old Carlisle.

"No, indeed! I have so much at least, and no one can ever take away from me what I have learned.

"But, oh! oh! this horrid smoke!

"This dreadful air. My head! my head! It will surely burst."

I tossed and turned from one side of my hard bed to the other, thinking one minute that schools were a good thing for the Indians, and the next moment thinking they were not.

"Yes, they are of use, especially those far away from our homes," I concluded.

"I never in the world would have learned to be disgusted at this way of living, had I not been taken clear away from it, where I could not see it, nor hear anything about it for years.

"Some people think for that very reason schools away from home are not so good as schools at home.

"They think we ought to stay near to this filth, this dirt. I suppose they think it is good enough for us. Thank God, however, there are some people who think we should have as good a chance as children of other races.

"I am thankful I had a chance to get away from this, if only for a little while.

"We *must* learn to feel disgust for these things. If we have no disgust for them we will never try to make them better.

"We MUST be disgusted, I say, and I *am* thoroughly disgusted this moment at the way the Indians live, if *this* is the way they live. I know, however, that some live in great deal worse houses than this.

"I can make this place better.

"I must make home more pleasant.

"But, pshaw! What is the use?

"My mother don't care. My father is satisfied with things as they are.

"I don't care if he is satisfied, *I* am not, and there MUST be a change. I will show them a better way of living than this."

[. . .]

Chapter 15: True Courage

My mother arose, and went to the door.

"I hear nothing and see nothing of him," she said. "Why doesn't he come back?"

Going also to the door, I laid my arm gently over her shoulder, while we both stood peering out into the night.

[. . .]

Should I go in search of him?

I went back for my coat, but when in the room my better judgment said:—

"Foolish girl! go to bed!"

I did so, but could not sleep.

Hour after hour passed, and finally the morning began to dawn.

"Oh, father, father; where are you?" I was saying, when he entered the door.

I sprang to my feet and rushed into his arms, crying, "Where have you been? I have not slept a wink, fearing that harm had come to you; and mother, too, has been anxious. Why, how black your face is, and your hands! Father, dear, what have you been doing?"

His eyes fairly glistened with pleasure as he answered, "Shoveling coal."

I could scarcely believe my ears.

"Shoveling coal? Why, father, where is there any coal around here to shovel? Who has coal to shovel?" I asked.

"The man at the station," he replied.

"Where? the railroad station ten miles away?"

"Yes," he said.

"You walked all that distance, then shoveled coal, and after that walked back? It is too much, and I am afraid you will get sick."

"I have danced all night many a time, and didn't get sick. I ought to be able to work as well as dance, eh? And here is a dollar to help pay for the new house," said he, proudly holding up the money.

"I remember the man at the station. He has a kind face," said I.

"But you should have seen him look at me when I went in last night and asked for work," said my father.

"What, you?" he said.

"Yes," I replied. "Can't you hire me to help shovel coal, like the man I see working out in the shed?"

"I thought you cared for nothing but dancing."

"I have given that up."

"What does all this mean?" he asked.

"My daughter has come home from Carlisle. I want to make money quick. I must have a better house for her to live in."

"You never shoveled coal, did you?"

"No," I replied, "but I believe I can."

"I need a man," he said. "I will pay you well if you work well."

"That was all I wanted," and he took a lantern, and showed me what to do. Train after train came in and took the coal from the bin, and it was my work to fill up. Here is the dollar I earned last night. Put it in your trunk, and to-night I will get another, maybe. We shall soon have our new house, shan't we?" said he, looking as delighted as any boy.

And to think that it was *my father* talking such good common sense,— the man whom I did not want to own as father when I first met him on my return home, at that very station!

I did not see his Indian dress now. Not even his coal-blacked face disturbed me.

My father had never been to school a day, yet behind his black eyes and down deep in his heart, I saw in him the spirit which we at Carlisle had been so earnestly advised to cultivate,—COURAGE!

Chapter 16: Results

We had many other seemingly insurmountable difficulties to encounter in our progress up the hill of Right, but we soon found friends to help us conquer some of our troubles.

My father continued to work and save his money until he had earned enough to build a comfortable adobe house with three rooms.

He adopted the civilized dress, with the exception of wearing short hair.

Although my mother never would change her Indian dress for one like mine, she was pleased to work as I did, and kept her house and the dishes nice and clean.

I worked with the trader's family until I had enough money saved to buy necessary furnishings for the house.

A few years after we were in the new home, two of my Carlisle teachers came out to New Mexico upon business for the school.

They stayed in our house, slept in my bed, now an ash wood double-bed, and made up with as clean white sheets as they had at Carlisle.

My teachers praised the Carlisle pictures and others which adorned the wall, and spoke well of the appearance of our best room, with its centre-table and rocking-chair and other furniture.

When they saw my cousin's little girls wearing nicely made dresses and aprons, and the little boys in good fitting suits, all made by me on my new sewing-machine; when they ate the bread and cake and pie I baked, and the meat and eggs and potatoes and cabbage and other good things I prepared and set before them on a table, spread with a clean tablecloth (a real one), and had napkins, too, they seemed so delighted that I felt more than repaid for the hard times I had passed through.

And, indeed, I have never regretted having braved the first hard steps that led me out of the accursed home slavery and made me a free woman.

If every returned girl could resist the first efforts of her home friends to drag her back into the old Indian ways, and make them feel in a kind but decided way that they were no longer right for her, she would eventually enjoy untold satisfaction and happiness.

Who Am I?

BLACK BEAR

Who am I? I am a Blackfeet Indian from Montana. I am more Cree than Blackfeet, and I hardly look Indian, but I am an enrolled Blackfeet. I am not quite half Indian—some French, Irish, and Scottish too. I was my Grandpa's Blackfeet Indian boy. That is all I ever knew.

I am a little boy who grew up with drinking and fighting all around him. I remember the sounds of beer bottles hitting the wall. I remember my father thrusting his fist through a glass door in a drunken rage because my mother had tried to lock him out—shattered glass and blood were all over the floor. I remember loud angry voices and the terror of silence, waiting, for the next act of violence. My mother was beautiful with dark brown hair and hazel eyes. She liked laughter, hot jazz, and good times. She dressed in expensive clothes and preferred Chanel #5— most say she was a very classy lady. My father was good looking and a star basketball player. He liked pretty women and he lived fast and fought hard. My mother and father drank and partied all the time. Pretty soon they drank and fought each other. Then I had many step-fathers and stepmothers. Drinking and fighting is what I remember most about growing up. That is all I ever knew.

I developed a bone disease in my right hip when I was six. I was in and out of hospitals, on crutches and braces. I spent two years in a hospital in Helena, Montana. I wasn't sick; I had all the energy of any six-year-old. They strapped me to a metal frame with a canvas covering to keep the weight off my hip. The nurses were mostly kind, but they could not nurture me. I don't remember my mother coming to visit very often, and I never remember my father coming at all. I remember looking out the window, watching other kids play, and crying. Dying cancer and tuberculosis patients were in the next wing. I remember the screams at night. I remember being scared, and my skin yearned for a comforting, loving, and nurturing touch. I remember going inside to entertain myself, for eternity. That is all I ever knew.

I am a boarding school Indian. When I say this, you *know* something about me already. I had work details, slopped dishes, mopped and polished floors. I scrubbed toilet bowls and scoured sinks. Memories of nights on hard bunks still haunt me—a scared little kid, eyes wide open in the dark. One night a big boy came to my bed. He told me that if I told, he would hurt me good. He did—pain of penetration, stifled screams, and "lost innocence." The dorm attendant kicked our asses up the stairs if we didn't move fast enough. The kind war vet with the slow mind used to take us upriver and show us how to make fire and boil coffee—the best I ever tasted. That is all I ever knew.

I survived on the streets of Portland, Spokane, Cut Bank, and Browning. My parents still drank. I lost count of how many stepfathers and stepmothers I had. I lived in many foster homes, mostly with white folk. Some were good to me, and some were not. They needed money, and a few needed an extra hand with the work. They did not teach me about being a good Indian boy, but they did teach me how to survive in the cities among non-Indian peoples. Once my father came home drunk and beat up a woman he was with. She whacked him with a vacuum cleaner hose. I knocked on the ceiling with my crutches to signal the neighbors upstairs to call the police. The police came. They took my father away to jail. The woman took off. The neighbors went home. The social workers put me in a detention home for six months, because they didn't know what else to do with me. My father came to see me once. He was drunk. I told him that I didn't want to see him anymore when he was drunk. That is all I ever knew.

I went back to boarding school in Montana. I was older now, but it was the same old stuff. Only now the fights were over whether I could speak Blackfeet or whether I knew my Indian ways—and I was teased because I did not. The ones who did know were called blanket-asses and teased or beat up anyway. You weren't supposed to know your ways or speak your language in those days. I went to high school in Browning. I began to drink and party and found I liked women just like my father did. I stayed in town on weekends with my dad at the old Yeagan Hotel. He was still drinking. He slapped me once when I told him that I hadn't been drinking that night. "Don't lie to me, boy!" he said with stale booze breath. During my sophomore year I met a pretty girl at a river party in Cut Bank. We got real interested in each other. When I told my dad, he said "No. No. She is your sister!" "Oh!" I said, "you never told me about my sister." That is all I ever knew.

I left Browning and went to Haskell when it was still a high school. It was pretty good: three squares and a roof over my head for more than a year at a time were new to me. There were over a thousand students from many different tribes at Haskell. Today I have relatives anywhere I go. It feels good. I received a full National Merit Scholarship to the University of Kansas. I felt lucky as I had no other hope of going to college. My father had a year's sobriety when he came down to my graduation. I was very happy and proud that he was there, but he got drunk and thrown in jail. He didn't come to the graduation. That is all I ever knew.

At Kansas, they gave me all of my scholarship money at the beginning of each semester! I learned how to shoot pool pretty well, and I learned how to play a good hand of cards. I liked to party, and I still liked women. I ran out of money before I flunked out. After I left school and worked for a while, I came back to Kansas and played even harder. Then I got a rancher's daughter pregnant. That is all I ever knew.

As a new father, I tried to be responsible for the first time in my life. I worked at whatever I could find for eight years before returning to Kansas. This time I worked for my degree during the day and worked at night to support my family. I graduated—first in my family! I became a bureaucrat with the federal government. I had muttonchop sideburns and wore wingtip shoes and pinstripe suits. That was the American dream, wasn't it? I drank more and more and ran around on my wife. For me, "Indian affairs" wasn't about politics or the BIA. I played and drank hard. I hurt many people and lost wives number one and number two and three wonderful children. Now I was just like my parents. That is all I ever knew.

I quit drinking in Tucson, many years later. I had gone to a four-day Indian golf tournament in Phoenix. Stayed drunk the whole time. When I drove home, my bones ached. I quit cold. They call me a dry-drunk because I never went to treatment. I was sober, but not healed. I looked around me. I didn't like my job. I didn't like my friends; we just drank together. I didn't like myself. I knew that I had hurt many people and was not a responsible person—to myself, to my family, as an Indian person, or to my community. I realized that the world would be a sorry place to live in if everyone was like me. That is all I ever knew.

I quit a promising career and good money and left Tucson to start over in life—sober. I consulted for different tribal groups for several years. I married a Pueblo woman and went back to school. Also, I learned how to make pottery. I sat on the plaza in Santa Fe for four years selling my wares and *paying my dues*. But I still had not dealt with my addictive behaviors. I was still toking so I wasn't clean, nor had I lost my love for women. I lost wife number three. This time I *felt* the loss. That is all I ever knew.

I met some Lakota friends who began taking me to sweats and teaching me about spirituality and responsibility. I stopped toking and got clean. I went home to Montana to learn about my own ways. It is not easy to humble yourself in your mid-forties and tell "elders" who are fifteen years younger, "I am ignorant but I want to learn!" I learned about Blackfeet teachings, language, and songs. I was brought out from behind the barrier at the Sun Dance and given my Blackfeet name in ceremony. I now had a Blackfeet identity. The name was given to my father by his father. I have the right to give the name Black Bear to my son, and it has dignity. Today I have a good relationship, a garden, and a *home*. Yes, I know what the Gallup drunk tank smells like. I experienced and survived boarding school. I understand the pain of abandonment. I know the terror of sexual abuse. I understand the shame of not being a good parent. However, now I try to be a good person and use my experience and understanding to help others. *Now I know what I never knew.* I know who I am, and it is all I ever knew.

Thank you, Creator.

As It Was in the Beginning

E. PAULINE JOHNSON

They account for it by the fact that I am a Redskin, but I am something else, too—I am a woman.

I remember the first time I saw him. He came up the trail with some Hudson's Bay trappers, and they stopped at the door of my father's tepee. He seemed even then, fourteen years ago, an old man; his hair seemed just as thin and white, his hands just as trembling and fleshless as they were a month since, when I saw him for what I pray his God is the last time.

My father sat in the tepee, polishing buffalo horns and smoking; my mother, wrapped in her blanket, crouched over her quill-work, on the buffalo-skin at his side; I was lounging at the doorway, idling, watching, as I always watched, the thin, distant line of sky and prairie; wondering, as I always wondered, what lay beyond it. Then he came, this gentle old man with his white hair and thin, pale face. He wore a long black coat, which I now know was the sign of his office, and he carried a black leather-covered book, which, in all the years I have known him, I have never seen him without.

The trappers explained to my father who he was, the Great Teacher, the heart's Medicine Man, the "Blackcoat" we had heard of, who brought peace where there was war, and the magic of whose black book brought greater things than all the Happy Hunting Grounds of our ancestors.

He told us many things that day, for he could speak the Cree tongue, and my father listened, and listened, and when at last they left us, my father said for him to come and sit within the tepee again.

He came, all the time he came, and my father welcomed him, but my mother always sat in silence at work with the quills; my mother never liked the Great "Blackcoat."

His stories fascinated me. I used to listen intently to the tale of the strange new place he called "heaven," of the gold crown, of the white dress, of the great music; and then he would tell of that other strange place—hell. My father and I hated it; we feared it, we dreamt of it, we trembled at it. Oh, if the "Blackcoat" would only cease to talk of it! Now I know he saw its effect upon us, and he used it as a whip to lash us into his new religion, but even then my mother must have known, for each time he left the tepee she would watch him going slowly away across the prairie; then when he was disappearing into the far horizon she would laugh scornfully, and say:

"If the white man made this Blackcoat's hell, let him go to it. It is for the man who found it first. No hell for Indians, just Happy Hunting Grounds. Blackcoat can't scare me."

And then, after weeks had passed, one day as he stood at the tepee door he laid his white, old hand on my head and said to my father: "Give me this little girl, chief. Let me take her to the mission school; let me keep her, and teach her of the great God and His eternal heaven. She will grow to be a noble woman, and return perhaps to bring her people to the Christ."

My mother's eyes snapped. "No," she said. It was the first word she ever spoke to the "Blackcoat." My father sat and smoked. At the end of a half-hour he said:

"I am an old man, Blackcoat. I shall not leave the God of my fathers. I like not your strange God's ways—all of them. I like not His two new places for me when I am dead. Take the child, Blackcoat, and save her from hell."

The first grief of my life was when we reached the mission. They took my buckskin dress off, saying I was now a little Christian girl and must dress like all the white people at the mission. Oh, how I hated that stiff new calico dress and those leather shoes! But, little as I was, I said nothing, only thought of the time when I should be grown, and do as my mother did, and wear the buckskins and the blanket.

My next serious grief was when I began to speak the English, that they forbade me to use any Cree words whatever. The rule of the school was that any child heard using its native tongue must get a slight punishment. I never understood it, I cannot understand it now, why the use of my dear Cree tongue could be a matter for correction or an action deserving punishment.

She was strict, the matron of the school, but only justly so, for she had a heart and a face like her brother's, the "Blackcoat." I had long since ceased to call him that. The trappers at the post called him "St. Paul," because, they told me, of his self-sacrificing life, his kindly deeds, his rarely beautiful old face; so I, too, called him "St. Paul," though oftener "Father Paul," though he never liked the latter title, for he was a Protestant. But as I was his pet, his darling of the whole school, he let me speak of him as I would, knowing it was but my heart speaking in love. His sister was a widow, and mother to a laughing yellow-haired little boy of about my own age, who was my constant playmate and who taught me much of English in his own childish way. I used to be fond of this child, just as I was fond of his mother and of his uncle, my "Father Paul," but as my girlhood passed away, as womanhood came upon me, I got strangely wearied of them all; I longed, oh, God, how I longed for the old wild life! It came with my womanhood, with my years.

What mattered it to me now that they had taught me all their ways?— their tricks of dress, their reading, their writing, their books. What mattered it that "Father Paul" loved me, that the traders at the post called me pretty, that I was a pet of all, from the factor to the poorest trapper in the service? I wanted my own people, my own old life, my blood called out for it, but they always said I must not return to my father's tepee. I heard them talk amongst themselves of keeping me away from pagan influences; they told each other that if I returned to the prairies, the tepees, I would degenerate, slip back to paganism, as other girls had done; marry, perhaps, with a pagan—and all their years of labor and teaching would be lost.

I said nothing, but I waited. And then one night the feeling overcame me. I was in the Hudson's Bay store when an Indian came in from the north with a large pack of buckskin. As they unrolled it a dash of its insinuating odor filled the store. I went over and leaned above the skins a second, then buried my face in them, swallowing, drinking the fragrance of them, that went to my head like wine. Oh, the wild wonder of that wood-smoked tan, the subtilty of it, the untamed smell of it! I drank it into my lungs, my innermost being was saturated with it, till my mind reeled and my heart seemed twisted with a physical agony. My childhood recollections rushed upon me, devoured me. I left the store in a strange, calm frenzy, and going rapidly to the mission house I confronted my Father Paul and demanded to be allowed to go "home," if only for a day. He received the request with the same refusal and the same gentle sigh that I had so often been greeted with, but *this* time the desire, the smoke-tan, the heartache, never lessened.

Night after night I would steal away by myself and go to the border of the village to watch the sun set in the foothills, to gaze at the far line of sky and prairie, to long and long for my father's lodge. And Laurence— always Laurence—my fair-haired, laughing, child playmate, would come calling and calling for me: "Esther, where are you? We miss you; come in, Esther, come in with me." And if I did not turn at once to him and follow, he would come and place his strong hands on my shoulders and laugh into my eyes and say, "Truant, truant, Esther; can't *we* make you happy?"

My old child playmate had vanished years ago. He was a tall, slender young man now, handsome as a young chief, but with laughing blue eyes, and always those yellow curls about his temples. He was my solace in my half-exile, my comrade, my brother, until one night it was, "Esther, Esther, can't *I* make you happy?"

I did not answer him; only looked out across the plains and thought of the tepees. He came close, close. He locked his arms about me, and with my face pressed up to his throat he stood silent. I felt the blood from my heart sweep to my very finger-tips. I loved him. O God, how I loved him! In a wild, blind instant it all came, just because he held me so and was whispering brokenly, "Don't leave me, don't leave me, Esther; *my* Esther, my child-love, my playmate, my girl-comrade, my little Cree sweetheart, will you go away to your people, or stay, stay for me, for my arms, as I have you now?"

No more, no more the tepees; no more the wild stretch of prairie, the intoxicating fragrance of the smoke-tanned buckskin; no more the bed of buffalo hide, the soft, silent moccasin; no more the dark faces of my people, the dulcet cadence of the sweet Cree tongue—only this man, this fair, proud, tender man who held me in his arms, in his heart. My soul prayed to his great white God, in that moment, that He let me have only this. It was twilight when we re-entered the mission gate. We were both excited, feverish. Father Paul was reading evening prayers in the large room beyond the hallway; his soft, saint-like voice stole beyond the doors, like a benediction upon us. I went noiselessly upstairs to my own room and sat there undisturbed for hours.

The clock downstairs struck one, startling me from my dreams of happiness, and at the same moment a flash of light attracted me. My room was in an angle of the building, and my window looked almost directly down into those of Father Paul's study, into which at that instant he was entering, carrying a lamp. "Why, Laurence," I heard him exclaim, "what are you doing here? I thought, my boy, you were in bed hours ago."

"No, uncle, not in bed, but in dreamland," replied Laurence, arising from the window, where evidently he, too, had spent the night hours as I had done.

Father Paul fumbled about for a moment, found his large black book, which for once he seemed to have got separated from, and was turning to leave, when the curious circumstance of Laurence being there at so unusual an hour seemed to strike him anew. "Better go to sleep, my son," he said simply, then added curiously, "Has anything occurred to keep you up?"

Then Laurence spoke: "No, uncle, only—only, I'm happy, that's all."

Father Paul stood irresolute. Then: "It is—?"

"Esther," said Laurence quietly, but he was at the old man's side, his hand was on the bent old shoulder, his eyes proud and appealing.

Father Paul set the lamp on the table, but, as usual, one hand held that black book, the great text of his life. His face was paler than I had ever seen it—graver.

"Tell me of it," he requested.

I leaned far out of my window and watched them both. I listened with my very heart, for Laurence was telling him of me, of his love, of the new-found joy of that night.

"You have said nothing of marriage to her?" asked Father Paul.

"Well—no; but she surely understands that—"

"Did you speak of *marriage?*" repeated Father Paul, with a harsh ring in his voice that was new to me.

"No, uncle, but—"

"Very well, then; very well."

There was a brief silence. Laurence stood staring at the old man as though he were a stranger; he watched him push a large chair up to the table, slowly seat himself; then mechanically following his movements, he dropped on to a lounge. The old man's head bent low, but his eyes were bright and strangely fascinating. He began:

"Laurence, my boy, your future is the dearest thing to me of all earthly interests. Why, you *can't* marry this girl—no, no, sit, sit until I have finished," he added, with raised voice, as Laurence sprang up, remonstrating. "I have long since decided that you marry well; for instance, the Hudson's Bay factor's daughter."

Laurence broke into a fresh, rollicking laugh. "What, uncle," he said, "little Ida McIntosh? Marry that little yellow-haired fluff ball, that kitten, that pretty little dolly?"

"Stop," said Father Paul. Then, with a low, soft persuasiveness, "She is *white*, Laurence."

My lover started. "Why, uncle, what do you mean?" he faltered.

"Only this, my son: poor Esther comes of uncertain blood; would it do for you—the missionary's nephew, and adopted son, you might say— to marry the daughter of a pagan Indian? Her mother is hopelessly uncivilized; her father has a dash of French somewhere—half-breed, you know, my boy, half-breed." Then, with still lower tone and half-shut, crafty eyes, he added: "The blood is a bad, bad mixture, *you* know that; you know, too, that I am very fond of the girl, poor dear Esther. I have tried to separate her from evil pagan influences; she is the daughter of the Church; I want her to have no other parent; but you never can tell what lurks in *a caged animal that has once been wild.* My whole heart is with the Indian people, my son; my whole heart, my whole life, has been devoted to bringing them to Christ, *but it is a different thing to marry with one of them.*"

His small old eyes were riveted on Laurence like a hawk's on a rat. My heart lay like ice in my bosom.

Laurence, speechless and white, stared at him breathlessly.

"Go away somewhere," the old man was urging; "to Winnipeg, Toronto, Montreal; forget her, then come back to Ida McIntosh. A union of the Church and the Hudson's Bay will mean great things, and may ultimately result in my life's ambition, the civilization of this entire tribe, that we have worked so long to bring to God."

I listened, sitting like one frozen. Could those words have been uttered by my venerable teacher, by him whom I revered as I would one of the saints in his own black book? Ah, there was no mistaking it. My white father, my life-long friend who pretended to love me, to care for my happiness, was urging the man I worshipped to forget me, to marry with the factor's daughter—because of what? Of my red skin; my good, old, honest pagan mother; my confiding French-Indian father. In a second all the care, the hollow love he had given me since my childhood, were as things that never existed. I hated that old mission priest as I hated his white man's hell. I hated his long, white hair; I hated his thin, white hands; I hated his body, his soul, his voice, his black book—oh, how I hated the very atmosphere of him!

Laurence sat motionless, his face buried in his hands, but the old man continued, "No, no; not the child of that pagan mother; you can't trust her, my son. What would you do with a wife who might any day break from you to return to her prairies and her buckskins? *You can't trust her.*" His eyes grew smaller, more glittering, more fascinating then, and leaning with an odd, secret sort of movement towards Laurence, he almost whispered, "Think of her silent ways, her noiseless step; the girl glides about like an apparition; her quick fingers, her wild longings—I don't know why, but with all my fondness for her, she reminds me sometimes of a strange—*snake.*"

Laurence shuddered, lifted his face, and said hoarsely: "You're right, uncle; perhaps I'd better not; I'll go away, I'll forget her, and then—well, then—yes, you are right, it *is* a different thing to marry one of them." The old man arose. His feeble fingers still clasped his black book; his soft white hair clung about his forehead like that of an Apostle; his eyes lost their peering, crafty expression; his bent shoulders resumed the dignity of a minister of the living God; he was the picture of what the traders called him—"St. Paul."

"Good-night, son," he said.

"Good-night, uncle, and thank you for bringing me to myself."

They were the last words I ever heard uttered by either that old archfiend or his weak, miserable kinsman. Father Paul turned and left the room. I watched his withered hand—the hand I had so often felt resting on my head in holy benedictions—clasp the door-knob, turn it slowly, then, with bowed head and his pale face wrapped in thought, he left the room—left it with the mad venom of my hate pursuing him like the very Evil One he taught me of.

What were his years of kindness and care now? What did I care for his God, his heaven, his hell? He had robbed me of my native faith, of my parents, of my people, of this last, this life of love that would have made a great, good woman of me. God! how I hated him!

I crept to the closet in my dark little room. I felt for a bundle I had not looked at for years—yes, it was there, the buckskin dress I had worn as a little child when they brought me to the mission. I tucked it under my arm and descended the stairs noiselessly. I would look into the study and speak good-bye to Laurence; then I would—

I pushed open the door. He was lying on the couch where a short time previously he had sat, white and speechless, listening to Father Paul. I moved towards him softly. God in heaven, he was already asleep. As I bent over him the fulness of his perfect beauty impressed me for the first time; his slender form, his curving mouth that almost laughed even in sleep, his fair, tossed hair, his smooth, strong-pulsing throat. God! how I loved him!

Then there arose the picture of the factor's daughter. I hated her. I hated her baby face, her yellow hair, her whitish skin. "She shall not marry him," my soul said. "I will kill him first—kill his beautiful body, his lying, false heart." Something in my heart seemed to speak; it said over and over again, "Kill him, kill him; she will never have him then. Kill him. It will break Father Paul's heart and blight his life. He has killed the best of you, of your womanhood; kill *his* best, his pride, his hope—his sister's son, his nephew Laurence." But how? how?

What had that terrible old man said I was like? A *strange snake*. A snake? The idea wound itself about me like the very coils of a serpent. What was this in the beaded bag of my buckskin dress? this little thing rolled in tan that my mother had given me at parting with the words, "Don't touch much, but some-time maybe you want it!" Oh! I knew well enough what it was—a small flint arrow-head dipped in the venom of some *strange snake.*

I knelt beside him and laid my hot lips on his hand. I worshipped him, oh, how, how I worshipped him! Then again the vision of *her* baby face, *her* yellow hair—I scratched his wrist twice with the arrow-tip. A single drop of red blood oozed up; he stirred. I turned the lamp down and slipped out of the room—out of the house.

I dream nightly of the horrors of the white man's hell. Why did they teach me of it, only to fling me into it?

Last night as I crouched beside my mother on the buffalo-hide, Dan Henderson, the trapper, came in to smoke with my father. He said old Father Paul was bowed with grief, that with my disappearance I was suspected, but that there was no proof. Was it not merely a snake bite?

They account for it by the fact that I am a Redskin.

They seem to have forgotten I am a woman.

Black Robes

LEE MARACLE

The children of our people must seek knowledge wherever life presents it. Black Robe was a new thing; thus, she was there in the green meadow where Mexica horses lolled about, clipping grass and enjoying the soft warmth of mother sun. Here, indeed, was something different. Wordlessly, she absorbed its newness.

Black Robe seemed agitated. He spoke fast, and later the girl learned from her father's account to her mother that he never repeated his listeners' words as we do (very rude). She heard everything Black Robe said only because her father spoke in the old way. He was careful to repeat Black Robe's words verbatim, to show respect for the speaker's vision of truth and to ensure that no misunderstanding or distortion of his words occurred. Then, her father answered him.

"There is only learning and knowledge, Black Robe. We do not deny our children knowledge. You say that you have teachers who will show my children how to live. Can you not see? Behind me sits my daughter, who is neither blind nor deaf nor imprisoned. She is free to seek knowledge among whomever she chooses to learn from. Her presence among adults indicates her desire to know. Hence, are we not obligated to give her our knowledge whenever she walks among us? You see her. She will have no need of interpreters if we continue to counsel, you and I. What need, then, has she of this place called 'school'?

"Her brothers and she can learn things that we cannot teach them, like medicine, sanitation, housekeeping and flight, you say." Her old father laughed. "When she grows wings and learns to fly, will she also acquire the beauty and sense of freedom of the eagle, the brazenness and wit of raven? Will her eyes see at night like owl? Black Robe, show me how you fly and my daughter will fly tomorrow; then, she will have no need of canoes. It takes a long time to build a bridal canoe.

"You say she will learn not flying, but different things than her brothers; that her brothers will learn about flying in something of their own making, not by themselves. In a glider, you say. That they will not actually make such a thing but only know of its existence. Of what use is such knowledge? You will fill my young men's minds with useless knowledge, Black Robe. You say my daughter will learn how to be a good Christian wife, to do a thing called read from deadwood leaves. What need has she to be a woman different than what she is? To kill trees and put marks on the deadwood leaves to remind her of how she must conduct herself? She is not lazy, nor is she forgetful. She is a good girl and will become a good woman. She will make a good wife—maybe Pierre's wife," he teased. She blushed and looked at the ground. Her old father chuckled sensuously.

Black Robe sucked in his breath. (I should not say this, nor even think it, but written on his face was exasperation, like when a young girl weaves her first basket and her fingers disobey the heart and will not weave it right.) The interpreter interjected, trying to bring depth to Black Robe's shallow vision of life. He tried to make the father and Black Robe see each other's point of view; to make them understand that there is no disagreement over the value of different (new) knowledge, but only a difference in how to learn—at home, or far away, with children from many different villages.

The interpreter is not speaker or listener, so neither Black Robe nor the father responded. But his words stayed with the young woman. She looked hard at the interpreter. She knew that her father would not relent. Her eyes tried to tell the interpreter that Black Robe was wasting his time. She wanted to save him more embarrassment. Soon the father would look upon his pleas as begging. No woman should sit and watch a man reduce himself to a beggar without first warning him. Black Robe was blind to the young woman's eyes and the interpreter dared not say what he thought he saw in the young woman's eyes.

Black Robe did not stop talking.

In the end, the father did not relent, but he invited Black Robe to counsel whomever he pleased. "Turn anyone around that you may, Black Robe." It was for her father a great and generous concession.

His prophecy about the young woman and the interpreter came to be. Pierre Deneuve, a man whose father came from a place called France and his mother from her own people, came to be her partner.

Partner. Husband in English. She learned to understand this immodest and mean language which has so many names for the same man; as though they were the land, not men from such-and-such a land. She never bothered to speak the language much, and, by the time I came to be it was hard for her to speak English.

In the warmth of her kitchen the soft tones of her voice touched my ears and gentled my raucous spirit. She brought me sadness but once in the multitude of after-school days I spent in her kitchen. I had learned not to query uselessly before I learned to speak. This day I mentioned all my great-grandmothers and how I would like to see them. She could not give me their presence; instead she gave me her story.

"Pierre tried to teach me all the new things he knew, but they never made sense." She winced and laughed mischievously. "He said that he was a Christian, a Catholic, an interpreter, a Half-breed, a worker, and not just Pierre. To me, he was always Pierre. The funniest thing he said was that he was a Roman Catholic. Rome is in a place called Italy—far away. How could he be from here and from Italy?"

She stopped laughing. Silent, gentle tears flowed from her tired eyes. "He made me send my children to school. All my babies, I knew them only while they were small. They came home men and women. So different were they from me. So many of their words grated on my being, foreign words, like Pierre's. So little did they speak their own language. Today, I am surrounded by the faces of our people speaking as the Black Robes spoke. In the faces of the children are written the characters of the people of the Black Robes. The laughter of my ancients died in the house that Pierre built.

" 'My brothers, my sisters are all dead from the Black Robes' disease or killed in their wars. How can you ask me to send my little ones to grace their presence and not shorten my own life with their smiles and their growth? Will you call me wife, yet deny me motherhood?' I asked him."

She said that Pierre had said a lot of nice things to ease her pain, but he sent the children. "Of what use were nice words? Was he standing at the precipice of our son's grave—my son—alcohol-crazed, screaming insane words at a room with deaf walls, in a dirty hotel, while alcohol ate the life from his body? No. The Black Robes' disease had already taken his life and it was I who had to bury my son. All mothers ever ask of life is to die before their children. I have buried four of mine. Worse, now I must bury my tiny little grandchildren."

She whispered in the language of the old people, a language she forbade me to speak lest the craziness of her sons and daughters who had died overtake me. Lest I have no one language but become a crippled two-tongue.

"Master their language, daughter; hidden within it is the way we are to live among them. It is clear that they will never go away. Every year more of them come. England, France, Wales—all must be terrible places, for they keep coming here to get away from there. I do not begrudge them a place here, but why do they have to bequeath to us the very things they escape from?"

It was like that in the 1950s in the wood-smoked kitchens of our grannies. I thought then that I would join the lonely march of six-year-old children going to grow up in the convent, missing my mom and unable to speak to my brothers. What a shock when school arrived and I was thrown not among Native children, but Europeans. The teacher was not a nun, but an ordinary white woman.

Back in my granny's kitchen I was in tears, complaining about not being with the other children. She watched me weep until a deep sense of the foolishness overtook me and stopped the flow of my tears. "You are fortunate. How else will we ever master the language and keep our ways unless we can learn among them and still live with our mothers and grandmothers? You are fortunate. How else will we learn to master their ways and still master the ancient art of motherhood unless we are schooled by them and our mothers too? Further, it is not our way to bring misery to others. Better to teach them to treat you as a human being ought to be treated than to come here making gifts of misery to an old woman who has done you no harm." Her silence spelled dismissal.

At age ten I stood at the edge of my granny's grave, surrounded by Europeans, and witnessed the burial of our ancient ways. I wondered if the birth of a new world founded on the coming together of both our histories was really possible. Would Europeans ever look at me and see an equal, not an aborted cripple but a human being with all my frailties, my separate history, and our common future? I would not have had such thoughts if the grandmothers of this land had not battered themselves with the question, mused aloud in the presence of their granddaughters.

Had mass death, tuberculosis, and the loss of our grandmothers' right to raise their young not have accompanied the development of Canada, the settlers would not have thought thus. Should we have been invited not as inferior sub-humans, but as people with a great contribution to make to the creation of a next nation, death would not haunt us as it does. More, our disappearance from the realm of history—the lingering realization that to most Canadians we do not exist—would not be our intimate agony.

Racism is an essential by-product of colonialism. That Europeans came here to escape something may be true, but it was not the real reason for erecting a colonial colossus all over the world. It was not the reason for the enslavement and importation of millions of African citizens to work our lands and build a meaner system than the world had ever known.

Europeans today see Natives without being able to imagine our grandmothers. They never see the old women who shaped our lives: the ankle-length flowered and paisley cotton skirts; the warm earth colours of their clothes; the kerchiefs and laughing eyes are lost to Europeans. They can never hear the soft tones of our grandmothers' ancient languages.

Europeans are blinded by Hollywood images. How sad. Not for me, but for them, as humanity is forever lost to those who would object to the colours and voices of the people of the past that have left their mark on the hearts and minds of the people of the present.

As a child I was humiliated by a string of teachers wearing brothel-tinted sunglasses. I was accused of sluttish behaviour by a moralizing principal whose assessment of me was guided by the colour of my skin rather than my character. Now that line of teachers looks pathetic and the poetry of T.S. Eliot burns new meaning onto the pages of my own book: "We are the hollow men / the stuffed men . . ."

I no longer weep for myself or the lost Europeans, but rather insist on writing myself into a new book that counts all of humanity on its tender, warm and colourful pages.

We are not an integrated people. We do not even co-exist peacefully. The reality of death still mangles our existence.

Black Widow-maker

Death hangs over us
like a black widow-maker
on a treeless mountainside.

A beleaguered army
caught in a valley
we thought green, lush
and teeming with life
        suddenly becomes a swamp
        full of alligators
        leeches, filth and disease

DIS-EASE

Caused more by the shame
of being fooled one more time.

In the darkness of our own
confusion we have forgotten
our reason for being.

In our grannies' kitchens, where the scent of wood smoke and sumptuous meals cooked over a thousand fires lingered in the unpainted walls and cupboards, that is where I learned the laws which enabled me to love my children. In my granny's kitchen, the sweet smells and gentle words soothed the aches and pains of a six-year-old growing up in a schizophrenic situation. Unlike in school, in my granny's kitchen I was not made to memorize or even contemplate the meaning of her words.

"You will remember what you need to know when the time comes."

Right then, it was the sunshine of her presence that I needed. Her radiance was neither finite nor momentary. It is this shower that I bequeath to my children.

Her love was not without discipline, but it did preclude violence. I searched her story for some parable, and after many years realized there was none. She could not give me my ancestors. I would have to find them myself. Not to let me walk away empty-handed, she gave me herself. She must have known I was desperate, for she never shamed me for begging. I was desperate, so desperate.

Before the fires of maddened Blacks burned their anger onto the face of a frightened white America and made it forever impossible to erase African-Americans, there was sleep. The sleep of fools who know what they do but don't think of the consequences of their actions. It was the sleep of an insipid historical continuum that repeated its idiocy, not just by force of habit, but because no one raised any objections.

Force is the midwife of historical change.

"It was the best of times and the worst of times . . ." We need only add, "and the stupidest of times," and we will have painted the prosperous '50s in the bleak colours of mass insensitivity and righteous, redneck practice. In the '50s there was no challenge. The Red "man" was vanquished—consigned to a kind of living purgatory in curio shops and tourist-trap trading posts. The Black "man" was reduced to a toe-tapping bundle of rhythm. (Black and Red women did not exist for anyone, yet.) All the Natives were happy, and working-class Europe-cum-CanAmerica was movin' on up.

> Before Rusty and Alexander Street,
> skid row and my children
> there was my grandmother.
> On the shore by the lakes
> and in the hills of our heritage,
> our grannies sat on deadwood logs
> behind the Black Robes
> and their fathers.

The Prisoner of Haiku

GORDON D. HENRY, JR.

He never saw himself as a prisoner, at least as far as I can know. And of course he carries another name, but I use the name "the prisoner" as a reference to the years he spent in prison for idealistic crimes. He received ten years for burning down liquor stores, federally funded enterprises, and other imposing white structures, on and around the Fineday reservation. Apparently, he lost his voice many years before that in a distant government boarding school. A few teachers in the school didn't like the way he continuously spoke his own native language in school, so they punished him. Two strong men with the force of God and Jesus who knows what else dragged him outside on a bitter wind-chilled Minnesota day and tied him to an iron post. They left him then without food, without water, through the night. Somehow the men believed the force of the cold, the ice hand of winter would reach out and take the boy by the throat and silence his native language. The other boys looked out the windows of their quarters, but they saw only tree shapes through snow slanting, as far as the light of the building let their eyes reach. Even so, they heard the punished boy screaming in defiance all night, defending the language, calling wind, calling relatives, singing, so he wouldn't forget. The screaming went on all night, and in the morning, on a bright winter day, when the school fathers went out to untie him, the boy could speak no more. No matter how fiercely or how often they beat him, the boy would not, could not speak. The teachers' tactic worked on the boy: He no longer spoke his native language. But the punishment went further, deeper than the imposition of social structure: The boy couldn't speak English either. When he opened his mouth to try, less than a whisper stirred air in an inaudible act of diminished physical volition. Boys who were close to him then said that though they heard nothing, they felt something: a coolness floated out of his mouth and went directly to their ears to the point where—the boys claimed—their hearing was frozen in time. That is, though they walked away from the boy with the frozen words, they felt the breath-held syllables melt in their heads later, in words of the Anishinaabe language, and still later in Native translations of circumstances and relationships that they never would have thought of without remembering the cold in their ears. Moreover, boys who went to the same boarding school, years later, testified to hearing Native words whirling up with every snow from sundown to sunrise in their winters at that place.

I know this: I slept in the ruins of the boarding school last December, waiting four nights for snow, and I heard the voice of the boy. What was spoken is untranslatable, immutable, subject to semantic contexts of pain most people can't fathom in the world in which they hear and speak. Yet the voice had a strength, a powerful resilience.

As for the boy, he drifted back to the reservation where he became a silent man of hands, a sculptor, then a political artist, an invidious communicator of visual forms. He made a living that way until he turned to acts of sabotage, for him another form of art. For the sabotage was never performed without the grace and idealism of an artist. When he burned liquor stores, when he burned federally funded structures, he mixed flammables so magnificently the buildings burned in colors and fireworks that left the reservation and nearby communities gasping "oh [incredulous] mys." One time his fire left a smoke that drifted into the shape of a human face. People who saw it swear the face was of an old one, the first bringer of light, or of one who floated in a stone white canoe. On another occasion his fireworks illuminated the night with the words "The Treaty of 1837." On the night of his greatest political burning, on the night of his seventh fire, on the night in which the flames reached up, exploding bottles, licking the dark with colors and room cracklings, on the night people gathered to see in the flames an old lodge, ancestors within the lodge, throwing melted clocks into the air, burning the country-and-western ambiance, of chairs and wall hangings, pointing to the melting jukebox, singing instead healing songs through that wasting machinery, to tell the people the lodge is still open, on that night the FBI found the silent man and arrested him among his cache of art materials in an abandoned barn near the state game refuge.

What could he do? Speak in his own defense? Nod his head with his hand on the Bible and convey the truth in a series of still-lifes, or antlered sculptures, for a jury who didn't understand his artistic aims? For a jury who had been selected by two lawyers, one of whom would represent him without knowing what he could say? He resorted to one last symbolic act. He made a shirt and painted the words "guilty" and "not guilty" on the front and back. Then just before he entered the courtroom, he put a cigarette in his mouth, gestured to his lawyer and pointed at the tip of the cigarette. When the lawyer gave him a light, however, he took off his shirt and crushed the tobacco of the cigarette onto the shirt and set it on fire with his lawyer's lighter. He went to Deepwater Prison after a one-week trial.

For years prison meant a series of drawings to this artistic warrior. With the permission of prison officials, the man made a series of historical murals on the walls of his cell. After two years and a few changes in the mural, prison officials pushed for inmate education. A lovely white humanist came into the school and taught a class on Oriental poetry. She explained the conceptual foundations of such work, the cultural orientation, the affinities between form and image, between isolation and universal vision. She taught the prisoners how to read and write haiku. The political artist adopted the form and wrote graceful passages that he passed on to the professor one evening before class. The professor carried the works with her on the commuter train the next morning and wept thick silver tears on a brown autumn day as the train passed through smoking urban neighborhoods. She advocated the prisoner's release, based on the beauty of his words. She passed his words on to poets and scholars, lawyers and radical political activists and the prison board. "The unusual nature of the man's crime," she was informed by the prison board, "stems from his unusual methods of producing forms that illustrate his personal conceptions of beauty, and to release him on the basis of his ability to produce beautiful words might reinforce his use of art to commit philosophically grounded crimes." For the final week of class the professor prepared a lesson aimed specifically at the Native prisoner. She introduced the class to translations of tribal dream songs. According to her, these songs carried the same intense brevity of some haiku and Zen koans. She hoped to make a connection for the prisoner: He could write haiku and they could be like dream songs for him; a culturally, politically appropriate act could be generated in a foreign form, from language to language, image to form. Obviously, the professor didn't understand the nature of the Native prisoner's criminal acts. What she hoped the prisoner would understand in the relationship between haiku and dream songs was deeply embedded in the prisoner's history. A partial loss of language, new forms, old forms were part of his existence before the professor gave him a final farewell kiss. This was the last connection she made with the prisoner since she failed to win his release. But the time in the class, the education the professor had given him, inspired the prisoner to write haikus and dream songs. And he wrote only in those forms, as he understood those forms. When he wrote letters home he wrote haiku letters; when he wrote prison officials he wrote in the language of dream songs; when he wrote editorials in Indian newspapers he wrote haikus; when he wrote old girlfriends he wrote in one form or the other. This went on for two years and became the prisoner's only form of communication. Still, he could not speak.

Then, through a cultural coup, a group of Native advocates for religious freedom convinced state prison authorities to allow Native spiritual leaders to come into the prison and conduct traditional ceremonies. Since the education program had been scrapped, the officials agreed. For over a year, spiritual leaders came into Deepwater to discuss Native culture and perform ceremonies. One elder spoke about oral history and prophecy; another discussed dancing and drumming; one talked of prayer and the sacred pipe. A fourth elder brought the sweat lodge into the prison. In time, the elders and one or two helpers from the outside conducted monthly sweat lodge ceremonies for the prisoners.

The Native prisoner participated in the ceremonies from the beginning. But in the first lodge when it came his turn to speak, another inmate had to explain to the elder, Samuel Little Boy, that the man could not speak, that he would pray in silence and pour water on the rocks, then pass the water bucket to signify the end of his personal prayer. At the end of that first sweat lodge ceremony, Little Boy spoke to the group, outside the sweat lodge. "This man," he said, nodding toward the prisoner of haiku, "he had to pray in silence here. And I know his story, why he doesn't speak, why he's in here, in this prison. A little while ago after we came out he handed me a note and he gave me tobacco. He wants to speak again. So in one month we will begin healing sweats for this man. Offer prayers for him until that time."

When Little Boy returned a month later, the sweat went on as planned, but the voice didn't come back then. So the group went on with Little Boy sponsoring one sweat a month, and each time they prayed for healing for the prisoner who could not speak. After three more ceremonies, he spoke, but the words were brief and breath soft.

> The earth embraces
> in song the blue sky
> moves one face after another.

Apparently the healing wasn't complete. And for four more healing sweats nothing changed. The prisoner spoke, but briefly, softly, always with the same syllabic rhythm, always in strange poetic words. Finally, another prisoner who had been in the poetry class remembered the haikus and the dream songs, and he realized those were the forms the man spoke in. When one of the Indian prisoners informed Little Boy about the ways and reasons for the political artist's speech, Little Boy suggested that the healing sweats continue until the prisoner could speak freely, beyond the limits of the literary forms he'd learned. Four more sweats produced nothing more, and Little Boy never came back to the prison. A Native newspaper ran Little Boy's obituary in January. He died on New Year's Day bringing wood into his home on the Fineday reservation.

No other elder picked up the spiritual traditions program for Deepwater Prison, and the Native prisoner spoke only in haikus and dream songs.

I made a point to find the man, to read his words, to hear his voice. Four years after he was granted parole, I met him on the reservation, at the Strawberry Inn bar. It took some time for me to adjust my vision when I entered the bar, but when I did my first glances stopped just short of amazement at the Indian artifacts and artwork in the place. Old photographic prints and drawings hung on the walls above booths at the rear end of the room. A variety of red pipestone pipes hung above the bar, reflected in a wide mirror behind a stand of hard liquor. Some pipes were carved into animal shapes of eagles and buffalo; some had plain red bowls with carved twisted stems; some stems were ornamented with feathers and beadwork. On both sides of the mirror simulated treaty documents covered the wall in glass cases. Human clay figures, about a foot tall—each unique, in facial features and physique, each marked with an engraved pictograph on the forehead—lined shelves above the treaties. Except for the bartender, there was only one other person in the place. He sat drinking at a stool, a few feet from a murmuring jukebox, examining the positions of balls on a pool table.

I spoke first. "I know you," I said. He looked my way for a moment, then lifted the bottle between his legs. "I'm here to see your writings, your drawings. I want to put them into a book," I went on. "I've talked to your brother, he said he would let you know that I was coming to see you."

> When the church bells ring
> the road to Rush Lake breaks off
> one cold crow calls there.

That was all he said before he got up from his stool and walked away. I didn't understand the meaning of it until later, when I watched the smoke gliding away from an introspective cigarette. I met him the next morning on the road to Rush Lake. He handed me a birchbark bundle and walked away on the road to the old grave houses.

Haikus and Dream Songs of Elijah Cold Crow

> The red horse eats
> from blowing weeds in human
> indulgence at dusk.

The river with a
missionary's name wears an
ice face at dawn.

Walls leave no company:
a man's shadow grows solitary
moon songs in a cell

So many sundown dogs
improvise on a bark fugue
running for machines

Names travel autumn
wind under the formation
of white cranes passing

Flammables in air
sculpted moment to moment
a heart hungry for home

A sky full of shapes
animals of days above
animals below

A dried flower lifts
then you too are gone away
wind over concrete

Let the girls sleep deep
in dandelion grass, let boys
explode from their skin

An old woman cries son
under uniformed photographs
the red hawk keens out

A leader mouths peace
on the bright road from Yellowhead
one thousand trees fall

Who will sing for whom
when he who sings for no one
must die singing

An old dancer whirls
on his bustle feathers shake
surrounding a cracked mirror

What has fallen to earth
this time has fallen to earth
in a whole fog.

Deer measures silence
between words and guns going off
again and again

The road to eternity
is closed by x's and y's
a roof between the eye and cloud

Prison guards sleepwalk
in a cancerous vista
of domestic quarrels

Travelers come out
of sun looking for Indian-
made real crafts real cheap

This one-eared woman
whose father slept with crow once
saw him turn to steel

The sweet upside-down
cake the radical's wife made
changes the dialogue

Anger comes and goes
one fire ant walking the tongue
to the back of the head

Tired of windows
the dull dead dream of cities
Santa Claus lights go out

Eagles nest in the refuge
uncle returns from Vietnam
a drunken shortstop misses a pop fly

A museum with two doors
one door out into the rain
a dark full bus leaves

He of the golden hand
metallurgical carnivore,
carnival god of grease

and meat grows great
until trickster finds
his racing heart.

Oh, you must agree
the words will hold to the end
meaning what they must

Save the fish with beer
one can funds anti-Indian
underprivileged drunks

Now the blue heron moves
striding twice over wet stones
lifting, twisting snakes

Two old ones in this
doorway of light calling come
down come down come down
from that high wall

Two crows rise from a
squashed possum breakfast
cawing in sun bands

Lips to skin under
squash-blossom necklace the day
holds no more for us

Bezhig, neezh, Andaykug
Awkeewanzee neeba, gee
weesinnin wabun

Church women speak out
Flower drives a new galaxy
to her father's funeral

Under the iron tracks
through dwindling space of closing eyes
(a bridge of panted names and years)

Then mother reaches out
picks up the golden cross on
the red Formica table

Winter comes for her
sings her death in the guild hall
a boy receives a blanket

In the moon of the
frozen doorknob, what looks good
takes part of your tongue

With many fathers
I leave my voice of the past
not speaking is not knowing

Hands gesture open
the space around the stone form
man, woman, child

Descended from stone
before the merging of clans
into treaty bands

In black and white, words
coordinates, rivers, lakes, mark
lines over red earth

Signatures, names, the
undersigned, with marks and lines
anglicized in print

Clan leaders, head men
scripted identities so
many with an x.

Andayk, Flatmouth, Sweet,
Minogeshig, Broken Tooth,
an x by the name.

On 59 a moose
lopes through wisps of prairie snow
lost but not afraid

Tracks of birds in dirt
hieroglyphs around stumps are
filling with warm rain

An oar in water
a hand lit by moonlight
journeys holding sky

The dream x of man
the woman in the chromosome
shadow into light

Smell of autumn smoke
trachoma drags away a child
in a fevered village

Name energy repose
before the blue gun reports
death on a distant hill

Winter lasts and kills
and graves can't be dug
by ordinary hands
with ordinary shovels

The heart runs on from an
essential terror, the news is
there is always news

Days are numbered
like numbered suns
sunlight gestures
into dust to a picture
near a radio

The dream x, old man
an immigrant at a station
waiting for his wounded son
an American shadow

Bear ascends the stairs
one golden glass from oblivious
to women problems

A boy painted himself
white and ran into a river

A boy painted himself black
and fasted out in the sun

A boy painted himself
yellow and rolled in the mud

A boy painted himself
red and white and black and yellow

Crossing Wind's stick is
invisible at the Megis Lake drum

Abetunge he who
inhabits his X mark
in the presence of ———.

The dream x draws us on. I cannot speak for Cold Crow, but his words have forced me from the page. I see how he returns to old forms, and in my references to documents, I hammer away at myself for thinking of myself, and an old drunken shadow builds another wall. In the dark I look for my hands and find windows beyond the fringes of light around my fingers. On the road a few memories wander away singing, their tracks filling with falling snow. This is who I am, a few photographs taken for a moment of truth, a few belongings wrapped in brittle paper, a few dead relatives away from my own road into the sun. And I don't want to think of Cold Crow anymore. He died where we all die, on the way to death, run down by a vehicle out of control. I went to find him on the road where he gave me his haiku manuscripts, and I found him there, frozen in a ditch, beyond wild wheel tracks. He was the subject of his own name, covered with winter crows feasting on his body. Of course they whirled away when I discovered him; of course I discovered him when they whirled away in great numbers. He had no eyes then. What I had to ask him ran wild with tears from my own eyes. "Cold Crow," I said to the dead body, "I understand now your name. I understand the dream songs, the haiku attempts. I understand this frozen road; the words will come back. They will return from the air and reform on distant lips." But Cold Crow had no lips; these too were taken by the voracious birds in a thousand bloody painful kisses. So I looked to the rest of the body. Everything was there. One hand rested on one breast, the fingers of that hand pinched at the tips, near an opening in his long black coat, as if Cold Crow stopped in oratory, gesturing to his heart as he referred to some deep truth without words. But there under his hand, inside the coat, were words on yellow notepaper.

A Final Dreamsong

a note to hold
the eyes open a hole
in the Fineday earth

make an x in the snow
where you saw me standing last

I am on this road
to town to find a gun
for my lips

make a circle in the snow
a prayer offering of tobacco

make this place
a prayer place

to each of the four directions
put flags of different colors
when the wind turns warm.

The Snakeman

LUCI TAPAHONSO

The child slid down silently and caught herself at the end of the fire escape. She eased herself down until she felt the cold, hard sidewalk through her slippers, then let go.

The night was clear and quiet. The only noise that could be heard was the echo of the child's footsteps in the moonlit alley behind the old brick buildings.

The little girls, watching her from the top floor of the dorm, swung the window screen in and out, catching it before it struck the window frame. They always talked about what would happen if the top hinges suddenly gave way, but they hadn't yet.

"Good thing it's spring," one of them said.

"She would freeze her toes off for sure," another answered.

"Shhh!" the biggest one hissed.

They whispered in lispy voices and someone on the other side of the room would only hear, "Ss . . . ss," hissing, and an occasional "Shut up!" The room was large with windows on three sides. The fire escape the child slid down was in the center of the north windows, which faced a big dark hill, its slope covered with huge round rocks and dry tumbleweeds.

Sometimes the dorm mother, who lived at the other end of the hall, would hear them giggling or running around. She would walk down the dark, shiny hall so fast that her housecoat would fly out behind her in billows. The girls would scurry to their beds, tripping over their long nightgowns, finally faking snores as she turned on the harsh, bright lights in each room. After she went back to her room, the children jumped up and down and laughed silently with wide, open mouths, and pounded little fists into their beds.

One of the girls whispered loudly, "She's coming back!" They all ran noiselessly to the window and watched the small figure coming. The little girl walked briskly with her hands in her housecoat pockets. She wore the soft wool slippers all the girls made for their sisters or mothers at Christmas. She didn't have sisters or a mother, so she wore them herself.

"Seems like she floats," one girl commented.

"How could she? Can't you hear her walking?" the biggest retorted.

The girls went back to their beds, and the ones closest to the fire escape opened the window and held it up until she was in. Then they all gathered at one bed and sat in the moonlight telling ghost stories or about how the end of the world was *really* going to be. Except for the girl who walked. She was quiet and always went right to sleep when she returned.

Sometimes late at night or toward morning when the sun hadn't come up completely, everything was quiet and the room filled with the soft, even breathing of the children; one of them might stand at the window facing east and think of home far away, tears streaming down her face. Late in the night, someone always cried, and if the others heard her, they pretended not to notice. They understood how it was with all of them— if only they could go to public school and eat at home everyday.

In the morning before they went downstairs to dress, two girls would empty their pockets of small torn pieces of paper and scatter them under the beds. The beds had white ruffled bed skirts that reached the floor and the paper bits weren't visible unless the bed skirt was lifted. This was how they tested the girl who swept their room. In the evenings, they checked under the beds to see if the paper was gone. If it wasn't, they immediately reported it to the dorm mother, who didn't ask how they were so sure their room hadn't been cleaned.

The building was divided into three floors and an attic. The youngest girls, who were in grade school, occupied the top and bottom floors, and the junior high girls had the middle floor. The bedrooms were on the top floor and all daytime activity took place on the bottom floor. The building was old, like all other buildings on campus, and the students were sure that the buildings were haunted. How could it not be? they asked among themselves. This was especially true for the little girls in the north end of the dorm because they were so close to the attic door. There was a man in there, they said in hushed voices, who kept the attic door open just a little, enough to throw evil powder on anyone who walked by. For this reason, they kept out of the hallway at night.

Once they had heard him coming down the stairs to the hallway door and the smaller girls started crying. They all slept two-to-a-bed, and the bigger girls made sure all the little ones had someone bigger with them. They stayed up later than usual, crying and praying. No one woke early enough to get everyone back to their own beds, and the dorm mother had spanked all of them. It was okay because nothing had happened to any of them that night, they said.

Once when the little girl went on one of her walks, the others were waiting for her as usual. Two girls were trying to figure out how to get to the bathroom down the hall when they heard scratching noises outside on the sidewalk.

"You guys! Come here! He's over here!" they whispered loudly. They ran to the west window and saw a dark figure go around the corner, and the biggest girl took control.

"You two get over by that window. You, on that side. Someone get on the fire escape, in case he tries to come up here."

They watched the man below and tried to get a description of him, in case someone asked them. They couldn't see him very well because he was on the shaded side of the building. Some of the girls started crying and others crawled quietly back into bed. Two of the bigger girls waited to open the window for the other girl. When she came back, they huddled around her and told her, crying a little. She said he was probably a father trying to see his daughter and maybe the mother won't let him see her. Then the girls calmed down and tried to figure out whose parents were divorced or argued a lot. They finally decided that he was the boyfriend of a junior high girl downstairs.

When a new girl came, she asked why the girl always walked at night and the biggest one had answered,

"Wouldn't you if you could see your mother every night, dummy?"

"Well, where's her mom? Can't she see her on weekends like us? That's not fair."

"Fair? *Fair?*" they had all yelled in disbelief.

Then the girl who walked explained that her parents had died years ago when she was six and that they were buried at the school cemetery. That's why she walked over to see them. Although she saw her mother more.

"How is she? Can she talk?"

"Can you really see her?" the new girl asked.

"Yeah," she answered patiently. "She calls me and waits at the edge of the cemetery by those small fat trees. She's real pretty. When she died, they put a blue outfit on her. A Navajo skirt that's real long, and a shiny, soft blouse. She waves at me like this, 'Come here, shiyázhí, my little one.' She always calls me that. She's soft and smells so good."

The girls nodded, each remembering their own mothers.

"When it's cold or snowing, I stand inside her blanket with her. We talk about when I was a baby or what I'll do when I grow up. She always worries about if I'm being good or not."

"Mine, too," someone murmured.

"Why do mothers always want their kids to be goody-good?"

"So you won't die at the end of the world, dummy!"

"Dying isn't that bad. You can still visit people like her mom does."

"But at the end of the world, all the dinosaurs and monsters that are sleeping in the mountains will bust out and eat all the bad people. No one can escape, either," said the oldest girl with confidence.

Then the little girl who talked to her mother every night said quietly, "No one can be that bad." She went to her bed and lay there looking at the ceiling until she fell asleep. The other girls gathered on two beds and sat in a circle and talked in tight, little voices about the snakeman who sometimes stole jewelry from them.

"You can't see him," one said, "'cause he's like a blur that moves real fast and you just see a black thing go by."

"He has a silver bracelet, and if he shines it on you, you're a goner 'cause it paralyzes."

They talked until they began looking around to make sure he wasn't in the room. The bigger girls slept with the little ones, and they prayed together that God wouldn't let the man in the attic or the snakeman come to them. They prayed that the world wouldn't end before their parents came to visit.

As the room became quiet and the breathing even and soft, the little girl got up, put on her housecoat, and slid soundlessly down the fire escape.

The Woman Who Fell from the Sky

JOY HARJO

Once a woman fell from the sky. The woman who fell from the sky was neither a murderer nor a saint. She was rather ordinary, though beautiful in her walk, like one who has experienced freedom from earth's gravity. When I see her I think of an antelope grazing the alpine meadows in mountains whose names are as ancient as the sound that created the first world.

Saint Coincidence thought he recognized her as she began falling toward him from the sky in a slow spin, like the spiral of events marking an ascension of grace. There was something in the curve of her shoulder, a familiar slope that led him into the lightest moment of his life.

He could not bear it and turned to ask a woman in high heels for a quarter. She was of the family of myths who would give everything if asked. She looked like all the wives he'd lost. And he had nothing to lose anymore in this city of terrible paradox where a woman was falling toward him from the sky.

The strange beauty in heels disappeared from the path of Saint Coincidence, with all her money held tightly in her purse, into the glass of advertisements. Saint Coincidence shuffled back onto the ice to watch the woman falling and falling.

Saint Coincidence, who was not a saint, perhaps a murderer if you count the people he shot without knowing during the stint that took his mind in Vietnam or Cambodia—remembered the girl he yearned to love when they were kids at Indian boarding school.

He could still see her on the dusty playground, off in the distance, years to the west past the icy parking lot of the Safeway. She was a blurred vision of the bittersweet and this memory had forced him to live through the violence of fire.

There they stood witness together to strange acts of cruelty by strangers, as well as the surprise of rare kindnesses.

The woman who was to fall from the sky was the girl with skinned knees whose spirit knew how to climb to the stars. Once she told him the stars spoke a language akin to the plains of her home, a language like rocks.

He watched her once make the ascent, after a severe beating. No one could touch the soul masked by name, age and tribal affiliation. Myth was as real as a scalp being scraped for lice.

Lila also dreamed of a love not disturbed by the wreck of culture she was forced to attend. It sprang up here and there like miraculous flowers in the cracks of the collision. It was there she found Johnny, who didn't have a saint's name when he showed up for school. He understood the journey and didn't make fun of her for her peculiar ways, despite the risks.

Johnny was named Johnny by the priests because his Indian name was foreign to their European tongues. He named himself Saint Coincidence many years later after he lost himself in drink in a city he'd been sent to to learn a trade. Maybe you needed English to know how to pray in the city. He could speak a fractured English. His own language had become a baby language to him, made of the comforting voice of his grandmother as she taught him to be a human.

Johnny had been praying for years and had finally given up on a god who appeared to give up on him. Then one night as he tossed pennies on the sidewalk with his cousin and another lost traveler, he prayed to Coincidence and won. The event demanded a new name. He gave himself the name Saint Coincidence.

His ragged life gleamed with possibility until a ghost-priest brushed by him as he walked the sidewalk looking for a job to add to his stack of new luck. The priest appeared to look through to the boy in him. He despaired. He would always be a boy on his knees, the burden of shame rooting him.

Saint Coincidence went back to wandering without a home in the maze of asphalt. Asphalt could be a pathway toward God, he reasoned, though he'd always imagined the road he took with his brothers when they raised sheep as children. Asphalt had led him here to the Safeway where a woman was falling from the sky.

The memory of all time relative to Lila and Johnny was seen by an abandoned cat washing herself next to the aluminum-can bin of the grocery story.

These humans set off strange phenomena, she thought and made no attachment to the thought. It was what it was, this event, shimmering there between the frozen parking lot of the store and the sky, something unusual and yet quite ordinary.

Like the sun falling fast in the west, this event carried particles of light through the trees.

Some say God is a murderer for letting children and saints slip through his or her hands. Some call God a father of saints or a mother of demons. Lila had seen God and could tell you God was neither male nor female and made of absolutely everything of beauty, of wordlessness.

This unnameable thing of beauty is what shapes a flock of birds who know exactly when to turn together in flight in the winds used to make words. Everyone turns together though we may not see each other stacked in the invisible dimensions.

This is what Lila saw, she told Johnny once. The sisters called it blasphemy.

Johnny ran away from boarding school the first winter with his two brothers, who'd run away before. His brothers wrapped Johnny Boy, as they called him, with their bodies to keep him warm. They froze and became part of the stars.

Johnny didn't make it home either. The school officials took him back the next day. To mourn his brothers would be to admit an unspeakable pain, so he became an athlete who ran faster than any record ever made in the history of the school, faster than the tears.

Lila never forgot about Johnny, who left school to join the army, and a few years later as she walked home from her job at Dairy Queen she made a turn in the road.

Call it destiny or coincidence—but the urge to fly was as strong as the need to push when at the precipice of any birth. It was what led her into the story told before she'd grown ears to hear, as she turned from stone to fish to human in her mother's belly.

Once, the stars made their way down stairs of ice to the earth to find mates. Some of the women were angry at their inattentive husbands, bored, or frustrated with the cycle of living and dying. They ran off with the stars, as did a few who saw their chance for travel and enlightenment.

They weren't heard from for years, until one of the women returned. She dared to look back and fell. Fell through centuries, through the beauty of the night sky, made a hole in a rock near the place Lila's mother had been born. She took up where she had left off, with her children from the stars. She was remembered.

This story was Lila's refuge those nights she'd prayed on her knees with the other children in the school dorms. It was too painful to miss her mother.

A year after she'd graduated and worked cleaning house during the day, and evenings at the Dairy Queen, she laughed to think of herself wearing her uniform spotted with sweets and milk, as she left on the arms of one of the stars. Surely she could find love in a place that did not know the disturbance of death.

While Lila lived in the sky she gave birth to three children and they made her happy. Though she had lost conscious memory of the place before, a song climbed up her legs from far away, to the rooms of her heart.

Later she would tell Johnny it was the sound of destiny, which is similar to a prayer reaching out to claim her.

You can't ignore these things, she would tell him, and it led her to the place her husband had warned her was too sacred for women.

She carried the twins in her arms as her daughter grabbed her skirt in her small fists. She looked into the forbidden place and leaped.

She fell and was still falling when Saint Coincidence caught her in his arms in front of the Safeway as he made a turn from borrowing spare change from strangers.

The children crawled safely from their mother. The cat stalked a bit of flying trash set into motion by the wave of falling—

or the converse wave of gathering together.

I traveled far above the earth for a different perspective. It is possible to travel this way without the complications of NASA. *This beloved planet we call home was covered with an elastic web of light. I watched in awe as it shimmered, stretched, dimmed and shined, shaped by the collective effort of all life within it. Dissonance attracted more dissonance. Harmony attracted harmony. I saw revolutions, droughts, famines and the births of new nations. The most humble kindnesses made the brightest lights. Nothing was wasted.*

I understood love to be the very gravity holding each leaf, each cell, this earthy star together.

PART 3

Child Welfare and Health Services

Patrick Johnston wrote that, after 1950, the child welfare system replaced the residential school system as an instrument of colonial control in Canada (24). Child welfare, health care, and education have "obvious parallels" as colonial institutions, according to Brad McKenzie and Pete Hudson, in serving to maintain decision-making authority within the dominant society, which continues to benefit from holding Native people in subjugation (130–34).

Such an analysis for the United States in the same period would include the BIA's Indian Adoption Project (see the introduction), the Mormon placement program (see the preface and part 4), and the Indian Health Service (IHS) sterilization campaign (United States, *Indian Child Welfare Program* 167). As Bruce E. Johansen has noted, the IHS remains underfunded, understaffed, and hard pressed to combat high infant mortality and low life expectancy, but it had enough resources to sterilize 3,406 Native American women in four of the seven IHS regions from 1973 to 1976 (44), including ten percent of Native women of childbearing age in Oklahoma (46–47).

As McKenzie and Hudson remind us, "it is important to recognize that what is happening to a total group has a much more focused impact on an individual child who is taken into care and placed in a [non-Native] environment" (132). The stories that individuals tell of their childhood and of their children translate institutional politics and practices into intensely human terms.

In part 3 some of the more damaging aspects of Native American child welfare and health care come out in testimony, autobiography, and fiction. In the selection from the 1974 US Senate hearings on Indian child welfare, Margaret Townsend, Mrs. Alex Fournier, and Cheryl DeCoteau narrate abuses of parental/child rights by local social services. Their stories, told in response to and sometimes in spite of senators' questions, emerge as what committee chairman Senator James Abourezk called "horror stories" in retrospect at the 1977 ICWA hearing (44).

The horror genre is apt for the legal kidnapping in the selection from Sherman Alexie's novel *Indian Killer* (1996). The paramilitary raid on a reservation to abduct a newborn child ultimately creates a monster: a stalking serial revenge-killer.

The silence that harms the adoptive family can also harm the birth family. The "code of family silence" that excluded Virginia Woolfclan ("Missing Sister") and her brother and sister from knowing about another sister's existence ruined her mother's mental well-being and her subsequent marriage.

A fundamental means of impairing the ability of Indian families to continue is the involuntary sterilization of women, as noted above. Lela Northcross Wakely courageously and chillingly testifies to her experience in "Indian Health."

Mary TallMountain's poetry explores having been an adoptive child whose imagination recreated the world she had been excluded from, the world she carried in her blood and distant memory, which compelled her poetry and prose.

Many individual voices gather in Milton and Jamie Lee's broadcast radio script "The Search for Indian," each searching for an Indian identity that had been disrupted by adoption, a foster home, residential school, or a family history of disowning such identity. Tom Porter's plan for a reverse-Carlisle "survival school" at Kanatsiohareke in New York's Mohawk Valley, Loretta Williams's enrollment difficulties, Rick Hill's rediscovery of his multiple Iroquois roots, and the adoption stories of Alan Michelson, Rita Pyrillis, and Milton Lee are forms of the search for Indian identity that has endured despite discontinuity and uncertainty.

Problems That American Indian Families Face in Raising Their Children

Hearings Before the Subcommittee on Indian Affairs of the Committee on Interior and Insular Affairs, United States Senate, April 8 and 9, 1974

Statement of Margaret Townsend, Fallon, Nev.

SENATOR ABOUREZK: The next witnesses will be Mrs. Margaret Townsend and her children from Fallon, Nev. Mrs. Townsend, would you please step forward, and give us the name of your children and their ages?

MRS. TOWNSEND: Kim Townsend, she's 14, and Alma Townsend, she's 9 and the little boy that's over there is Ira Walker and he's 7.

SENATOR ABOUREZK: Do you have something that you would like to say to the committee this morning? I understand you didn't bring a prepared statement.

MRS. TOWNSEND: No.

SENATOR ABOUREZK: Is this the first time you've ever been to Washington?

MRS. TOWNSEND: Yes.

SENATOR ABOUREZK: Were you nervous when you first came in?

MRS. TOWNSEND: No, but I am now.

SENATOR ABOUREZK: Why, because the television lights are here and so on, in front of all the people? I just want to try to make you at ease as much as possible because I think you probably have a lot of good information to give to the committee. I want to thank you on behalf of the Indian Affairs Subcommittee for making this trip in from Nevada. We appreciate it very much. And, I just want to say that you are performing a great service by coming here to testify because, hopefully, it will help Indian families and Indian children to stay together by providing information which, of course, is made public and will be part of our consideration when we try to make legislation and try to pass laws on this subject. Feel free, you and your children, to say what you came here to say and don't be nervous. Go right ahead, Mrs. Townsend, and say what you wish.

MRS. TOWNSEND: My children were taken out of my home because of the harassment of the police department in Fallon, Nev. The chief of police told me that he was going to make it hard for me to get my children and that I was going to lose my driver's license and that it was going to be hard for me to keep out of jail. So, he turned my children over to the juvenile probation officer and they went into my home and took my children and placed them in a foster home. And, I think they were abused in the foster home. I was beat up.

SENATOR ABOUREZK: Beat up by whom, Mrs. Townsend?

MRS. TOWNSEND: By the police.

SENATOR ABOUREZK: While you were in jail?

MRS. TOWNSEND: When they picked me up, they took me to the office and they argued with me and then they said I resisted arrest.

SENATOR ABOUREZK: If I may just interrupt you for a moment. What were you arrested for?

MRS. TOWNSEND: I was arrested for drunken driving and resisting arrest.

SENATOR ABOUREZK: How much was the bail they set on you?

MRS. TOWNSEND: It was $500.

SENATOR ABOUREZK: Were you able to raise the bail money to get out of jail?

MRS. TOWNSEND: I pleaded not guilty and I called an attorney and he got me out with a bail bond.

SENATOR ABOUREZK: How long did you stay in?

MRS. TOWNSEND: Well, after my children were gone, the next day, I knew they were gone, I just stayed in there for a week.

SENATOR ABOUREZK: You stayed in jail for a week?

MRS. TOWNSEND: Yes.

SENATOR ABOUREZK: When was this arrest, I don't think I asked you that?

MRS. TOWNSEND: January 4.

SENATOR ABOUREZK: Of this year?

MRS. TOWNSEND: Yes.

SENATOR ABOUREZK: While you were in the jail, who came and got the children?

MRS. TOWNSEND: I think the police department picked them up the next day.

SENATOR ABOUREZK: Where did they take them?

MRS. TOWNSEND: They placed them in a temporary foster home.

SENATOR ABOUREZK: Do you know who the foster parents were?

MRS. TOWNSEND: They wouldn't tell me, but later on I found out who they were.

SENATOR ABOUREZK: The father of the children is not living in the house with you at all?

MRS. TOWNSEND: No. I'm alone.

SENATOR ABOUREZK: How long did the children stay in the foster home and how long were they kept away from you?

MRS. TOWNSEND: About 3 weeks.

SENATOR ABOUREZK: How did you eventually get them back?

MRS. TOWNSEND: I had to call the Intertribal Council lawyer. They wouldn't let me make a phone call or anything. I had to sneak and ask one of the trustees to take a note to somebody that I knew who would call the Alcoholics Anonymous and he, in turn, called the Intertribal Council lawyer.

SENATOR ABOUREZK: And, the lawyer got them back for you?

MRS. TOWNSEND: Yes, and they communicated with Mr. [Bertram] Hirsch, here, in New York. The welfare tried to send me to an alcoholic rehabilitation center in Tucson, Ariz., for 6 months, and I don't drink at bars a lot, see, and everytime I'm downtown, about 6 to 8 times in the last 2 years, I seem to be harassed by the policemen, everytime I've been down there, about three times, and they'd say some terrible things to me. And, they said they would assault my daughter, my oldest daughter, and how fat this little girl was and she's just like me; and they just made fun of my children. They just said terrible things to me and intimidated me. So, I wouldn't go back to the police department. I had to get me an attorney.

SENATOR ABOUREZK: Did the welfare try to take your children away from you permanently while you were in jail?

MRS. TOWNSEND: Yes. They said I couldn't get them back for at least 6 months unless I went to the alcoholic center.

SENATOR ABOUREZK: In other words, they tried to force you to go to the alcoholic center by saying that?

MRS. TOWNSEND: Yes, and they tried to make me pay for their foster home care.

SENATOR ABOUREZK: That was Nevada State Welfare Department?

MRS. TOWNSEND: Yes. And, it's very hard for the Indian women to communicate with these people because they do look down on Indians, I think. My daughter had a bad time with the social worker that we had, and I tried to stay on the good side of her so that I could get my children back, but I don't think they had any excuse to take them. They said they would just take them temporarily, that's all.

SENATOR ABOUREZK: Is the social worker who handled your case an Indian?

MRS. TOWNSEND: No.

SENATOR ABOUREZK: Is it a male or female?

MRS. TOWNSEND: She's a female.

SENATOR ABOUREZK: Let me ask you this. Do your children have anything that they want to say this morning about the care that they received in the foster home?

MRS. TOWNSEND: This little girl.

SENATOR ABOUREZK: Which one?

MRS. TOWNSEND: The 9-year-old.

SENATOR ABOUREZK: You mean Anna?

MRS. TOWNSEND: Yes, that my 20-month-old baby was mistreated. She said the man in the foster home slapped my little baby and forced him to eat a whole plate of food and kept the baby penned up all the day. And, she said that the diaper was never changed until the girls got home.

SENATOR ABOUREZK: Would Anna want to testify about that?

MRS. TOWNSEND: I think so, she was real hurt.

SENATOR ABOUREZK: Anna, do you want to say anything?

ANNA TOWNSEND: Yes, I would like to. My brother, he was mistreated by Mr. Kelly. He slapped him and he smoked right in his face and puffed right in his face.

SENATOR ABOUREZK: Just a minute, Anna. If that's too hard for you to talk about, you don't have to. Perhaps it is better if she didn't, Mrs. Townsend. Mrs. Townsend, have you ever been arrested before at all, before that incident?

MRS. TOWNSEND: Yes.

SENATOR ABOUREZK: For the same charge?

MRS. TOWNSEND: I had a previous experience with the police where, I don't know why stories used to follow me around, but I used to live in Elton, Nev., and the police used to follow me around and aggravate me and say dirty things to me. I got in an argument with them and my baby, when he was a month old, he was in a cradle board, he was hit, and three policemen just laughed because they had a great time. I pleaded guilty because I worried about my baby. These stories followed me around and they had threatened me about my daughter, and I was worried about her all the time. I was trying to be overprotective, and they just think it's great fun just because I'm Indian, they can beat me up with handcuffs and chip my elbows where I couldn't pick my baby up. I had to let my brother and his wife take him for awhile, and it's just been hard on my kids. Them doing that to me just because they have a grudge on the Indian boys. It is just hard to communicate with them, that's all.

SENATOR ABOUREZK: I guess it would be a fair statement that the foster home experience was pretty rough on the kids, then?

MRS. TOWNSEND: Yes; and my daughter, I think they took her out of that home and they placed her with an Indian family, with some of her friends, and she said she liked it over there better.

SENATOR ABOUREZK: With the Indian family?

MRS. TOWNSEND: Yes.

SENATOR ABOUREZK: I would suppose that it would be fair to say that the kids would rather be with you?

MRS. TOWNSEND: Yes, they do.

SENATOR ABOUREZK: Is there anything else that you would like to say to the committee?

MRS. TOWNSEND: I think that most of the Indian women are usually overwhelmed by people who think their children should be taken away from them and they really don't stand up to anybody and they don't have anybody to tell.

SENATOR ABOUREZK: Does this happen to a lot of other Indian people in your community?

MRS. TOWNSEND: Oh, yes; it does. They just think that it is the right thing for the welfare to be doing and they just never say or have anything to say. They just let them do whatever they want to, let them adopt them out or whatever.

SENATOR ABOUREZK: In other words, it is a general practice for the welfare people who are handling families in your community to take children out of the home, in a lot of cases that is, and not advise parents of their rights with regard to getting them back? Does that happen quite a bit?

MRS. TOWNSEND: Oh, yes; it does.

SENATOR ABOUREZK: Senator Bartlett.

SENATOR BARTLETT: Thank you, Mr. Chairman. What do you think the reasons were that the police wanted to take your children?

MRS. TOWNSEND: Because he wanted to get even with some of the Indian boys that I know and they are just being hateful because I'm Indian. There's no other reason, because I don't resent white people. They don't bother me at all, except the people in authority. Sometimes they get a little too overwhelming.

SENATOR BARTLETT: Were there any particular people who wanted to adopt your children, that you know of?

MRS. TOWNSEND: No. I wasn't going to let them keep them that long.

SENATOR BARTLETT: The lawyer that you used was a lawyer that you obtained. Did he help you?

MRS. TOWNSEND: He is part of the intertribal agency. He is the attorney for the intertribal agency in Nevada.

SENATOR BARTLETT: Do you happen to know whether he is going to testify before this hearing?

MRS. TOWNSEND: No. He's not here. His name is Mr. Pope.

SENATOR BARTLETT: How do you spell that?

MRS. TOWNSEND: Pope, P-o-p-e.

SENATOR BARTLETT: Do you have employment?

MRS. TOWNSEND: No.

SENATOR BARTLETT: Thank you very much. We appreciate your testimony very much.

SENATOR ABOUREZK: Thank you very much, Mrs. Townsend. The committee wants to thank you very much.
[. . .]

SENATOR ABOUREZK: The next witness will be Mrs. Alex Fournier from Fort Totten, N. Dak. Mrs. Fournier, would you like to come up to the witness stand, and I think it might be better if your grandson not come up to the stand itself. I think that was a rough experience on Anna Townsend, and I don't want us to repeat that. Is this the first time you've been in Washington?

Statement of Mrs. Alex Fournier, Fort Totten, N. Dak.

MRS. FOURNIER: This is the second time.

SENATOR ABOUREZK: So you have flown on an airplane before and you aren't as nervous about the Capitol here and all these buildings and the television lights and so on?

MRS. FOURNIER: No.

SENATOR ABOUREZK: Good. Would you tell us your name and where you are from?

MRS. FOURNIER: I'm originally from Holliday, N. Dak.

SENATOR ABOUREZK: Do you live there now?

MRS. FOURNIER: I'm living there now. I used to live there, and then I moved to Devils Lake in Fort Totten.

SENATOR ABOUREZK: What tribe are you enrolled in?

MRS. FOURNIER: The Mandan Tribe.

SENATOR ABOUREZK: You have living with you your grandson, and his name is Ivan Brown?

MRS. FOURNIER: He isn't my grandson. This child is no relative of mine, but I have taken him since his mother died.

SENATOR ABOUREZK: Are either of his parents living?

MRS. FOURNIER: He takes me as his mother, and I take him as my own.

SENATOR ABOUREZK: Is his father living?

MRS. FOURNIER: They were not legally married. They were just living together, the mother and father.

SENATOR ABOUREZK: How long have you had Ivan in your home?

MRS. FOURNIER: He's 9 now. He was only about 3 weeks old when I started babysitting and raised him from there on.

SENATOR ABOUREZK: Did you have an experience with the county welfare people in North Dakota?

MRS. FOURNIER: Yes. In Benson County, I did.

SENATOR ABOUREZK: Do you want to tell us about the experience you had? When was it, first of all?

MRS. FOURNIER: It was around 1968, I think.

SENATOR ABOUREZK: 1968?

MRS. FOURNIER: Yes. When I first got the child.

SENATOR ABOUREZK: What happened in 1968 with the welfare?

MRS. FOURNIER: That was when they were trying to take my little boy away. When I first took him, he was small and I kept him there and he didn't have anything. He didn't have hardly any clothing or anything and I went to the mission to get clothing for him. I barely got clothes for him. Then, his mother burnt up the day she was supposed to come and pick him up. So, from there on, I had him. His grandmother is still living, yet; but she did not want the child.

SENATOR ABOUREZK: By the way, I wanted to ask how old you are?

MRS. FOURNIER: I'm 69 now.

SENATOR ABOUREZK: You are now 69?

MRS. FOURNIER: Yes.

SENATOR ABOUREZK: What happened between you and the welfare department?

MRS. FOURNIER: They wanted to take him as soon as his mother burnt up. They said they were going to take him, so I agreed to it. I was just babysitting at that time. They said they were going take him. I agreed to it and I said OK. They never came. They said, in about a week; and when the week was up, they never showed up. Then they finally came about a month later. They came back and wanted to take the child. I agreed to it.

SENATOR ABOUREZK: Even the second time, they never came?

MRS. FOURNIER: The second time they came they wanted to take him again, and they said they were going to put him up for adoption. I thought it was OK. It went on and on until he was over a year old. Then I was attached to him and he took me just like his own mother. Then they took us to Devils Lake to a clinic and they had him checked over.

SENATOR ABOUREZK: That's the welfare that took him?

MRS. FOURNIER: Yes, the welfare from Benson County. They were trying to find a place where they could adopt him out, and it went on further and they never came around again for so many months. Finally, one day they came. I had everything marked down but I have been . moving so much, I lost everything. They tried to take him, and when they came after him I said no. He started crying and hanging on to me. He was 2 years old then.

SENATOR ABOUREZK: That was over a year after the first set up?

MRS. FOURNIER: Yes. Then they tried to take him and he hung on to me and he cried. They took us to court because I wasn't going to let him go, the BIA.

SENATOR ABOUREZK: Did you have a lawyer?

MRS. FOURNIER: I really didn't. They just had Indian court there. It was just an Indian court.

SENATOR ABOUREZK: It was tribal court?

MRS. FOURNIER: Yes, and they took me and the welfare people took me in and they wanted to take the child and I said no, I can't let him go. This man jumps up, my little boy was out in the hall, and he went out and he grabbed the child and he was going to walk out with him, and the little boy fought.

SENATOR ABOUREZK: Who was that?

MRS. FOURNIER: He was from Milwaukee. I don't know if he still works there.

SENATOR ABOUREZK: He is with the welfare?

MRS. FOURNIER: Yes. He's a welfare worker.

SENATOR ABOUREZK: During the court, he tried to take Ivan with him then?

MRS. FOURNIER: He [The child] was playing out by the entrance, and he went out and took the child and he was going to walk out with him. The little boy cried and started fighting back. So, the judge in the courtroom said, Margaret Ironheart was the judge then, and she said look they're taking him. I looked back and I ran out and he was screaming and crying and hollering "momma." He yelled out that he was taking him away and I said, no you're not going to take him. The way he's crying, you're not going to take him. I took the child and I took him in.

SENATOR ABOUREZK: What did the court decide on the issue?

MRS. FOURNIER: They fixed out papers there that I could keep the child.

SENATOR ABOUREZK: Have you had any trouble with the welfare since then?

MRS. FOURNIER: Not very often, but they're sort of peeved at me, so they don't come around much any more like they used to.

SENATOR ABOUREZK: They never tried to take him again?

MRS. FOURNIER: No, they never tried to.

SENATOR ABOUREZK: Before the court hearing, did the welfare people ever just come to you and talk to you to find out whether Ivan was happy there, or whether that was the best home for him?

MRS. FOURNIER: They never hardly come around anymore.

SENATOR ABOUREZK: I mean before the trial.

MRS. FOURNIER: Yes.

SENATOR ABOUREZK: Did they talk to you a lot and try to find out whether Ivan was happy living with you?

MRS. FOURNIER: No. They didn't say much of anything.

SENATOR ABOUREZK: They just decided on their own to take him and that was it?

MRS. FOURNIER: Yes.
[. . .]

SENATOR ABOUREZK: Do you have anything more that you would like to say, Mrs. Fournier?

MRS. FOURNIER: No, I don't think so.

SENATOR ABOUREZK: On behalf of the committee, I'd like to thank you very much for coming out here to testify. As I told Mrs. Townsend, what you have to say here today, I hope will be very helpful in trying to correct what we see is a very bad situation. We're very grateful to you and to Ivan and we want to wish you the best of luck. We again thank you.

Statement of Cheryl DeCoteau, Sisseton, S. Dak.

SENATOR ABOUREZK: Cheryl, first of all, I'd like to welcome you to the subcommittee hearings and ask you if this is your first trip into Washington to testify like this?

MRS. DECOTEAU: Yes.

SENATOR ABOUREZK: Your first time?

MRS. DECOTEAU: Yes.

SENATOR ABOUREZK: Do you have any of the children here with you today?

MRS. DECOTEAU: Yes; two.

SENATOR ABOUREZK: Are they here in the room?

MRS. DECOTEAU: Yes.

SENATOR ABOUREZK: Cheryl, we want to ask you to go ahead and testify any way that you would like to so you don't feel nervous about it. I just want to tell you that we appreciate you coming in all the way from Sisseton to provide testimony. As I told the other witnesses, we are hopeful that what you have to tell us today will help other people and prevent the things that happened to you from happening to other people. Your testimony will be very important to the committee and we are very grateful for you coming. You can tell your story any way that you like. First, it might be good to give your name, your age, and exactly where you live, and so on.

MRS. DECOTEAU: Cheryl Spider DeCoteau, I'm 23.

SENATOR ABOUREZK: From where?

MRS. DECOTEAU: I'm not originally from Sisseton, but from Minnesota.

SENATOR ABOUREZK: You are living in Minnesota right now?

MRS. DECOTEAU: Yes. Herbert John Spider is 5, and Robert Lee is 3, and Joseph there, is 10 months.

SENATOR ABOUREZK: Ten months?

MRS. DECOTEAU: Yes.

SENATOR ABOUREZK: Only the two oldest ones with you today?

MRS. DECOTEAU: Yes.

SENATOR ABOUREZK: Who is keeping the baby?

MRS. DECOTEAU: I have a babysitter in Minnesota. I had a babysitter watching the kids, in 1970, and I went to them and they wouldn't let me take them.

SENATOR ABOUREZK: I have to stop you for just a minute and tell you that I can hardly hear you, because I suspect that what it is, is you're bashful and little bit scared because of all the lights, and you're afraid to talk. I know you can talk a lot more clearly than that. I know that's because you're a little bit nervous. If you just talk as loud as you can.

MRS. DECOTEAU: I'll start with my oldest boy, John. I had a babysitter watching him and I went to get him, and they wouldn't give him back to me. So, I went to my social worker and I asked him if he would come with me up there.

SENATOR ABOUREZK: I have to ask you a couple of questions. When did this take place? Can you tell us the month and the year? Do you want to wait a minute before you start testifying?

MRS. DECOTEAU: Yes. That was in December 1970, and I asked him—

SENATOR ABOUREZK: You asked the social worker?

MRS. DECOTEAU: Yes. Asked him to meet me at the store. He didn't come. So, I left, and I called from that store, and I said that they already went and they took John, and they took him to a foster home, and that I couldn't get him back.

SENATOR ABOUREZK: They had taken John without your permission or without your knowledge?

MRS. DECOTEAU: Yes. They took him, and I went back up there, and I tried to get him back, and they said "No," that they couldn't. I don't know if they had a court hearing or something. I didn't get any papers or nothing.

SENATOR ABOUREZK: Did you go to the court hearing?

MRS. DECOTEAU: No, I didn't. I didn't know they had a court hearing.

SENATOR ABOUREZK: They had a court hearing without your knowledge?

MRS. DECOTEAU: They had a petition or something. I didn't know anything about it, and when I did go, they had to appoint me a lawyer. The welfare appointed me a lawyer, so I went to see him. The judge appointed me a lawyer. I went to see him, and he didn't try to help me or anything. All he did was just ask me my age, name and address, and the name of my first boy and my other one. Then he asked me how old they were, and that was all. Then he said he was going to go talk to the judge and the welfare workers. He didn't do anything because I didn't know anything that happened until July of 1971.

SENATOR ABOUREZK: Did they keep John all that time?

MRS. DECOTEAU: Yes. They had John all that time in a foster home.

SENATOR ABOUREZK: Did you know where he was?

MRS. DECOTEAU: No; I didn't know where he was. I kept asking, but they wouldn't tell me where he was or anything.

SENATOR ABOUREZK: I'd like to ask you to back up just a minute. Did this happen in South Dakota or Minnesota?

MRS. DECOTEAU: It was in Sisseton.

SENATOR ABOUREZK: Did the welfare department ever, to your knowledge, prove that you weren't being the best mother for that child at all, and perhaps your lawyer, Mr. Hirsch, can answer if you're unable to?

MRS. DECOTEAU: The man said that I wasn't a very good mother and everything, and that my children were better off being in a white home where they were adopted out, or in this home, wherever they were. They could buy all this stuff that I couldn't give them, and give them all the love that I couldn't give them.

SENATOR ABOUREZK: They said that, but did they really prove that in court, or did they give any specific examples of why you weren't a good mother?

MR. HIRSCH: The answer to that is "No."

[. . .]

SENATOR ABOUREZK: Is it true that you found out about the original hearing accidentally and that she was given no notice of the hearing?

MR. HIRSCH: The original hearing was one of the grossest violations of due process that I have ever encountered. Unfortunately, I find it is quite commonplace when you're dealing with Indian parents and Indian children.

SENATOR ABOUREZK: Did you get notice?

MR. HIRSCH: She did not get notice of either the first hearing or the second hearing. The first hearing was a hearing on the petition of the social worker stating that there was a need for emergency custody in the department of welfare over Mrs. DeCoteau's children. The judge issued an order placing that child in the custody of the department of public welfare without informing Mrs. DeCoteau that such a hearing was taking place, and without allowing her an opportunity to come before the court and submit testimony that such an order should not be issued. So, the child was placed in a foster home and the judge appointed an attorney for Mrs. DeCoteau and set a hearing date on the issue of dependency and neglect. Pending the hearing the child was to remain in a foster home. In other words, you were talking before about burden of proof. They already took the child away from her prior to having any hearing on unfitness and the burden of proof was very clearly shifted on Mrs. DeCoteau to prove that she was fit, rather than the State proving that she was unfit. Then the hearing was scheduled for about 7 months after the child was originally taken from her. Then the hearing was scheduled. They notified Mrs. DeCoteau by publication in the local Sisseton paper, despite the fact that her social worker knew exactly where to find her. This is another problem where the State quite frequently uses the publication notice when, in fact, they know very clearly where the person can be found and how to serve that person directly. They use publication notices instead. Needless to say, these people don't usually make a habit of reading the local paper. She found out entirely by accident that there was a hearing on the merits because another tribal member happened to pick up the paper the day before the hearing and noticed that the hearing was scheduled for the next day.

SENATOR ABOUREZK: All right. Cheryl, then, did you have a subsequent experience with the welfare people with regard to your second son, Bobby?

MRS. DECOTEAU: Yes.

SENATOR ABOUREZK: I wonder if you could tell us what happened there?

MRS. DECOTEAU: I was pregnant with Bobby and the welfare came there and asked me if I would give him up for adoption.

SENATOR ABOUREZK: While you were pregnant with him?

MRS. DECOTEAU: Yes.

SENATOR ABOUREZK: Before he was even born?

MRS. DECOTEAU: Yes. They just kept coming over to the house. They came every week. On a certain day they come and they kept talking to me and asking if I would give him up for adoption and said that it would be better. They kept coming and coming and finally when I did have him, he came to the hospital. After I came home with the baby, he would come over to the house. He asked me if I would give him up for adoption and I said no. He'd go back again and he'd come the next week and ask me again and I'd say no. He let me alone for awhile until I moved into Sisseton and moved in town. He kept coming over and asking if I would give him up for adoption. Then he called me one afternoon and said if I wanted to give him up, and I said no; and the next morning, real early he came pounding on the door and I let him in and he asked me if I'd come up to the office. He had something to talk to me about. So I went up to the office and there were a whole bunch of papers there. I was kind of sick then too and I didn't know what I was signing. He just asked me if I would sign my name on this top paper, and I signed it and he sealed it or something. I signed it and he signed it, and sealed it or something.

SENATOR ABOUREZK: Do you know what that paper was?

MRS. DECOTEAU: No; I didn't know what that paper was. But, then they took the baby and I asked him what he was doing, and he said it was too late now, that I gave him up for adoption. I signed the papers. Then, they took him. They told me to wait a week. Before all this happened, when I did sign the paper, he told me to come back and see him in a week and he would tell me if I could have him back or not. When I did go back in 1 week, that's when he told me it was too late, that I had signed the papers for adoption and I couldn't get him back.

SENATOR ABOUREZK: How old was the baby when he took him?

MRS. DECOTEAU: He was 4 months.

SENATOR ABOUREZK: Can you describe how they came and took him, or how that happened?

MRS. DECOTEAU: When they came to the house there, I just had the baby with me. My grandmother took John home the day before. I had the baby with me and then I took him with me when I went up there. Before I signed the paper, one of the social workers came there and took him to the next room. When they did that, I signed the papers and stuff and they wouldn't give him back to me. They wouldn't let me take him home and all that. They told me that they'd give me 1 week and to come back and see him in 1 week.

SENATOR ABOUREZK: You mean you took the baby with you when you signed the papers and they kept the baby right there?

MRS. DECOTEAU: When they took me in the office there, the social worker went and called another lady in to watch the baby in the next room until I got done. When he got through talking with me, when they took the baby and I signed the papers, they just took him right out the doors and they took him right to the foster home the same day. Afterwards, I went to see an attorney and he said that he would help me, and that was in March 1970. And, it took me until February. No, this all happened in March 1970. I went to this lawyer and he said that he would help me and I filled out all kinds of papers and answered all the questions he wanted to know and then he said he'd let me know. I didn't hear nothing from him for awhile and I think it was in August he called me and I went to see him. He said that a date was set in September 1970, to have a court hearing. We went to that, but I lost that. This was before John was taken away, because they took Robert and then John was taken away. My grandfather notified me and said that I had to go to court for both kids. They were going to give them up for adoption and that's when Bert here, he was my lawyer.

SENATOR ABOUREZK: Did you eventually get Bobby back?

MRS. DECOTEAU: I got him back last April.

SENATOR ABOUREZK: How long did you and your lawyer have to fight that in court before you got him back?

MRS. DECOTEAU: About 10 months, 7 months for Johnny and 10 for Robert.

SENATOR ABOUREZK: It was almost a year and a half for both kids?

MRS. DECOTEAU: Yes.

SENATOR ABOUREZK: Do you have custody now of all three of the children?

MRS. DECOTEAU: Yes.

MR. HIRSCH: That was 10 months, Senator, after I became involved in the case. She had been trying for quite some time before that to get the kids back.

SENATOR ABOUREZK: Yes. Cheryl, did you have anything more to say?

MRS. DECOTEAU: No.

SENATOR ABOUREZK: I want to thank you very much. Senator Bartlett probably has some questions.

SENATOR BARTLETT: Thank you, Mr. Chairman. I wonder if, Mr. Hirsch, in either case, was there any indication of black market for adoption?

MR. HIRSCH: As close as I can come to answering affirmatively to that question is to describe to you an incident that occurred in the county welfare office when I went to serve papers for tribal intervention. The tribe felt very strongly about this case and the tribe wanted to intervene in the case on behalf of Mrs. DeCoteau and to assert a tribal right to maintain custody of these children within the tribe. I went to serve intervention papers upon the State's attorney and he was with one of the supervisors, codirectors of the county welfare department. When I served those papers we had the following exchange: I gave him the papers. He said why is the tribe so interested in this case? What is the big issue here? I said that the tribe was concerned that if many more of their children were taken, because there's been quite a history of taking these kids from this reservation, that they were afraid that their very survival would be at stake. And, the codirector of this county welfare office responded to that by shrugging his shoulders and saying, "So, what?"

SENATOR BARTLETT: Mr. Hirsch, has there been any indication by the large number of adoptions that there is a black market for children for adoption?

MR. HIRSCH: I would say you could describe it as a gray market, rather than a black market. Although, there have been in the past, I suppose, quite a few cases that might be more accurately described as black market cases. Recently, they've only had a few of those types of cases that I know of. I think it is more accurately described as a gray market. I think there's tremendous pressure to adopt Indian children, or have Indian children adopted out. I think that local welfare workers in Indian communities feel this pressure intensely. They have long lists of non-Indian applicants for Indian children, and they feel obliged for a whole variety of social reasons to comply with the orders that they receive.

SENATOR BARTLETT: You say long lists for adopting Indian children. Is that a relative term? Is there more interest in adopting Indian children than other children?

MR. HIRSCH: I think so. I think there's more interest in adopting Indian children primarily because non-Indian potential adoptive parents are white. They do not want to have a black child, as a generalization.

White children are unavailable, there are just a few; and they are generally now settling on either Indians or orientals.
[. . .]

SENATOR BARTLETT: Thank you very much. Thank you very much Mrs. DeCoteau.

SENATOR ABOUREZK: I want to thank you very much Mrs. DeCoteau, especially for your testimony, which is very revealing and which, again, I hope will be very helpful. Thanks for coming.

Five Poems

MARY TALLMOUNTAIN

The Light on the Tent Wall
For Mary Joe, my mother

There was light. Suffused
onto canvas through mother's womb.
Her round belly turned the
tent wall pink. There was humming,
soft talk about the baby coming.
Women, mothers, warm by the
Yukon stove, visiting Mary Joe
and her child, I who lay unborn
in her cradle of light.

Years came. I was taken
where there were no tent walls,
where I had to dream my own,
and as time passed, often
I saw the light on the wall.
No longer pink, it was
fire, its tongues licking

the tent wall.
Fire of our life, flickering.

Light returned where I was,
moving through far places, years.
Not suffused now. Gone
the voices, singing. Useless,
wind plucked with
chill fingers at the wall.
Often the sound was angry,
hasty, wanted to speak
but could not find words.

I overtook it, brought back
my dream. Light dyed the canvas
the color of mother's blood
gliding through her womb,
through labored lungs,
through death, and I
remembered the color of her blood,
light on the tent wall,
painted by my infant dreams.

Sometimes I still hear
angry winds plucking mutely
at the wall. The light is there too,
and thinking of the watching women
I wonder whether they
saw the light on the tent wall.
I saw it plain before my birth
and held it a half century.
I will hold it forever.

Indian Blood

On the stage I stumbled,
my fur boot caught
on a slivered board.
Rustle of stealthy giggles.

Beendaaga' made of velvet
crusted with crystal beads
hung from brilliant tassels of wool,
wet with my sweat.

Children's faces stared.
I felt their flowing force.
Did I crouch like *goh*
in the curious quiet?

They butted to the stage,
darting questions; pointing.
        Do you live in an igloo?
        Hah! You eat blubber!

Hemmed in by ringlets of brass,
grass-pale eyes,
the fur of *daghooda-aak*
trembled.

Late in the night
I bit my hand until it was
pierced
with moons of dark
Indian blood.

Beendaaga': Mittens
Goh: Rabbit
Daghooda-aak: Caribou parka

Going Home

I started on the road of the silent, secret drinker. Therapy was hush-hush
in those days. Into my forties I stumbled along, my work suffering. One
day I went out in a haze to the corner for my morning stinger at
the Brown Dog Bar, and suddenly realized everything was darker than
usual. Why was traffic heavy? Why was it all going west? Then I knew. It
was evening, and I didn't know where the day had gone. I made up my
mind to quit drinking, cold turkey. It took a long, sweating time, but it
worked.

Shyly, tentatively, I began in the mid-60s to continue my early efforts at writing. Fate brought me a wonderful friend and tutor, who honed my unskilled talent into the great gift of word-smithing. I discovered that I had an obligation to myself and my peers to use this talent constructively to rebuild, perhaps, some part of the world I live in. My friend urged me to return to Nulato and on the very day I was to leave for Alaska, I located my father, Clem, in Phoenix. I returned to Nulato to discover what I could about my beginnings, and went to Phoenix to be with my 86-year-old father. I stayed with him for the last two years of his life and I learned much from him about how to forgive, to sharpen my perceptions. Much of my long lingering bitterness faded away in his gentle and tender presence. He told me about his life with Mary Joe, and about my brothers. He gave me her message: "Tell my girl I love her. I wanted her to have the best life she could have, that is why I adopted her out."

—A revised excerpt from the anthology *I Tell You Now*

A Song for My Mother

Owl spoke gravely of winter.
I walked out with you
to see whether ptarmigan
and snowshoe rabbit
had turned white.

Sky wore a purple mantle
With you I saw through snow
and rough backs of malemutes,
your shadow against the
silver spike of moon.

You slid Salmon to the table
raised the fishknife, and
your hands honored
the holiness of all things.

Always do this with care,
you said, and the knife
traced a flashing crimson

stripe along the
soft white belly, baring
massed luscious eggs.

I looked into a million faces
afterwards, but found
none like yours,
none anywhere.
I stood different, knowing.

So I went the alien ways
but held my life with you apart,
gripped tight my soul,
waited, wrapped in
the cloak of your strength.

My Wild Birds Flying

When bayonet cactus thrusts its
Blossomy cap into desert sky,
A white cry announcing winter,
I remember my father.

Lost in my childhood, Clem
Perched forever, a wild bird
Fluttering in the cage of my head.
I could not set him free.

Years of search. I found him—
Old soldier, spiny as ocotillo.
A few years left for laughter,
Return to our Alaskan youth.

He thought I was Mary Joe
Stepping across the years,
Hair tossed in a scarlet band,
Dancing to his fiddle.

He was frail and ancient,
Flickered like fireflies of summer

In dreams he drove the
malemutes
Through the land with Mary Joe.

In a fleece-bright dawn
He cried out to her.
She came, bent into the light,
And took his hand.

Now in the silences of night
They come to me,

My wild birds flying.

Missing Sister

VIRGINIA WOOLFCLAN

I grew up on the rez during a turbulent time for our people and families, as we were going through a major battle with the government over land, and a lot of our community's parents were working with our tribe to fight the government's decision. There were three of us kids, our mother, grandparents, and great uncle living together then, and Mom was rarely around—in other words, a pretty standard extended family situation. Since our parents had split before I was born, the youngest of three, this is the only way of life I knew. Mom would sometimes be at long meetings and we would either be left at home, in the car, or to play with the kids of others working on the land project.

During the summer before I went into fourth grade and my sister into fifth, my grandparents packed us up and we moved to my maternal aunt's house two counties over. My brother went to live with a ninth-grade classmate of his in our hometown. Mom disappeared, and we were eventually told she was sick and we'd need to stay with the aunt for a year or so, until she could recover. My sister and I were stunned, but kids were supposed to be seen and not heard, so we just lived with it. We adjusted to another school, and never heard from our brother. We also never heard from our mom the whole time. We wondered if she was getting well. We wondered if we'd ever see her again.

It ended as abruptly as it started. The next summer we moved back in with our mom, as if nothing had happened. Not long after, my mom came home married to this guy we only sort of knew. My brother would never return home, and lived with our grandparents until he graduated from high school and went to college.

It was during these first years of a very violent and abusive marriage that we first had an inkling of what went on in that year we lived away. During one of their beat-each-other-up arguments, my step-dad accused her of having a kid by some married guy and giving it away. My sister and I were stunned that he would accuse her of such a thing. We didn't believe him because we didn't like him or the way he treated us and her. But over the years as the fights continued, the accusation began to ring true. We'd overhear hushed little bits and pieces from other family members, too, which seemed to support this idea. But no one ever told us anything, and not until my sister and I had finished college, gone our separate ways, and come back home much later, were we able to break the code of family silence.

Finally, one of our family members confirmed what we'd long wondered: Mom had a baby girl that year and immediately gave her up for adoption.

The knowledge flooded us with grief and anguish, as we had long felt such an empty and unexplainable feeling about that time. We were relieved finally to know the truth, and saddened not to know what became of her. Few days go by that we don't think about her, where she might be, and what she looks like, and wish we could find her and introduce ourselves and let her know she has family that cares and wants to connect. She was said to resemble me a lot at birth, and probably resembles the three of us kids in recognizable ways.

But we can't even pursue finding her, because Mom is a highly respected community member who kept this secret all these years and has denied it ever happened; she truly believes it never did. I've wondered over the years if that put Mom's mind over the edge a bit as well. It was probably traumatic and certainly life-changing, if only temporarily. I say it this way because my mom has sincerely blocked it out. It never happened, and any suggestion of such a horrible abandonment of a child or sexual indiscretion is tantamount to slander. The sad thing is that she's an intelligent and well-read woman, strong, a fluent speaker, and very knowledgeable about her culture. But even more sadly, she's been mentally damaged. It boggles the mind, I'll tell you.

None of the family knows what happened to our sister either, nor were they allowed to have any part, except to take us kids away during that time. So while my mom's alive, we can't pursue it, and we live with that inexplicable emptiness, wondering if we'll ever find her or if we've already seen her and don't know it. We have been deprived of knowing each other. We feel the emptiness and loss at never having known her or been told about her and the helplessness of not even being able to look for her. And we also live with the knowledge that, because it was the mid-1960s, she was most likely raised in a non-Native home without connection to our people or culture and has thereby been robbed of the richness of her heritage. So we hold on to the prospect of someday finding her and filling a void in both our and her lives.

Indian Health

LELA NORTHCROSS WAKELY

The big reason women hesitate to come forward is: who would believe them? Some, such as my sister, don't even know for certain. She had children at the ages of sixteen and eighteen. She never used or asked for birth control, but after her second child was delivered by C-section, she didn't conceive again until she was in her thirties. Tubal ligations have histories of not being one hundred percent complete, and that's a long time to go without conceiving. Doctors told her not to worry—she had two kids, why have any more?

My mother had ten children. I was the only one born in a hospital. The seventh and eighth were born in doctors' offices in Tulsa. A doctor offered my mother one thousand dollars for Joseph. He said she had six children and could use the money more than another baby. This was in 1953. My mother never went back to that doctor.

I was removed from my family when I was fifteen and sent briefly to foster care, then to state-run facilities. At the time, my niece was four and extremely gifted, and my sister feared losing her. She became very religious and rigid, and made the two- and four-year-olds take separate baths and stay fully dressed even in the house in summer. As for me, I didn't know the meaning of the word *abuse* until I was sent to the

Diagnostic and Evaluation Center. I didn't know the meaning of the word *rape* until I was placed in state-run homes.

At twenty years of age I was just a young girl. I didn't know what was wrong with me. I can ignore pain up to a point, but after I fainted for the first time in my life, friends took me to the emergency room of a small town hospital. I was asked if I was pregnant. I had no idea that I was, or that it was an ectopic pregnancy about six weeks along that was causing internal bleeding and the pain I had been ignoring.

I was admitted and taken to a room where I continued to bleed internally. A doctor on call came to examine me. I was in the beginning stages of shock from loss of blood. This doctor took the time to tell me what he thought of me. He told me I wasn't fit for decent society. He told me I was just like all those other unwed girls who have children and go on welfare to leech off the good folks who work for a living. He told me I didn't deserve to have children. He said he wasn't going to lie for me and was disgusted to have to tell my parents of my shameful diagnosis. He said he would take care of me only because of the oath he had taken as a doctor. "But I'll take care of you. I'll take care of you."

I'll take care of you were the last words I heard him speak to me before my operation.

Six years later and in a different town with different doctors, I had surgery to determine the cause of my infertility. The assisting surgeon later came to talk with my husband and me about the results. She apologized for the great length of time it had taken and explained, "There was all that wire we had to remove." I was never told wire had been used to suture my reproductive system or even my abdomen. The doctor just passed it off by saying, "Well, some doctors tried wire as suture material back then. Don't worry about it."

I dismissed it from my mind, but the following years of heartbreaking disappointment left me wondering: Why?

In 1993, after my seventh and last miscarriage, I started researching on my own. In the University Medical Library are documents that show just what can happen if wire is used as suture material in the reproductive system. Crying, shaking, at last I found the reason why.

The continued pain I complained of, the low-grade fever, and the slightly elevated white cell count after my first surgery now made perfect sense: my body was rejecting all that wire that was in me, poisoning my body, my reproductive system. The doctor kept telling me to "Ignore it. It will go away." Months later, I was admitted with a massive pelvic infection and finally treated with antibiotics by a different doctor.

Wire sutures run as a continuous coil, winding around and around, very much like the razor wire used on top of prison walls. Even after it is removed, the wire leaves scars that interfere with an embryo implanting properly. At least prison inmates have their day in court. My unborn were never given a chance to speak for themselves, just sentenced to die without trial, without just cause, without justice. Who would be a jury of their peers? Or of mine? My birthright to have children was taken from me and can never be replaced.

Although it may make no difference to the first doctor, I'd just like to tell him that I have never been on welfare, that I wouldn't change my ethnic identity even if I could, and that being "poor" is less about how much money you have in your pocket and more about how much love you have in your heart.

from *Indian Killer*

SHERMAN ALEXIE

Chapter 1: Mythology

The sheets are dirty. An Indian Health Service hospital in the late sixties. On this reservation or that reservation. Any reservation, a particular reservation. Antiseptic, cinnamon, and danker odors. Anonymous cries up and down the hallways. Linoleum floors swabbed with gray water. Mop smelling like old sex. Walls painted white a decade earlier, now yellowed and peeling. Old Indian woman in a wheelchair singing traditional songs to herself, tapping a rhythm on her armrest, right index finger tapping, tapping. Pause. Tap, tap. A phone ringing loudly from behind a thin door marked PRIVATE. Twenty beds available, twenty beds occupied. Waiting room where a young Indian man sits on a couch and holds his head in his hands. Nurses' lounge, two doctor's offices, and a scorched coffee pot. Old Indian man, his hair bright white and unbraided, pushing his I.V. bottle down the hallway. He is barefoot and confused, searching for a pair of moccasins he lost when he was twelve years old. Donated newspapers and magazines stacked in bundles, months and years out of date, missing pages. In one of the examining rooms, an Indian family of four, mother, father, son, daughter, all coughing blood quietly into handkerchiefs. The phone still ringing behind the PRIVATE door. A cinderblock building, thick windows that distort the view, pine trees, flagpole. A 1957 Chevy parked haphazardly, back door flung open, engine still running, back seat damp and bloodstained. Empty now.

The Indian woman on the table in the delivery room is very young, just a child herself. She is beautiful, even in the pain of labor, the contractions, the sudden tearing. When John imagines his birth, his mother is sometimes Navajo. Other times she is Lakota. Often, she is from the same tribe as the last Indian woman he has seen on television. Her legs tied in stirrups. Loose knots threatening to unravel. The white doctor has his hands inside her. Blood everywhere. The nurses work at mysterious machines. John's mother is tearing her vocal cords with the force of her screams. Years later, she still speaks in painful whispers. But during his birth, she is so young, barely into her teens, and the sheets are dirty.

The white doctor is twenty-nine years old. He has grown up in Iowa or Illinois, never seeing an Indian in person until he arrives at the reservation. His parents are poor. Having taken a government scholarship to make his way through medical school, he now has to practice medicine on the reservation in exchange for the money. This is the third baby he has delivered here. One white, two Indians. All of the children are beautiful.

John's mother is Navajo or Lakota. She is Apache or Seminole. She is Yakama or Spokane. Her dark skin contrasts sharply with the white sheets, although they are dirty. She pushes when she should be pushing. She stops pushing when they tell her to stop. With clever hands, the doctor turns John's head to the correct position. He is a good doctor.

The doctor has fallen in love with Indians. He thinks them impossibly funny and irreverent. During the hospital staff meetings, all of the Indians sit together and whisper behind their hands. There are no Indian doctors, but a few of the nurses and most of the administrative staff are Indian. The white doctor often wishes he could sit with the Indians and whisper behind his hand. But he maintains a personable and professional distance. He misses his parents, who still live in Iowa or Illinois. He calls them often, sends postcards of beautiful, generic landscapes.

The doctor's hands are deep inside John's mother, who is only fourteen, and who is bleeding profusely where they have cut her to make room for John's head. But the sheets were dirty before the blood, and her vagina will heal. She is screaming in pain. The doctor could not give her painkillers because she had arrived at the hospital too far into labor. The Chevy is still running outside, rear door flung open, back seat red and damp. The driver is in the waiting room. He holds his head in his hands.

Are you the father?

No, I'm the driver. She was walking here when I picked her up. She was hitchhiking. I'm just her cousin. I'm just the driver.

The phone behind the PRIVATE door is still ringing. His mother pushes one last time and John slides into the good doctor's hands. Afterbirth. The doctor clears John's mouth. John inhales deeply, exhales, cries. The old Indian woman in the wheelchair stops singing. She hears a baby crying. She stops her tapping to listen. She forgets why she is listening, then returns to her own song and the tapping, tapping. Pause. Tap, tap. The doctor cuts the umbilical cord quickly. There is no time to waste. A nurse cleans John, washes away the blood, the remains of the placenta, the evidence. His mother is crying.

I want my baby. Give me my baby. I want to see my baby. Let me hold my baby.

The doctor tries to comfort John's mother. The nurse swaddles John in blankets and takes him from the delivery room, past the old Indian man dragging his I.V. down the hallway, looking for his long-lost moccasins. She carries John outside. A flag hangs uselessly on its pole. No wind. The smell of pine. Inside the hospital, John's mother has fainted. The doctor holds her hand, as if he were the loving husband and father. He remembers the family of four coughing blood into handkerchiefs in the examining room. The doctor is afraid of them.

With John in her arms, the nurse stands in the parking lot. She is white or Indian. She watches the horizon. Blue sky, white clouds, bright sun. The slight whine of a helicopter in the distance. Then the violent *whomp-whomp* of its blades as it passes overhead, hovers, and lands a hundred feet away. In the waiting room, the driver lifts his head from his hands when he hears the helicopter. He wonders if there is a war beginning.

A man in a white jumpsuit steps from the helicopter. Head ducked and body bent, the man runs toward the nurse. His features are hidden inside his white helmet. The nurse meets him halfway and hands him the baby John. The jumpsuit man covers John's face completely, protecting him from the dust that the helicopter is kicking up. The sky is very blue. Specific birds hurl away from the flying machine. These birds are indigenous to this reservation. They do not live anywhere else. They have purple-tipped wings and tremendous eyes, or red bellies and small eyes. The nurse waves as the jumpsuit man runs back to the helicopter. She shuts the rear door of the Chevy, reaches through the driver's open window, and turns the ignition key. The engine shudders to a stop.

Suddenly this is a war. The jumpsuit man holds John close to his chest as the helicopter rises. The helicopter gunman locks and loads, strafes the reservation with explosive shells. Indians hit the ground, drive their cars off roads, dive under flimsy kitchen tables. A few Indians, two women and one young man, continue their slow walk down the reservation road, unperturbed by the gunfire. They have been through much worse. The *whomp-whomp* of the helicopter blades. John is hungry and cries uselessly. He cannot be heard over the roar of the gun, the chopper. He cries anyway. This is all he knows how to do. Back at the clinic, his mother has been sedated. She sleeps in the delivery room. The doctor holds her hand and finds he cannot move. He looks down at his hand wrapped around her hand. White fingers, brown fingers. He can see the blue veins running through his skin like rivers. The phone behind the PRIVATE door stops ringing. Gunfire in the distance. Nobody, not even the white doctor, is surprised by this.

The helicopter flies for hours, it could be days, crossing desert, mountain, freeway, finally a city. Skyscrapers, the Space Needle, water everywhere. Thin bridges stretched between islands. John crying. The gunner holds his fire, but his finger is lightly feathering the trigger. He is ready for the worst. John can feel the distance between the helicopter and the ground below. He stops crying. He loves the distance between the helicopter and the ground. He feels he could fall. He somehow loves this new fear. He wants to fall. He wants the jumpsuit man to release him, let him fall from the helicopter, down through the clouds, past the skyscrapers and the Space Needle. But the jumpsuit man holds him tight so John will not fall. John cries again.

The helicopter circles downtown Seattle, moves east past Lake Washington, Mercer Island, hovers over the city of Bellevue. The pilot searches for the landing area. Five acres of green, green grass. A large house. Swimming pool. A man and woman waving energetically. Home. The pilot lowers the chopper and sets down easily. Blades making a windstorm of grass particles and hard-shelled insects. The gunner's eyes are wide open, scanning the tree line. He is ready for anything. The jumpsuit man slides the door open with one arm and holds John in the other. Noise, heat. John cries, louder than before, trying to be heard. Home. The jumpsuit man steps down and runs across the lawn toward the man and woman, both white and handsome. He wears a gray suit and colorful tie. She wears a red dress with large, black buttons from throat to knee.

John cries as the jumpsuit man hands him to the white woman, Olivia Smith. She unbuttons the top of her dress, opens her bra, and offers John her large, pale breasts with pink nipples. John's birth mother had small, brown breasts and brown nipples, though he never suckled at them. Still, he knows there is a difference, and as John takes the white woman's right nipple into his mouth and pulls at her breast, he discovers it is empty. Daniel Smith wraps his left arm around his wife's shoulders. He grimaces briefly and then smiles. Olivia and Daniel Smith look at the jumpsuit man, who is holding a camera. Flash, flash. Click of the shutter. Whirr of advancing film. All of them wait for a photograph to form, for light to emerge from shadow, for an image to burn itself into paper.

Chapter 2: The Last Skyscraper in Seattle

When no baby came after years of trying to conceive, Olivia and Daniel Smith wanted to adopt a baby, but the waiting list was so long. The adoption agency warned them that white babies, of course, were the most popular. Not that it was a popularity contest, they were assured. It was just that most of the couples interested in adopting a baby were white, so naturally, they wanted to adopt a white child, a child like them, but there were simply not enough white babies to go around.

"Listen," the adoption agent said. "Let's be honest. It's going to take at least a year to find a suitable white child for you. Frankly, it may take much longer than that. Up to eight years or more. But we can find you another kind of baby rather quickly."

"Another kind?" asked Olivia.

"Well, of course," said the agent. "There's always the handicapped babies. Down's syndrome. Children missing arms and legs. Mentally retarded. That kind of kid. To be honest, it's very difficult, nearly impossible, to find homes for those children. It's perfectly understandable. These children need special care, special attention. Lots of love. Not very many people can handle it."

"I don't think we want that," Daniel said. Olivia agreed.

"There are other options," said the agent. "We have other difficult-to-place children as well. Now, there's nothing wrong with these babies. They're perfectly healthy, but they're not white. Most are black. We also have an Indian baby. The mother is six months pregnant now."

"Indian?" asked Daniel. "As in American Indian?"

"Yes," said the agent. "The mother is very young, barely into her teens. She's making the right decision. She'll carry the baby to full term and give it up for adoption. Now, ideally, we'd place this baby with Indian parents, right? But that just isn't going to happen. The best place for this baby is with a white family. This child will be saved a lot of pain by growing up in a white family. It's the best thing, really."

Olivia and Daniel agreed to consider adopting the Indian baby. They went home that night, ate a simple dinner, and watched television. A sad movie-of-the-week about an incurable disease. Daniel kept clearing his throat during the movie. Olivia cried. When it was over, Daniel switched off the television. They undressed for bed, brushed their teeth, and lay down together.

"What do you think?" asked Olivia.

"I don't know," said Daniel.

They made love then, both secretly hoping this one would take. They wanted to believe that everything was possible. An egg would drop, be fertilized, and begin to grow. As he moved inside his wife, Daniel closed his eyes and concentrated on an image of a son. That son would be exactly half of him. He saw a son with his chin and hair. He saw a baseball glove, bicycle, tree house, barking dog. Olivia wrapped her arms around her husband, pressed her face to his shoulder. She could feel him inside her, but it was a vague, amorphous feeling. There was nothing specific about it. During the course of their married life, the sex had mostly felt good. Sometimes, it had been uncomfortable, once or twice painful. But she did not feel anything this time. She opened her eyes and stared at the ceiling.

Olivia knew she was beautiful. She had been a beautiful baby, little girl, teenager, woman. She had never noticed whether it was easy or hard to be that beautiful. It never really occurred to her to wonder about it. All her life, her decisions had been made for her. She was meant to graduate from high school, get into a good college, find a suitable young man, earn a B.A. in art history, marry, and never work. Somewhere between reading a biography of van Gogh and fixing dinner, she was supposed to have a baby. Except for producing that infant, she had done what was expected of her, had fulfilled the obligations of her social contract. She had graduated with honors, had married a handsome, successful architect, and loved sex in a guarded way. But the baby would not happen. The doctors had no explanations. Her husband's sperm were of average count and activity. "In a swimming race," their doctor had said, "your husband's sperm would get the bronze." She had a healthy uterus and her period was loyal to the moon's cycles. But it did not work. "Listen," the doctor had said. "There are some people who just cannot have babies together. We can't always explain it. Medicine isn't perfect."

Still staring at the ceiling, Olivia moved her hips in rhythm with her husband's. She wanted to ask him what he was thinking about, but did not want to interrupt their lovemaking. She lifted herself to her husband, listening to the patterns of his breathing until it was over.

"I love you," she whispered.

"I love you, too," Daniel said.

He lifted himself off her and rolled to his side of the bed. She reached out and took his hand. He was crying. She held him until they fell asleep. When they woke in the morning, both had decided to adopt the Indian baby.

Olivia was determined to be a good mother. She knew it was a complicated situation, that she would have to explain her baby's brown skin to any number of strangers. There was no chance that she would be able to keep her baby's adoption a secret. Two white parents, a brown baby. There was no other way to explain it. But she did not fool herself into thinking that her baby would somehow become white just because she and Daniel were white. After John arrived, she spent hours in the library. With John sleeping beside her, she would do research on Native American history and culture. The adoption agency refused to divulge John's tribal affiliation and sealed all of his birth records, revealing only that John's birth mother was fourteen years old. Olivia spent hours looking through books, searching the photographs for any face like her son's face. She read books about the Sioux, and Navajo, and Winnebago. Crazy Horse, Geronimo, and Sitting Bull rode horses through her imagination. She bought all the children's books about Indians and read them aloud to John. Daniel thought it was an obsessive thing to do, but he did not say anything. He had named the baby John after his grandfather and thought it ironic. His grandfather had been born in Germany and never really learned much English, even after years in the United States.

"Honey," Daniel whispered to his wife when John woke up crying. Three in the morning, the moon full and bright white. "Honey, it's the baby."

Olivia rose from bed, walked into the nursery, and picked up John. She carried him to the window.

"Look, sweetie," she said to John. "It's just the moon. See, it's pretty."

Daniel listened to his wife talking to their son.

"It's the moon," she said and then said the word in Navajo, Lakota, Apache. She had learned a few words in many Indian languages. From books, Western movies, documentaries. Once she saw an Indian woman at the supermarket and asked her a few questions that were answered with bemused tolerance.

"It's just the moon," whispered Olivia and then she softly sang it. "It's the moon. It's the moon."

Daniel listened for a few minutes before he rolled over and fell asleep. When he woke the next morning, Olivia was standing at that same window with John in her arms, as if she'd been there all night.

"We need to get John baptized," she said with a finality that Daniel didn't question.

Because the baby John was Indian, Olivia and Daniel Smith wanted him to be baptized by an Indian, and they searched for days and weeks for the only Indian Jesuit in the Pacific Northwest. Father Duncan, a Spokane Indian Jesuit, was a strange man. A huge man, an artist. He painted contemporary landscapes, portraits, and murals that were highlighted with traditional Spokane Indian images. His work was displayed in almost every Jesuit community in the country. He was a great teacher, a revered theologian, but an eccentric. He ate bread and soup at every meal. Whole grains and vegetable broth, sourdough and chicken stock. He talked to himself, laughed at inappropriate moments, sometimes read books backward, starting with the last page and working toward the beginning. An irony, an Indian in black robes, he took a special interest in John and, with Olivia and Daniel's heartfelt approval, often visited him. The Jesuit held the baby John in his arms, sang traditional Spokane songs and Catholic hymns, and rocked him to sleep. As John grew older, Father Duncan would tell him secrets and make him promise never to reveal them. John kept his promises.

On a gray day when John was six years old, Father Duncan took him to see the Chapel of the North American Martyrs in downtown Seattle. John found himself surrounded by vivid stained glass reproductions of Jesuits being martyred by Indians. Bright white Jesuits with bright white suns at their necks. A Jesuit, tied to a post, burning alive as Indians dance around him. Another pierced with dozens of arrows. A third, with his cassock torn from his body, crawling away from an especially evil-looking Indian. The fourth being drowned in a blue river. The fifth, sixth, and seventh being scalped. An eighth and ninth praying together as a small church burns behind them. And more and more. John stared up at so much red glass.

"Beautiful, isn't it?" asked Father Duncan.

John did not understand. He was not sure if Father Duncan thought the artwork was beautiful, or if the murder of the Jesuits was beautiful. Or both.

"There's a myth, a story, that the blood of those Jesuits was used to stain the glass," said Duncan. "But who knows if it's true. We Jesuits love to tell stories."

"Why did the Indians kill them?"

"They wanted to kick the white people out of America. Since the priests were the leaders, they were the first to be killed."

John looked up at the stained glass Jesuits, then at the Spokane Indian Jesuit.

"But you're a priest," said John.

"Yes, I am."

John did not have the vocabulary to express what he was feeling. But he understood there was something odd about the contrast between the slaughtered Jesuits and Father Duncan, and between the Indian Jesuit and the murderers.

"Did the white people leave?" asked John.

"Some of them did. But more came."

"It didn't work."

"No."

"Why didn't the Indians kill all the white people?"

"They didn't have the heart for it."

"But didn't white people kill most of the Indians?"

"Yes, they did."

John was confused. He stared up at the martyred Jesuits. Then he noticed the large crucifix hanging over the altar. A mortally wounded Jesus, blood pouring from his hands and feet, from the wound in his side. John saw the altar candles burning and followed the white smoke as it rose toward the ceiling of the chapel.

"Was Jesus an Indian?" asked John.

Duncan studied the crucifix, then looked down at John.

"He wasn't an Indian," said the Jesuit, "but he should have been."

John seemed to accept that answer. He could see the pain in Jesus's wooden eyes. At six, he already knew that a wooden Jesus could weep. He'd seen it on the television. Once every few years, a wooden Jesus wept and thousands of people made the pilgrimage to the place where the miracle happened. If miracles happened with such regularity when did they cease to be miracles? And simply become ordinary events, pedestrian proof of God? John knew that holy people sometimes bled from their hands and feet, just as Jesus had bled from his hands and feet when nailed to the cross. Such violence, such faith.

"Why did they do that to Jesus?" asked John.

"He died so that we may live forever."

"Forever?"

"Forever."

John looked up again at the windows filled with the dead and dying.

"Did those priests die like Jesus?" asked John.

Father Duncan did not reply. He knew that Jesus was killed because he was dangerous, because he wanted to change the world in a good way. He also knew that the Jesuits were killed because they were dangerous to the Indians who didn't want their world to change at all. Duncan knew those Jesuits thought they were changing the Indians in a good way.

"Did they die like Jesus?" John asked again.

Duncan was afraid to answer the question. As a Jesuit, he knew those priests were martyred just like Jesus. As a Spokane Indian, he knew those Jesuits deserved to die for their crimes against Indians.

"John," Duncan said after a long silence. "You see these windows? You see all of this? It's what is happening inside me right now."

John stared at Duncan, wondering if the Jesuit had a stained glass heart. Rain began to beat against the windows, creating an illusion of movement on the stained faces of the murderous Indians and martyred Jesuits, and on young John's face. And on Duncan's. The man and child stared up at the glass.

Father Duncan's visits continued until John was seven years old. Then, with no warning or explanation, Duncan was gone. When John asked his parents about Father Duncan's whereabouts, Olivia and Daniel told him that the Jesuit had retired and moved to Arizona. In fact, Duncan's eccentricities had become liabilities. After the strange Sunday when he had openly wept during Eucharist and run out of the church before the closing hymn, Duncan was summarily removed from active duty and shipped to a retreat in Arizona. He walked into the desert one week after he arrived at the retreat and was never seen again.

As he grew up, John kept reading the newspaper account of the disappearance, though it contained obvious errors. Anonymous sources insisted that Father Duncan had lost his faith in God. John knew that Duncan had never lost his faith, but had caused others to believe he did. His body was never found, though a search party followed Duncan's tracks miles into the desert, until they simply stopped.

For John, though, Father Duncan did not vanish completely. The Jesuit, exhausted and sunburned, often visited him in dreams. Duncan never spoke. He just brought the smell, sounds, and images of the desert into John's head. The wind pushing sand from dune to dune, the scorpions and spiders, the relentless yellow sun and deep blue sky, the stand of palm trees on the horizon. John always assumed it was a Catholic way to die, lost in the desert, no water, no food, the unforgiving heat. But the hallucinations must have been magical. John knew that real Indians climbed into the mountains to have vision quests. Stripped of their clothes, they ate and drank nothing. Naked and starved, they waited for a vision to arrive. Father Duncan must have been on a vision quest in the desert when he walked to the edge of the world and stepped off. Did it feel good to disappear? Perhaps Duncan, as Indian and Christian, had discovered a frightening secret and could not live with it. Perhaps Duncan knew what existed on the other side of the desert. Maybe he was looking for a new name for God.

John attended St. Francis Catholic School from the very beginning. His shoes always black topsiders polished clean. His black hair very short, nearly a crew cut, just like every other boy in school. He was the only Indian in the school, but he had friends, handsome white boys. And John had danced with a few pretty white girls in high school. Mary, Margaret, Stephanie. He had fumbled with their underwear in the back seats of cars. John knew their smell, a combination of perfume, baby powder, sweat, and sex. A clean smell on one level, a darker odor beneath. Their breasts were small and perfect. John was always uncomfortable during his time with the girls, and he was never sorry when it was over. He was impatient with them, unsure of their motives, and vaguely insulting. The girls expected it. It was high school and boys were supposed to act that way. The girls assumed the boys were much more complicated than they actually were. Inside, John knew that he was more simple and shallow than other boys, and less than real.

"What are you thinking?" the girls always asked John. But John knew the girls really wanted to tell him what they were thinking. John's thoughts were merely starting points for the girls to talk about mothers and fathers, girlfriends, ex-boyfriends, pets, clothes, and a thousand other details. John felt insignificant at those times and retreated into a small place inside of himself, until the girls confused his painful silence with rapt interest.

The girls' fathers were always uncomfortable when they first met John, and grew more irritated as he continued to date Mary, Margaret, or Stephanie. The relationships began and ended quickly. A dance or two, a movie, a hamburger, a few hours in a friend's basement with generic rock music playing softly on the radio, cold fingers on warm skin.

"I just don't think it's working out," she'd tell John, who understood. He could almost hear the conversations that had taken place.

"Hon," a father would say to his daughter. "What was that boy's name?"

"Which boy, daddy?"

"That dark one."

"Oh, you mean John. Isn't he cute?"

"Yes, he seems like a very nice young man. You say he's at St. Francis? Is he a scholarship student?"

"I don't know. I don't think so. Does it matter?"

"Well, no. I'm just curious, hon. By the way, what is he? I mean, where does he come from?"

"He's Indian, daddy."

"From India? He's a foreigner?"

"No, daddy, he's Indian from here. You know, American Indian. Like bows and arrows and stuff. Except he's not like that. His parents are white."

"I don't understand."

"Daddy, he's adopted."

"Oh. Are you going to see him again?"

"I hope so. Why?"

"Well, you know. I just think. Well, adopted kids have so many problems adjusting to things, you know. I've read about it. They have self-esteem problems. I just think, I mean, don't you think you should find somebody more appropriate?"

The door would shut with a loud and insistent click. Mary, Margaret, or Stephanie would come to school the next day and give John the news. The daughters would never mention their fathers. Of course, there were a few white girls who dated John precisely because they wanted to bring home a dark boy. Through all of it, John repeatedly promised himself he would never be angry. He didn't want to be angry. He wanted to be a real person. He wanted to control his emotions, so he would often swallow his anger. Once or twice a week, he felt the need to run and hide. In the middle of a math class or a history exam, he would get a bathroom pass and quickly leave the classroom. His teachers were always willing to give him a little slack. They knew he was adopted, an Indian orphan, and was leading a difficult life. His teachers gave him every opportunity and he responded well. If John happened to be a little fragile, well, that was perfectly understandable, considering his people's history. All that alcoholism and poverty, the lack of God in their lives. In the bathroom, John would lock himself inside a stall and fight against his anger. He'd bite his tongue, his lips, until sometimes they would bleed. He would hold himself tightly and feel his arms, legs, and lower back shake with the effort. His eyes would be shut. He'd grind his teeth. One minute, two, five, and he would be fine. He would flush the toilet to make his visit seem normal, slowly wash his hands and return to the classroom. His struggles with his anger increased in intensity and frequency until he was visiting the bathroom on a daily basis during his senior year. But nobody noticed. In truth, nobody mentioned any strange behavior they may have seen. John was a trailblazer, a nice trophy for St. Francis, a successfully integrated Indian boy.

There were three hundred and seventy-six students at St. Francis. Along with three black kids, John was one of the four nonwhite students in the school. He was neither widely popular nor widely disliked. He played varsity basketball for two years, but never started, and entered the game when the outcome, a win or loss, was already decided. He was on the varsity only because he was an upperclassman and over six feet tall. His teammates cheered wildly whenever he entered the game because teammates are taught to behave that way. John understood this. He cheered for his teammates, even during those games in which he never played. He never really cared if the team won or lost. But he was always embarrassed when he had to play, because he knew he was not very good. In fact, he only played because his father, Daniel, a St. Francis alumnus, had been a star player.

"You need to get your hand behind the ball when you shoot," Daniel Smith said to John during one of their driveway practices.

"Like this?" asked John, desperately trying to hold the basketball correctly.

"No," Daniel said, calmly, patiently. Daniel Smith never raised his voice, not once, in all the years. He would coach John for hours, trying to show him how to play defense, box out for rebounds, throw the bounce pass. No matter how poorly John played, and he was awful, Daniel never yelled.

One winter, when John was a sophomore, Daniel read about an all-Indian basketball tournament that was going to be held at Indian Heritage High School in North Seattle. Daniel and Olivia both looked for any news about Indians and shared the information with John. The sportswriter made the tournament into some kind of joke, but Daniel thought it was a wonderful opportunity. He had never seen Indians play basketball. Maybe John would improve if he saw other Indians play.

John had spent time at different Indian events. Olivia had made sure of that. But he had never seen so many Indians crammed into such a small space. The Indian Heritage gym was full of Indians. All shapes and sizes, tribes and temperaments. Daniel and John found seats in the bleachers and watched a game between a Sioux team and a local team of Yakama Indians. The game was fast-paced and vaguely out of control, with offenses that took the first open shot, from anywhere on the court, and defenses that constantly gambled for steals. Most of the players were tall and impossibly thin, although a few were actually fat. The best player on the court was a chubby guy named Arnold, a Yakama Indian. Daniel and John knew he was named Arnold because they heard his name announced over the loudspeaker.

"Arnold for two."

"Arnold with a three-pointer."

"Arnold with the steal, and a nice pass for two."

Daniel decided that Arnold was the best player he had ever seen. He could have played Division I basketball. God, Daniel thought, this Indian is fifty pounds overweight, closing in on forty years old, and still plays well.

"Watch," Daniel said to John.

John was watching Arnold, but he was watching the people around him too. So many Indians, so many tribes, many sharing similar features, but also differing in slight and important ways. The Makahs different than the Quinaults, the Lummi different from the Puyallup. There were Indians with dark skin and jet-black hair. There were Indians with brown hair and paler skin. Green-eyed Indians. Indians with black blood. Indians with Mexican blood. Indians with white blood. Indians with Asian blood. All of them laughing and carrying on. Many Indians barely paying attention to the game. They were talking, telling jokes, and laughing loudly. So much laughter. John wanted to own that laughter, never realizing that their laughter was a ceremony used to drive away personal and collective demons. The Indians who were watching the game reacted mightily to each basket or defensive stop. They moaned and groaned as if each mistake were fatal, as if each field goal meant the second coming of Christ. But always, they were laughing. John had never seen so many happy people. He did not share their happiness.

"Look at him," Daniel said. "Look at that guy play."

John watched Arnold shoot a thirty-five-foot jumper that hit nothing but the bottom of the net. A glorious three-pointer. The crowd cheered and laughed some more. Arnold was laughing, on the court, doubled over, holding his stomach. Laughing so hard that tears ran down his face. His teammates were smiling and playing defense. The other team worked the ball around, trying to shoot a long jumper of their own, wanting to match Arnold's feat. A big man caught the ball in the far corner, faked a dribble, then took the shot. An air ball, missing the basket and backboard completely, by two or three feet. The big man fell on his back, laughing. The crowd laughed and rolled all over the bleachers, pounding each other on the back, hugging each other tightly. One Yakama player grabbed the rebound and threw a long pass downcourt to Arnold. He caught the pass, fumbled the ball a bit, dribbled in for the layup, and missed it. So much laughter that the refs called an official timeout. John looked at his father. Daniel was laughing. John felt like crying. He did not recognize these Indians. They were nothing like the Indians he had read about. John felt betrayed.

John never did become a good basketball player, but he graduated from high school on time, in 1987. Since he was an Indian with respectable grades, John would have been admitted into almost any public university had he bothered to fill out even one application. His parents pushed him to at least try a community or technical college, but John refused. During his freshman year in high school, John had read an article about a group of Mohawk Indian steel workers who helped build the World Trade Center buildings in New York City. Ever since then, John had dreamed about working on a skyscraper. He figured it was the Indian thing to do. Since Daniel Smith was an architect, he sometimes flattered himself by thinking that John's interest in construction was somehow related. Despite John's refusal to go to college, his parents still supported him in his decision, and were sitting in the third row as he walked across the stage at St. Francis to accept his diploma. Polite applause, a few loud cheers from his friends, his mother and father now standing. John flipped his tassel from one side to the other, blinked in the glare of the flashbulbs, and tried to smile. He had practiced his smile, knew it was going to be needed for this moment. He smiled. The cameras flashed. John was finished with high school and would never attend college. He walked offstage and stepped onto the fortieth floor of an unfinished office building in downtown Seattle.

John Smith was now twenty-seven years old. He was six feet, six inches tall and heavily muscled, a young construction worker perfect for all of the heavy lifting. His black hair was long and tucked under his hard hat. When he had first started working, his co-workers used to give him grief about his hair, but half of the crew had long hair these days. Seattle was becoming a city dominated by young white men with tiny ponytails. John always had the urge to carry a pair of scissors and snip off those ponytails at every opportunity. He hated those ponytails, but he did not let them distract him at work. He was a good worker, quiet and efficient. He was eating lunch alone on the fortieth floor when he heard the voices again.

John swallowed the last of his cold coffee and gently set the thermos down. He cupped his hand to his ear. He knew he was alone on this floor, but the voices were clear and precise. During the quiet times, he could hear the soft *why-why-why* as Father Duncan's leather sandals brushed against the sand on his long walk through the desert. Once, just once, John had heard the bubble of the baptismal fountain as Father Duncan dipped him into the water. Sometimes there were sudden sirens and explosions, or the rumble of a large crowd in an empty room. John could remember when it first happened, this noise in his head. He was young, maybe ten years old, when he heard strange music. It happened as he ran from school, across the parking lot, toward the car where Olivia waited for him. He knew this music was written especially for him: violins, bass guitar, piano, harmonica, drums. Now, as he sat on the fortieth floor and listened to those voices, John felt a sharp pain in his lower back. His belly burned.

"Jesus," said John as he stood up, waving his arms in the air.

"Hey, chief, what you doing? Trying to land a plane?"

The foreman was standing in the elevator a few feet away. John liked to eat his lunch near the elevator so he could move quickly and easily between floors. He always liked mobility.

"Well," said the foreman. "What's up?"

John lowered his arms.

"On my break," John said. He could still hear voices speaking to him. They were so loud, but the foreman was oblivious. The foreman knew John always ate lunch alone, a strange one, that John. Never went for beers after work. Showed up five minutes early every day and left five minutes late. He could work on one little task all day, until it was done, and never complain. No one bothered him because he didn't bother anyone. No one knew a damn thing about John, except that he worked hard, the ultimate compliment. Not that the hard work mattered anymore, since there would be no more high-rise work in Seattle after they finished this job. They were building the last skyscraper in Seattle. Computers had made the big buildings obsolete. No need to shove that many workers into such a small space. After this last building was complete, the foreman would take a job for the state. He did not know what John had planned.

"Well," the foreman said. "Lunch is over. Get in. We need you down on thirty-three."

John was embarrassed. He felt the heat build in his stomach, rise through his back, and fill his head. It started that way. The heat came first, followed quickly by the music. A slow hum. A quiet drum. Then a symphony crashing through his spinal column. The foreman brought the heat and music. John looked at him, a short white man with a protruding belly and big arms. An ugly man with a bulbous nose and weak chin, though his eyes were a striking blue.

John knew if he were a real Indian, he could have called the wind. He could have called a crosscutting wind that would've sliced through the fortieth floor, pulled the foreman out of the elevator, and sent him over the edge of the building. But he's strong, that foreman, and he would catch himself. He'd be hanging from the edge by his fingertips.

In his head, John could see the foreman hanging from the fortieth floor.

"Help me!" the foreman would shout.

John saw himself plant his feet just inches from the edge, reach down, take the foreman's wrists in his hands, and hold him away from the building. John and the foreman would sway back and forth like a pendulum. Back and forth, back and forth.

"Jesus!" the foreman would shout. "Pull me up!"

John would look down to see the foreman's blue eyes wide with fear. That's what I need to see, that's what will feed me, thought John. Fear in blue eyes. He would hold onto the foreman as long as possible and stare down into those terrified blue eyes. Then he'd let him fall.

"Let's go, chief," the foreman said, loud and friendly. "We ain't got all day. We need you on thirty-three."

John stepped into the elevator. The foreman pulled the gate shut and pressed the button for the thirty-third floor. Neither talked on the way down. John could feel the tension in his stomach as the elevator made its short journey. He fought against the music.

"Chuck needs your help," the foreman said when they arrived.

John looked where the foreman pointed. The thirty-third floor was a controlled mess. Chuck, a white man with a huge moustache, was pounding a nail into place. He raised a hammer and brought it down on the head of the nail. He raised the hammer, brought it down again. Metal against metal. John saw sparks. Sparks. Sparks. He rubbed his eyes. The sparks were large enough and of long enough duration to turn to flame. The foreman didn't see it. The rest of the crew didn't see it. Chuck raised the hammer again and paused at the top of his swing. As the hammer began its next descent, John could see it happening in segments, as in a series of still photographs. In that last frozen moment, in that brief instant before the hammer struck again its explosion of flame, John knew exactly what to do with his life.

John needed to kill a white man.

The Search for Indian

MILTON LEE AND JAMIE LEE

Edited transcript of a radio documentary, with interviews of Loretta Williams (Shinnecock), Tom Porter (Mohawk), Leonard Prescott (Mdewaketon Sioux), Alan Michelson (Mohawk), Rick Hill (Tuscarora), Rita Pyrillis (Cheyenne River Sioux), Greg Borland (Cheyenne River Sioux), Mike Her Many Horses (Cheyenne River Sioux), and Gerald Clifford (Oglala Sioux).

READER: *Whitlock Crossing, Cheyenne Agency, South Dakota, February 4, 1948. Miss Kay, a twenty-eight- or twenty-nine-year-old Indian girl, was referred to a worker by Sister William, St. Luke's hospital in Aberdeen. Miss Kay entered the hospital the day before and had given birth that day, February 4, to a baby boy out of wedlock. Sister William said that Miss Kay had another child out of wedlock which she had kept.*

MILT: The pages of my birth records are blotchy, the print thick and irregular either from dirty keys or copies made from copies. The record was eight pages long and first came into my hands in 1986. When I looked up Whitlock Crossing on a South Dakota map, it was under water, flooded when the Oahe reservoir was formed.

READER: *Miss Kay supposed that her pregnancy is known to the agency, but she does not want them to know for sure that she has had a child. She did not tell the worker this, but Sister William had stated that Mr. and Mrs. Smith, who teach in the school, would like to have adopted the new baby. Miss Kay did not want them to have him, because she did not wish to know where he was.*

MILT: In truth this first inquiry into my heritage had little to do with any deep desire to know my birth family or my connection to these people. I just wanted to be an Indian so I could do the production work I seemed to be always doing in Indian Country without the constant question, "Are you a real Indian or not?" The records said that my birth mother looked "Indianish" and that she hadn't wanted to know where I was. She didn't sign the adoption papers until I was over three months old.

READER: *February 29, 1948. Worker later saw baby, who is called Joe by the nurses. He is very thin with small features. Worker did not think he showed his Indian blood particularly. March 24, 1948. Baby was moved from St. Luke's in Aberdeen to St. Mary's in Pierre and registered as Douglas Ford.*

MILT: I put the file away for several years making very few inquiries into the information it provided. Finally, a few years ago, a very important teacher in my life turned to me unexpectedly and asked, "Where are you from?" Her question became like a Zen koan for me. Where am I from? It led me back to that file and, in fact, it led me into this "Search for Indian." It prompted me to ask others, all over the county, what their idea of "Indian" was. The answers, like my travels, were all over the map.

RICK: I always used to tell people that the difference between being an Indian and not is that you got used to death very quickly. You lived with death. Everybody has got a cousin who committed suicide, a young guy killed in a car wreck, a baby that died.

TOM: There's no more really Indian, I don't care where you go in the United States. They're biologically Indian but they're not real Indian anymore.

LORETTA: No one has ever, ever challenged the fact that I have French ancestry. Isn't that wild? I mean, I don't look French, but I say French ancestry and everybody nods. I could say African American and most people do not blink, but look with a little confusion on their faces and I say Shinnecock and they go, *Really?*

GERALD: If I say I'm an Indian, I am letting the oppressors define me. If I say I am a Lakota, I am affirming who I am.

MIDGE: As long as we allow the networks to continue playing the old, stereotypical cartoons, and we allow the Disney studio to change the Pocahontas story to Barbie and Ken in the wilderness, and as long as we allow them to play the old John Wayne movies, I guess we're going to still be in that same bind.

RITA: Well, yeah, isn't that the million-dollar question?

LORETTA: Here's part of the dilemma. For me, it's an issue of identity. Can I say I am an Indian if I have never been enrolled in a tribe?

RITA: For me it's something that, in my heart, I feel I can't take off or change about myself. And I've wanted to.

GREG: It don't have nothing to do with blood quantum; it has everything to do with philosophy and heart.

RICK: A couple of months ago I asked my dad, "When you were a kid, what did you think about being an Indian?" He says, "We never thought about it. To tell you the truth, we didn't know we were Indians. All we knew is we were these families living on the reserve in Ontario and everybody farming, my dad's way. We were too busy working to worry about being Indian." He meant they were doing the Indian work, farming and trading, and he said it wasn't until he went to school that he realized that there is a non-Indian teacher talking about Indians. That happened probably when he was about five. My little girl, when she was about the same age, we were sitting there talking at the dinner table one night and I mentioned that word Indians and she looked and she says, "What do you mean we're Indians?" I says, "We're Iroquois Indians, we're Tuscaroras. Your mother's an Indian, your grandmother's an Indian, my mother's an Indian, my father, we're all Indians." And she looked at me and she says, "Daddy, I don't want to be an Indian," and I says "Yeah, but you are. Why?" And she says, "Indians are too mean, they're always hurting women." Now, where does a little five-year-old girl who grew up on the reservation get these ideas? Well, on the television. No wonder Indians kind of grow up a little confused sometimes, what it means to be an Indian.

MILT: Maybe this show is a map of Indian country; my story and the story of others, the route we have all taken to answer the question, What does it mean to be an Indian? In this day of mass identity confusion, the question is being asked, in individual minds, in courts, before tribal councils. I met Loretta Williams at a conference in Bismarck, North Dakota. For her, a LONG way from home.

LORETTA: I grew up in Oyster Bay, which is an upper-middle-class town, small town, still on Long Island, but there were no other folks that you would categorize Indian except for my relatives. It was such an assumption that that's what we were. Not until I left was it challenged. That's when I tried to enroll. You grow up with this assumption that this is what you are, and then someone comes along and says, "No, you're not . . ."

My father raised me to say that I was Shinnecock, and we'd go to powwows and I had been introduced to folks who I was told were my relatives. But my dad died when I was thirteen, and all the information about what connection I have to that tribe vanished with him. I'm almost forty. A few years ago, I called the tribe and I said, "Here are the names back to my great-grandfather. Do you have any records that would establish that I am part of this lineage, that I am Shinnecock?" They said they don't keep those kind of records and that it was up to me to prove it. That's painful. I want to be able to say that I am Shinnecock and not have to worry that I'm offending someone, worry that I'm a fraud, worry that I am deceiving someone. Right now, being Shinnecock seems to mean you live there, nothing else.

MILT: The Shinnecock reservation is on the very end of Long Island in New York State. On a recent trip, we abandoned the beach and opted to drive out to the rez to see Loretta's homeland. It was evening when we arrived. The reservation is a small boot of land jutting out into the sea, and you drive onto the rez and leave the Hampton communities behind; you feel you have definitely entered another country. Many reservations seem to have this same aura, a sense of longevity but also isolation and protection.

LORETTA: I just want to be, I just want to be Shinnecock.

MILT: Confusion, chaos, loss of identity. It is as if the European infiltration tore Indian communities into confetti—and the pieces continue to drift slowly to the ground. These stories reflect that confusion. Some, like Tom Porter, believe that being Indian is all about connection to the land, language and a way of thinking. He is a Mohawk who lives in a rich beautiful valley in New York State. It is the original homelands of the Mohawk people, but Tom is the first to return to live there on 400 acres that they bought. The grounds have a ragtag collection of outbuildings, a huge Amish barn, and two beautiful but dilapidated houses.

TOM: The Mohawk people had almost 150 years or more of fighting and just taking a stand to try to keep our lands and to keep our people together. But 150 years of struggle took their toll. Our ancestors went north to Akwesasne, which is our hunting and fishing grounds up there on the border, so they didn't have to fight the Europeans anymore. But when we left here, we said that some day our grandchildren will return to the valley, and again they will make a fire and again the sacred smoke will ascend into the Creator's land. It was prophesied like that when they left. In my youth I heard these stories from my grandmother and elders talking about our real homeland, so I been thinking about coming here for about thirty years to re-settle and start over again just with the traditional Mohawk people. Christianity took away our spirit and our soul that is Indian and put in garage-sale religion. It's not the one the Creator gave to us. Colonization—the school, the social systems, economic systems, all European origin—de-programmed the Indian. There's no more real Indian. I don't care where you go in the United States, they're biologically Indians but they're not real Indian anymore. They don't have the same values, they don't have the same history; it's like a made-over, colonized product of colonization.

It's that way because of Carlisle Indian School, Haskell, Spanish Indian School, Thomas Indian School—all those government schools took all the Indian kids over there to de-program them, to de-spirit them, to de-culture them. My great-grandfather went to Carlisle, so did my grandfather, and they kept them there ten to fourteen years, never seen their father or their mother, or their grandma or their grandpa, and been forbidden to talk their language too.

Is it any wonder why we got alcoholism? Is it any wonder why we got suicide, the highest of anybody else? Is it any wonder that we're going crazy and we're so stupid we don't even know what we're doing? That we're so confused and we got no hope and we got no dignity and we got no spirit and we got no courage?

The big dream we have here is to turn this place into a Carlisle School in reverse in the next couple of years. I'm going to have to fund-raise like you never seen fund-raising before. It's only on the drawing boards now, in the dream state, and we're going to try to take fifty kids at the maximum and have them board here for at least four years like Carlisle. Their families can come visit them, but everything will be immersed in Iroquois language.

All the history will be taught, all the treaties, broken or not, will be taught. All the true history will be taught. All the spiritual ceremonies will be taught so that we can find again our balance and our place relative to the universe as real Indians again.

MILT: Tom and the people with him welcomed us, fed us, told us their stories and dreams, and yet I left wondering to myself, can Indian be taught in a sort of reverse assimilation? Or is the process of defining Indian in this day and age more of a reaching out into the future rather than attempting to reclaim the past?

Leonard Prescott lives in Minneapolis and has been instrumental in helping start Indian casinos. The Little Six tribe in Shakopee has experienced monumental success—a fact that has created a sudden flurry of people trying to enroll in the Mdewaketon Sioux tribe.

LEONARD: My name is Leonard Prescott. I've been a tribal chairman for about seven years. I've been involved in a lot of Indian issues in the last ten years. I lived on the reservation in Morton, Minnesota until I was about five years old, when we moved into St. Paul. There, I was really out of touch with my culture, my people. We went back to visit every now and then and it really wasn't until I moved back to the Shakopee reservation in 1970 that I learned what it meant to be on that land, that that kind of identity started to come back to me.

My grandfather was traditional, but living in the St. Paul/Minneapolis area, I wasn't that traditional. I used to listen to my grandfather's stories, and some of the things I talked about in the years I worked for Little Six were from memories that he had given me. He used to always say that some day the Indian people of this country are going to come back and be strong again. I remembered that time when I wrote a story about this buffalo hunter from an Indian tribe a long time ago, and that buffalo hunter being alive today looked across the nation and he saw what has happened to his people. So I related that to the buffalo. The buffalo was everything to Indian people—it was their food, it was their clothing, it was their spiritual well-being, it was tools and weapons. This buffalo hunter goes home and he sees what is happening in the United States, and he prays to the grandfathers. He says, "Grandfathers, my people suffer because of alcohol and drugs."

MILT: Leonard tells a parable about the new white buffalo. The old weapons no longer work and today's warrior wears a different suit of clothes.

LEONARD: They all meet and they're thanking the grandfathers, and the grandfathers have a message for them that this buffalo is a fragile buffalo and he'll not be with you long. While he's here you should build your homes, you should take of his meat and become stronger, you should take of his clothing so you're warm and your houses are filled, you should take of his bones so that you're spiritually stronger. He says to create new buffalo of your own. So out of that, I said there is a new buffalo that needs to be created. The new buffalo is not the one that you get with a bow and arrow, it's one that you have to recognize if you want to be a fireman and get a fireman's suit. If you want to be an attorney, get an attorney's suit. If you want to be a doctor, get a doctor's suit. I mean education.

MILT: Porter and Prescott sit on opposite political poles, each with his own idea of what Indian is all about. Alan Michelson, an Indian living in Manhattan, floats in the middle waters of a more personal search. Ironically, I had trouble imagining Indians in New York City. A shadow of my own socialization I guess—and ironic because they once owned the entire island. Alan is another adoptee, an Iroquois baby who was placed in a Jewish family.

ALAN: I was 25 when my adoptive mother died. I had another wave of curiosity, because I'd lost my immediate family, but there's one on a reserve somewhere. I think I was just having a casual conversation with a cousin of mine—my sister talks to our cousin in Buffalo, Gert, all the time. At some point or other we had a phone conversation where I think Gert, very emotional, says something to the effect of, "Oh my God, Alan, you're Indian, or *she's* Indian." It was the farthest thing from my mind. So that just floored me. It floored her and it floored me and I said, "Well, where from, you know, what tribe?" And the information she had was, at that point, just Iroquois.

I still wasn't ready to meet her, but I was ready to see a picture. I got this sweet little letter from Carol with a Polaroid in it. I'll never forget opening that letter and taking out that Polaroid and just staring at this face that must have been no more than, you know, less than a half square inch in the picture of this beautiful, young-looking, smiling, very vivacious and happy-looking person who happened to be my natural mother (laughs).

All I can say is that my family has embraced me with open arms. If belonging to a tribe or a nation or band or whatever is really about relatives and about family, about an extended family, well, maybe there is a way of thinking about the way my family has welcomed me as an example for others to welcome, to welcome others.

MILT: On the tip of Manhattan is the National Museum of the American Indian. Just a few steps out and you can see the Statue of Liberty. The museum is housed, this makes me chuckle, in the Old Customs House. It was the gate through which millions of immigrants had to enter this county. In fact, the high domed ceiling of the museum boasts elaborate paintings of the colonization of the USA: Chris Columbus looking out over his dominions.

The Smithsonian invited people from many nations to be involved in the design of the museum. Rick Hill was the special assistant to the director when I first met him. He lives in upstate New York on the Tuscarora reservation.

RICK: I consider myself the Iroquois person who was the man without a country. I was born to an Iroquois family, my father's a Mohawk, my mother is Tuscarora, so right away you have that dual identity. My father's from Canada, my mother's from here. Right here where I live is where my mother grew up, this is her old homestead, used to have an old farmhouse here. I was born in Buffalo, my dad was an ironworker, as a lot of the Iroquois men were back then, living in the city. We spent our life going back and forth.

I was pretty much agnostic. I believed life was important but I didn't understand why I believed it. I grew up in kind of a nonsectarian Indian family. I wasn't pushed one way or another about religion. My parents were raised as Christian but didn't want to force us.

So when I began to look into things to satisfy my spiritual need, it was only in the traditional longhouse of the Iroquois that I found any kind of affinity, found my place and changed my life. Eventually, I decided I wanted to marry a Tuscarora, have Tuscarora kids and raise them on the reservation, and that's my master plan for myself and I've been doing that now for seventeen years.

I used to make a distinction between genetic Indians and cultural Indians. A lot of people are part Indian, genetically, whether they are enrolled or not. But not all of them believe in being an Indian. Like you say, this first stage of realization is that you are an Indian and then the rest of your life is measured to me by these certain rites of passage in the journey of life. But you got to make big decisions once you realize you're an Indian. Well, do you want to continue to explore what that means? Do you want to live like an Indian? Whatever that means. Do you want to live on the reservation? Do you want to learn your language, do you want to learn your traditional religion, are you going to marry an Indian, do you want to raise Indian kids?

When I was younger I used to go to Allegany (a Seneca nation reserve, New York), used to go down there hunting and I just used to really like it. But in the longhouse, there used to be these old men sitting there. They'd have work pants on but a suit coat, this little hat, cane, all speaking Seneca, and I used to sit there and say, "That's the kind of old man I want to be, I want to be just like those old guys." We used to love to hear them talk Seneca, you know, and they'd stand up. There was this one guy in particular, I always watched him. I just liked the way he moved, the way he acted, his presence. It wasn't charisma, it was just like here's a guy who knows what the world is all about and he does these ceremonies. Anyways, at his funeral, I was standing in line, to go up and walk around the body. The men go first and I was there with all the young men, and I would get closer up to the casket and I was feeling bad because I just hated to see this guy die. Finally this one behind me says, "Well, this is a lot of fuss for a white man." I looked at him and I said, "What are you talking about?" He says, "He's a white man." He was adopted by Senecas as a kid, raised on the reservation, and he spoke better Seneca than most of the Senecas. I had to confront, in my mind, my own internal racism, because I didn't like white people very much, and suddenly here's a guy, you know, a Caucasian, but he is a Seneca, so it was a good lesson there for me because the Senecas depended on him. They hated to see him go. They took him in and made him into a Seneca, made him into a good one. I always remember that when I get carried away too much about thinking about the genetic Indian and the cultural Indian. So that's why I made that distinction. However, in the art world I confront the other thing, artists who claim to be Indian because it will somehow advance their careers, compared to somebody like him who could say he's Seneca because he was. He was made one.

MILT: Last spring, a white woman and a black woman, visitors to the reservation, confronted me on my Indianness or lack of it. They said I was exploiting the people, that I had no right to do a story such as this one. A few weeks later I was enrolled as a member of the Cheyenne River Sioux tribe, and when the council meeting ended, several people shook my hand and said, "Welcome home." And about this same time I was invited to an Indians-only Sun Dance. In the middle of all these confusing messages, I wasn't really sure if I was an "Indian." Talking to all these people had not clarified the issue for me.

Rita Pyrillis was also searching out her connection to my tribe. She had been adopted by a Greek family.

RITA: I didn't have a whole lot of awareness of my Indian heritage or a lot of interest, quite frankly, until I got to college, and then I started to become curious. After journalism school, I was a reporter for the *Los Angeles Times*. I was doing a story on Indian health clinics, and I went down there to interview the dentist and the doctor and some of the people for a feature story. One woman came up to me and said, "Where are you from?" And I said, "Oh, I'm from Redondo Beach, I'm from LA, I'm from around here," and she said, "No, no, where are you from?" I said, "I'm from, well, I was born in Chicago," and she says, "No, where are you from?" And I said, "What do you mean, where am I from? I'm telling you, you know." And she said, "No, what's your tribe?" And that just totally blew me away because no one had ever asked me that question before, ever. And I was just shocked because even when I was growing up and I got teased in these white, suburban communities it was always for being dark. You know, they didn't know I was Indian. They would call me everything under the sun, but the racism wasn't directed at me because I was Indian, it was because they were really white and I was dark and I was just different; I looked different, I acted different. It had nothing to do with being Native American. It just had to do with being another color. So this was the first time anybody had ever identified me as Native American, and I looked at her and I said, I was sort of kidding, and I said, "No, no, no, I'm Greek. Don't you hear my last name, Pyrillis? That's a Greek last name." She laughed. "No, you're not Greek," she said. "I can tell you look Indian but you don't know your tribe, you don't know where you're from." I had never really told anybody this story and I wasn't going to start with this total stranger, so I just told her, "Well, you know, I was adopted out as a baby so I, I don't know." Her reaction was really interesting. She was joking around with me up until that point and then she looked really kind of solemn and said, "That's really sad, you know, Indian people need to know where they come from. . . ."

What got it started for me was being asked what tribe I was and not being able to answer and thinking about what that really meant. With the history of Indian people and, I thought, here I am, erased. I mean, I don't show up on any tribal rolls, I don't know what tribe I am, I don't know who my people are, I don't know anything. They succeeded in erasing me as an Indian person.

So that's what got me started going to powwows and getting involved with the Indian community in Los Angeles and meeting different people. I found acceptance, I felt really comfortable there. I remember my first powwow and looking at people who looked similar to me, and it was a mind-blower because nobody noticed me. I'm used to walking into a room and people noticing me, not because I'm striking but because I look different. There's the inevitable question: "What nationality are you, and oh, let me guess, let me guess, you're Mexican, no no no let me guess, you're Filipino, um, let me guess." I mean, people love to play this "what's your ethnic identity" with me and with us.

Finally here I was among a group of people and nobody cared who I was, nobody even looked at me. I thought, "Oh, I like this. I'm a nobody (laughs). I'm a nobody here, nobody knows who I am and nobody cares."

I have lost my culture to an extent, but I can always get that back, and that is what I'm in the process of doing right now. I was lost to my tribe and to my family, my Indian family, but now I'm back. I can't make up for the thirty-three years that I lost, but I can start to try.

MILT: Rita is now also an enrolled member. When I interviewed Greg Borland, our tribal chairman, at the Rapid City Airport, he thanked me for seeking enrollment into the tribe. This "search" continues to spin my mind around.

GREG: This situation goes back quite a ways. When our reservation was first formed, you have to remember that all you had to do was be enrolled into the agency back when the agency was run by the federal government, if you were Arikara, maybe Hidatsa, maybe even Mandan, or different mixtures of Sioux, French Indian—you know, they literally started the rolls. Then of course it became law in 1935, the Indian Recovery Act provided for a power of enrollment. Back then, it depended on your parents, though there was a big discussion over parents because to a Lakota, "parents" means also your grandparents, but to non-Indians, it means just your immediate parents. Then up to 1980, the Bureau of Indian Affairs started the issue of blood quantum, blood quantum, blood quantum—everyone was talking blood quantum. So they set forth a tribal constitutional amendment that was initiated by the Bureau of Indian Affairs that anyone born after the date of, I think it was like June 19, 1980, would have to be a quarter or more Cheyenne River Sioux. You could literally be four-fourths Indian, but if you didn't have one-quarter Cheyenne River, you weren't eligible for enrollment.

Just recently, we had a situation with a little girl, she's fourteen years old now. I'll tell you her tragic story. When she was a year and a half old her mom got run over by a car. Her mom had never been enrolled. Her grandma was a full-blooded Cheyenne River Sioux. But the mother had never been enrolled in any tribe. And the little girl, of course, couldn't get enrolled, since her mom got run over and her dad was unknown. They believed that he was Indian but nobody knew. So because she was a child without a country, and an orphan, her grandparents long since dead, and with no known relatives, she has been bounced from one foster home to the other for the last twelve and half years. All of the foster homes have been non-Indian. Nobody has ever been willing to adopt her. She's going through a lot of problems.

We took the big plunge and enrolled her based on the tradition, saying that her grandma was an enrolled member even though her mom wasn't enrolled, and we caught some flack, but we went ahead and did it anyway, and I stuck my neck out and said, "Look, this is the right thing to do. She is fourteen and an orphan, but at least now she has a family of 11,722 relatives because she can now claim us as a big giant *tiyospaye* [extended family], even though she has always been a member of our *tiyospaye*." Our council would have probably never done that two years ago, five years ago; I know they would have never done it seven years ago. So, it's a matter of growing.

MILT: The last people I chose to interview for this show are friends, people I have known for a long time, and who no longer question their own identity. In fact, Mike Her Many Horses lifted the issue of identity to a new level: what if racism itself is the result of a displaced European population whose own damaged roots have created a culture that is no deeper than dust?

MIKE: This country is very young in relationship to other established, western European countries and actually, it's even kind of a misnomer to use *country,* because you need to talk about one culture dealing with another. The culture that's evolved out of the United States in the last several hundred years is still growing, it's in its infancy yet. And sometimes it manifests itself as a really good and generous culture. They can be very giving and very open with their resources, and other times it can be as heartless as all git up. Its culture is still trying to find its legs. It doesn't understand older cultures because they want these older cultures to melt into theirs and to be like them. And that's possible to do but only in terms of economics; that's the playing field where our people are judged. If you make a certain income then you are truly an American, but that doesn't hold water here.

In trying to deal with the Native people, when they found out it became to expensive to kill us—I think the statistic was that every

Indian killed in open conflict cost them a million dollars, and a beginning country couldn't afford that kind of campaign—so they looked at education as a way of changing us, changing our attitudes and seeing the great benefits of this new society they created called America. Well, that didn't work either. So the way they've dealt with us is give us a number and try to identify us as a particular Indian of a particular tribe and then put some conditions on those. That worked for a time, but now it hasn't worked because we as Lakota people decide who is a Lakota, so we fight against that, we resist against that and we know that we're all distinct. You get comments working in public that "you don't look like some Indians I've seen before," or "you're not as dark as," or "you're lighter than," or you know, the American public has their perceptions. You're supposed to be whatever their notion is of that stereotype. Yeah, so you got to continually fight that as well. I use a lot of sarcasm in dealing with that. I will say you're not my idea of a stereotypical white man, you know. You're kind of half-way honest (laughs).

MILT: Gerald Clifford made me realize that identity is a question that people of all races struggle with, and that people of all races must answer for themselves. Those that have the answer no longer struggle.

GERALD: A group of folks, my folks included, formed the American Indian Leadership Council in 1969, maybe late '68. That group actually put that question exactly the same way: What does it mean to be an Indian? We had a series of meetings for about five weekends in a row. Out of that intense dialogue pretty much came a vision for the future by that group of people, and we decided that it doesn't mean anything to be an Indian.

We're Lakota. We're Oglala. We're Oglala Lakota. That's what we are. We're not Indians. What it means to be an Indian is to be viewed as a lesser human being than anybody else, and to be treated that way. It means to be viewed, as you walk into border towns, as being lazy and incompetent and probably drunk most of the time. When we adopt the notion that we're Lakota, then we stand straight because we know that we are a people. Particularly for those who have taken that back to traditional spirituality. When you affirm that you're Lakota, in your own way, you're affirming that you stood on a hill in Humblecha, and you're affirming that you pierced at the Sun Dance Tree, perhaps; you're affirming that you have adopted this view of reality; that means that you have a commitment to ensure that the people live. What does it mean to be a Lakota? That is what it means. What does it mean to be an Indian? It means nothing.

MILT: I have met a sister, and talked on the phone to another. I have a brother in Colorado who phoned the other day—turns out we actually spent two hours together a few years ago. I don't know what to think of this new family. They look a little like me. They live on reservations and are "Indian." Our parents are no longer alive but I have cousins, nephews, and nieces—so much family. And they have welcomed me with warmth and genuine pleasure. Charlie, my sister, played a tape for me of our father's AA testimonial and it is almost like his words finally penetrated the cat and mouse game I had been playing in my mind.

The search for Indian is about family. Indian family, in my case. It's about love. And looking for love. Nothing else. Nothing else matters at all. When I am square there, in my heart, that is what matters. I'll never know what my life would have been like had Miss Kay kept me, but of one thing I am sure—everything happens for the best.

PART 4

Children of the Dragonfly

The dragonfly poised a moment in the air over the head of the boy, then like a star seeking the house of a wife [meteor], he sped forth over the broad cornfields.

Hence to this day the dragonfly comes (the black, white, and red one) in early summer when the corn tassels bloom, humming from one plant to another, yet never content with his resting place.

And following him comes the beautiful green dragonfly, for of the green stalks of corn made the boy the companion of the first dragonfly, hence the green dragonfly is green with yellow light like a stalk of growing corn in the sunlight.

When eight days had passed, there came from over the northwestern hills the nation of Ha'wik'uh. Amongst them came many strangers from other tribes and countries. And when they entered the town through vast fields of ripening corn, they passed beneath the house of the great priest-boy, and breathed humbly upon his hands.

—Cushing, "The Origin of the Dragonfly" 121–22

In this epigraph from the Zuni story of the boy and girl who were separated from their people (see the introduction), Dragonfly, having carried the children's prayers to the spirit world, makes his ceremonial departure from the story into the present world, where his kind carry on their purpose. The reunion the Dragonfly has brought about restores and augments the nation's members, sustenance, and spiritual strength.

Dragonfly's first step toward restoration was to break the silence and isolation within which the children were withering. He carried their appeals and their story to the Corn Sisters, who sent food with him and brought comfort themselves to the children. The stories, poems, and autobiographical essays in part 4 all intend to break various silences, whether imposed through the suppression of language, culture, family history, or parentage, or created through the agency of law, education, or foster and adoptive homes. In conventional closed adoptions, according to Betty Jean Lifton, the adoptive child's social history is kept in a "conspiracy of silence" (36–37). Such silence is deeper for Native children in non-Native homes, where the facts of origin are often subject to the same devaluation as that imposed on Native America. "The metaphor of adoption serves the literature of dominance," wrote Chippewa author Gerald Vizenor (160). Subtracting the literary elements from his statement bares a political fact: adoption serves dominance as an instrument of colonial control. As a benign metaphor for assimilation, it propagates the "dominant" culture as normative while silencing the original birth culture of Native America. A post-immigrant culture that has severed itself from the past makes adoption a version of itself, severing the past from the adoptive child, but it does so at great risk of not knowing who the child is, even as it does not know its own origin.

Part 4 makes clear the destructiveness of such adoptions and the promise that adoption need not be practiced in those terms. Lifton argues for open adoptions that recognize that the child has two sets of parents and a "dual identity" (274–75). That duality is at greater extremes in transcultural than in same-culture adoptions, but openness in any arrangement allows all participants to listen and learn, as we will see in autobiographical narratives and essays by Joyce carlEtta Mandrake, Alan Michelson, Patricia Aqiimuk Paul, Terry Trevor, and others. As they show, the first step toward becoming whole is to find the voice to express the desire to become whole.

Whether the writers or their children or grandchildren are (or were) adoptive, foster-home, or boarding-school children, or children whose family heritage had been suppressed, they confront the disruption in their lives through the very act of writing, its pleasures and terrors, and through the creation of identities that are shaped by the effort to recover and carry on.

Peter Cuch ("I Wonder What the Car Looked Like") imagines again and again his father being taken as a child into the placement program of the Church of Jesus Christ of Latter-day Saints. For more than twenty years, the Church removed thousands of children from many tribes and placed them in Mormon foster homes (Heinerman and Shupe 223–27). At the moment of apprehension, Cuch's father's and his own future were set on a course, a course determined by the series of variously dysfunctional families from whom his father learned parenthood—a course that Cuch is determined his own children will not follow.

S. L. Wilde and Eric Gansworth have written poems about grandparents who had attended boarding school. Wilde's grandmother allowed her family to believe that she had lost her Anishnaabe language long ago in school, but Wilde ("A Letter to My Grandmother") treasures her childhood memories of her grandmother speaking when she thought no one could hear, and whispering to her in her native language at bedtime. In "It Goes Something Like This," Gansworth envisions his grandparents meeting as children on the train to boarding school and beginning a life together that they bring back to their people, even as their story, the writer admits, also brings him home.

Beyond the provisions of education that affected children, procedures such as allotment and enrollment could disrupt family heritage, as evident in the mixed-mode poems by Kimberly Roppolo and Phil Young (with the editor). In Young's "Wetumka," the consequences of his grandfather's decision not to enroll are sequenced with episodes from a traditional story of the separation of parents and children. Young's efforts to restore the broken and scattered paper trail of family documents back to the first tribal rolls evokes tribal and family history, and the personal complications of being an artist and a Cherokee. Roppolo's "Breeds and Outlaws" uses traditional lore to guide her recovery of family history and her developing sense of her modern Creek-Cherokee-Choctaw identity.

The final seven authors write of adoption from a range of experiences in the suppression or encouragement of connecting with Native birth heritage and in the ways that such connection can be made. In "The Long Road Home," Lawrence Sampson's adoptive parents hid him and poisoned his mind against his Cherokee father. But the boy intuitively came to know that he had been living under a lie, and both he and his birth father built a strong bond with determination and love.

In semi-autobiographical short fiction, both Beverley McKiver ("When the Heron Speaks") and Joyce carlEtta Mandrake ("Memory Lane Is the Next Street Over") find spirit helpers to bring them to a deeper understanding of their ancestry and heritage. In both stories, the adoptive parents are credited with an active interest in seeing their children successful in their pursuits.

Within the family silence concerning his birth, Alan Michelson ("Lost Tribe") toys with understanding himself as, at various ages, Peter Pan, half bison, Superman, Spanish, Jewish, as one exotic or another, until he discovers what he was born: Mohawk. And Sicilian. Raised Jewish. Michelson's humor displaces the silence about his past and underscores his need to discover and define his identity, a need that grows along with his vocation as an artist.

The opportunities of adoptive parenthood concern Patricia Aqiimuk Paul and Terry Trevor. In "The Connection," Paul reverses many of the conditions that had governed her early life as an adoptive child, by (with her adoptive parents' blessing) finding the dispersed members of her birth family through exhaustive searching, adopting a birth cousin's child, marrying into an American Indian family, and becoming a lawyer working for indigenous rights.

The excerpt from Terry Trevor's memoir *Pushing up the Sky* concerns two forms of adoptive motherhood: being counseled to surrender her yet unborn Indian child and later adopting two children of Korean ancestry. She advocates that parents "provide ties to the child's birth culture," an ideal that Trevor practices generously with her children.

The anthology ends with two of Annalee Lucia Bensen's dream songs that planted the seed of this book several years ago. Indian ancestry manifest in dream and vision does not invite interrogation, but prompts a pure poetry of unself-conscious expression that continues to lead to revelation after revelation of that ancestry and that self.

I Wonder What the Car Looked Like

PETER CUCH

I wonder if the car was one of those watermelons from the late fifties when my father was stolen. In 1958 somehow one of those old cars found its way through the Uintah Mountains to my father's home.

I wonder what color that car was. Who drove it? How did he find the small log cabin, hidden in a valley, over a mile above sea level? How did he avoid the ditches and ruts of the bumpy dirt road? Who led him to the site? It must have been one of those converted Indians, a social servant with the Book of Mormon in one hand and a willow in the other. Sometimes conversion of faith requires some added persuasion. I wonder if he honestly believed he was doing the right thing. That God had sent him to save these souls. That it was in these Indians' best interests to be placed in a non-Indian home.

It was common for Mormon and other churches to take Ute children from their impoverished families living on the Uintah and Ouray Indian reservation in the northeastern corner of Utah. It was part of a bigger plan of assimilation, a way of getting out of a debt. If you take the culture, religion, customs, and language from the children, then they could no longer be considered Indian, no longer grow up and have Indian children, and they could no longer claim the debt owed them.

That's why they invented boarding schools like the ones my grand-mother was raised in. The only picture I have seen of her as a child was one where she was standing in a long line of girls who had their hair cut short. They were all wearing the same dark dresses and black shoes. She is the girl who looks particularly miserable. It was that misery that she passed on to her children.

I wonder what was going through that eight-year-old's mind as he was kidnapped. He must have been kicking and screaming. Why else would they take his shoes, but to keep him from running away? But it's hard to run two miles, let alone two hundred or two thousand or two million miles, when you don't know where you're going. If he'd known, he wouldn't have needed shoes.

I'd run away. I'd give it a try. I would keep running until I was caught. Then I would run again. Again and again I would run, even if it were only in my mind. I would find a place they could not find me. I would lie hidden like a fawn, my spots blending with the background. I'm sure that's what happened. Then the inevitable punishments came. My fa-ther was beaten and locked in a closet when he spoke his own language. What else was he supposed to do? He knew no other language.

I think about being locked in a closet. I think about all the things a closet contains. I think about the young boy locked in a closet, in the suffocating darkness. The vast emptiness that such darkness contains. All that distance in such a small space. I bet it was like the eye of the storm. Calm surrounded by chaos, tears falling like rain. How many raindrops fell in that closet? Enough for a flood, enough for a lifetime. Did they pour out of the closet? Or did they stay locked within?

Why would they lock him in a closet? I bet they thought it would serve a purpose. I bet they thought they were helping him by locking the Indian in the closet, hoping only the boy would come out. That was one side of the Indian world in a time when being Indian was a crime, punishable by stares, glares, and bad service at restaurants. The other side of the Indian world was shrouded in darkness at the time; it is only now coming to light. It is the side where song and dance live, where feathers and bells have meaning. It is the side where a wooden hoop and piece of skin come together to form a drum, a living heartbeat, a prom-ise of a better life.

I keep imagining that scene when everything changed for my father, and so for us, his children-to-be, as well. It was the summer, average temperature, hot. If you cared to watch, you could see the heat waves rising from the baked red earth. The sky was blue and immense. Clouds were light and fluffy, offering no chance of rain, only temporary shade as they crossed the sky on their journey east. The clouds looked down at the earth from their vantage. What they saw was a rocky landscape with sparse, short vegetation. The earth was red between the plants, the soil consisting of clay, alkali, and sand. Not quite the desert, but not quite the mountain. It was the place in between. It was the mesas and plateaus, the sagebrush flats. It was a boy's paradise, home to birds and lizards, animals large and small. Coyotes sang all night long. Rabbits ran from bush to bush, trying to avoid the keen eyes of hawks as they rode the hot air currents, ever circling in search of prey. Prairie dogs stood at attention watching for any signs of danger. It was a vast expanse of natural beauty.

Three boys played under the hot sun, two brothers and a cousin. The brothers were like night and day. The younger was cute, short and stocky. The older was tall, slender and had bad skin. The younger one was loud and demanding; the older, quiet and accepting.

The boys loved to chase lizards, because they were fast and unpredictable. The boys occasionally would catch a lizard and hold it for a while until something else attracted their attention. Sometimes they didn't catch the lizard; sometimes the lizard left his tail, wiggling on the ground, one end pointed, the other rounded and bloody. The boys would watch fascinated, while the lizard escaped to grow another tail, lived to tell a tale, talk about the day he outsmarted three little boys, tell his children and their children. Some lizards weren't as fortunate. They were caught and held in a cage, where they slowly died. These three boys never did that. They didn't have a cage to keep a lizard in. They didn't wear shoes. They ran barefoot, all over the hills, the rocks, and the sagebrush flats. Their feet were so tough they could run across a dried riverbed or step on a cactus without piercing the skin.

A car bumped its way down a dirt road, an immense cloud of dust following closely behind.

The quiet calm of that hot, dusty, little house erupted into chaos. Children were screaming as strangers tried to drag them into the car. Men were yelling, urging the children to hurry, gather their meager possessions. They wanted to make this easy on everyone. The women were telling them to slow down, remain calm, everything is going to be all right. Two languages were being spoken, and no one understood both. The children couldn't understand the intruders, except for the old man in the shabby suit. They were scared, unable to understand what was happening, unable to know that their lives were being changed forever, that the lives of their children were being changed, all in that moment. That moment was a definite culture clash.

The Indian man with the old suit spoke to the boys in their own language, attempting to calm them down. In his mind it was better to act white, to dress white, to *be* white. In his mind he was a white man. He worked hard at being a white man. He acted twice as white as white men do. He had learned how at the boarding school. That is where he grew up. He learned a trade, like farming or carpentry. He also learned to survive. He learned that the whiter he acted, the fewer beatings he received. Eventually he was completely white. To a blind man.

There he was, an aging white man in an Indian skin, doing as was done to him, stealing another group of children, so he might improve their lives, turn them into dark little white people like himself. He wanted them to be as happy as he was, to live between two worlds, an outcast, neither world wanting you. White people don't want you because you look Indian. Indians don't want you because you act white. When faced with that situation what do you do? You simply create more people like you. You create a group of outcasts. After all, you have to belong somewhere.

So it was that the boys were taken away, placed in foster care, and bounced from one home to another, some bad, some not so good. They learned to survive.

The older one turned to paper and pencil. He became an artist. He drew pictures of the things he loved, the nature around him. The hills where he loved to run for hours on end. That is how he survived and maintained his identity.

The younger boy did as the old man with the shabby suit did. He adopted the white mentality and did as he was taught. He learned to stay out of trouble, but that took a long time and a lot of work. He had to be beaten often and almost beaten to death. Maybe they did kill the

Indian in him. Beaten to death, buried in a closet, right next to the hanging coat, the shoes, and the baseball bat that was used to beat him.

The first home my father went to was the worst. I imagine the first meeting, as my father seems unable, or unwilling to recall it. "*Mique*," my father said ("hello" in Ute). It must have angered the man, who was their foster father. His face contorted in anger, the veins on his neck and temple sticking out, throbbing with rage. He yelled and yelled in frustration, angry that these ignorant boys didn't understand him, that they didn't obey him like good boys should. He started to beat the Indian out of them.

Here, in this house, my father was locked in a closet after a fierce beating. For two years my father was beaten severely, continually. Here he was taught anger, uncontrolled rage. He was taught that when something went wrong, he was supposed to blame others. Never dare to accept responsibility. He and his brother were taught these lessons early and often. The first foster home he went to he nearly didn't survive. The neighbors could hear the cries; they knew what was going on. If it hadn't been for good-hearted neighbors, the boys surely would have died.

The neighbors took my father and uncle into their home. It was a small home filled with children. The neighbor was a no-nonsense steelworker, strict but fair. His wife was sickly. The neighbors wanted to adopt the boys, claim them as their own, but the state welfare had other plans. The neighbors didn't have enough money to care for the children. Not enough money, and not enough room. Love was all they had in any quantity, but love is not enough for the state.

Off they went again, this time a twelve-year-old boy and his fourteen-year-old brother. Moving again, motion, continual motion, never the quiet calm or stillness that children need to become comfortable, never any stability. They didn't move far, only about fifteen miles away. They stayed in the small town of Springville, Utah, where they could be near friends, though they didn't have any. Social Services cared about the boys. They didn't want to disrupt their lives.

At the next stop on the foster home merry-go-round, the boys found the best father figure they ever had. He was an honest man who genuinely liked them. He showed them what was expected of a man, and how to be disciplined. His wife, on the other hand, was a different type of person entirely. I remember thinking when I met her that she was living in her own reality. All the while I was there, she was singing hymns, talking, and quoting scripture. She wasn't talking to me, and I was the only other person in the room. In this home my father received his religious education.

The Mormons have a strange idea about Indians. They call us Lamanites, one of two lost tribes of the twelve original tribes of Israel. They believe that Indians brought their sacred texts, the Book of Mormon, written on gold sheets to the Americas. It was these sacred texts that Joseph Smith dug up and translated somewhere in Missouri. Mormons justified taking Indian children as a means of returning them to their true and original religion.

I met these foster parents years later, when they were old and decrepit. I remember our strange meeting. I thought that the woman was very odd. She had strange toys that I played with, old toys that looked the worse for wear. Apparently she was never able to have children of her own, so she did her best to raise the less fortunate. We stayed for a dinner of some type of food that I refused to eat. She yelled at me. But I was not her child. I did not react the way she expected. I was defiant. I didn't eat the food.

Both boys stayed with the good man and his wife until they graduated from high school. The oldest had good grades and few friends; the younger one had many friends and poor grades. The differences between the brothers grew into a deep rift, and the boys were separated. My father moved to his final foster home. Still in Springville, he was too old to beat, but not too strong to yell at. I met this family years later. They were old then, and fragile. When they spoke, I saw my father's posture change, not out of respect but from fear. I wondered why he was afraid of such frail people, but then, the visit did not induce in me the memories that must have flooded his mind, the images that swelled in his consciousness.

Unfortunately, both boys were drafted when the Vietnam War came around. The oldest boy was taken by the marines, the younger by the army's Special Forces, two years later. The older boy never made it back. He was killed in action. He gave his life for the country that had taken such good care of him.

After the conflict overseas, the younger brother continued his nomadic way of life. He wound up in Washington State, where he met a young woman and married her. Not long after that I arrived, and a few years after that, another child, then another and another—six in all.

We moved often. Whenever things seemed to be settling down, he would grow restless and need to move. My father seemed to be forever searching for himself. He needed to know if what people had been telling him all this time was true. He decided to see if he really was an Indian. Finally, after nineteen years, he decided to look to the place where he had been born. He did the best thing that he ever could have done for his children. He moved to the reservation.

I was eight years old. I had already learned to read the waves that were my father's emotions. I learned it was easy sailing when he was calm and everything was going well. I also learned that at any moment a tsunami might crash down on top of me and sweep me away. I learned to panic at the sight of gathering clouds, how to move to the highest ground and stay there until the storm passed. Interesting things they taught him in those foster homes. It was like they had some dysfunctional family manual on coping with self-created pressure and stress: When money is short, blame others. When you lose something, blame others, then make them search frantically even if they don't know what they are looking for. When you stub your toe, blame others. When you are unhappy with your job, blame others. When you are unhappy with yourself, blame others. When you make a mistake, blame others. When in doubt, hit the kids. If it doesn't work, hit the wife too. If that doesn't work, break something. Then blame someone for breaking what you just broke. Above all else, never accept responsibility.

I learned some interesting things growing up. I learned how to patch holes in the walls. By the time I was fifteen I had become pretty good at it. Before that, I had learned how to put the holes there myself. Since then, I've learned that it isn't very useful knowledge.

For years my father continually searched for himself everywhere, except in a mirror. He still hasn't found the life he was stolen from. The life of his stolen childhood, the life his grandparents lived. He dragged his children along with him, looking in different churches and sweat lodges. He looked to self-proclaimed medicine men. He looked at school, where he wound up with a master's degree. He was left searching, unable to see or understand what was right in front of him, unable to accept what he saw.

His search led him to and through dozens of jobs, good jobs that he didn't want, jobs he couldn't handle. The work was never the problem; it was the self-made, imagined pressures and stresses. Whenever things would get calm, his restless spirit felt confined and he would need to move, always staying one step ahead of himself. Maybe at first he wanted to find himself, but eventually the search became more important as a way of avoiding himself.

Eventually his searching led to another woman and two more children. The cycle began again. Again he became nomadic. He moved his young family all over the place. By this time, his older children had planted roots and did not want to leave. He was outnumbered and outgunned. He could no longer rule with an iron fist. The oldest fought back. And sometimes he even won.

Somehow through all his searching, his children were creating their own identity, learning who and what they were. He had managed to give his kids what he himself was unable to find. They had seen and heard the lessons that were invisible to him. They found out what it was to be an Indian. But for him the search continues. For him and hundreds of others like him. A small nation of people are searching for themselves, searching for what might still be locked in that closet, searching in a bottle. A whole generation, lost. My father is not unusual or unique. He continually ran across others on the same journey. Some of their kids did like his kids did. They found what was invisible to their parents. They found the Indian within.

I see my father for the man he is, the man he was, and the man he will never be. I look at the way he tried to raise my brothers and sisters and me. I realize now what I never could realize as a child—that he did the best that he knew how. He taught us as he was taught.

We learned to be contradictory. I grew proud to be ashamed of who I am. He'd tell us to be proud to be Indian, but then he'd say, "Those damn Indians are no good. They won't listen to reason. They won't listen to a damn thing I say. You can't teach them to do anything right." These things my father would say about his own people. Except he did not look at them as *his* people. They were always *those* people. I wondered at his frustration. How could I understand *those people* yet he could not?

My father took us to the Mormon Church to be good little Mormon children. We never fit in. I never understood the total unquestioned faith that was taught there. I always had questions that were never answered to my satisfaction. I was probably the biggest pain in the ass any of those teachers ever had. "How dare this ten-year-old boy ask questions that I can't answer?"

My father told us legends that he read from his college texts, so that we might know our history. He took us to powwows so that we might know our present. Later, right before he left, he took me to sweat lodges, where I learned a new way of thinking, a new type of spirituality that fit me like a glove. I don't think that my father was so comfortable in the lodge, being quiet and alone with himself. I don't think he liked his own company much.

He left when I was fourteen. Did he do all these things with me so that I might raise the rest of his children? Was it the passing of the torch? Was his job done? Did he intend for me to learn all of these things? Did he know that I would become a singer and dancer? Did he know that I would teach other people some day? I hope so, but I never asked. I didn't want to hear the answers.

My father was only doing what he knew. He learned most of his parenting techniques from the Army. Whenever one of us kids did something bad, like make a mess in the kitchen or take something of his, he would line us all up and spank us one at a time until the guilty one confessed, until the innocents pressured the guilty one into confessing. Sometimes I would confess right away so I wouldn't have to see my brothers and sisters get spanked, even if I didn't commit the offense.

I remember once when I was about five or six, I was acting like I was smoking a cigarette by holding a pencil in my mouth and puffing. My father cured me of that pretty quickly. He did what he knew, what was done to him. He bought a pack of cigarettes and made me smoke the whole thing one after another. Another time my dad caught me playing with matches. He asked me, "Have you ever seen a match burn twice?" I said no, because of course I hadn't. He lit a match and let it burn a while. He then blew it out and while the tip was still red and crackling, he touched it to my arm. The match burned twice.

For all the mistakes that my father made raising his children, he also did quite a few good things. He took us camping and fishing all summer long. He taught us how to hunt and how to get along with nature.

Looking back on it all he truly believes that he did a good job, even if he only did half the job he set out to do. He still did the best he could. He says things like "I must have done good. You turned out fine." Who can argue with that logic? What am I supposed to say, "No, I didn't"?

I wonder why things happened the way they did. Why didn't my grandmother raise my father? I realize that she was just doing what she was taught in the boarding schools.

I feel very fortunate that I was raised on a reservation. Yes, we were poor in material wealth, but we were surrounded by many Indian people who taught me what it meant to be an Indian. They taught me not through words or lessons, but by taking me into their homes, into their lives. They showed me through just being who they are. In so doing they instilled a sense of being in me. Just being who I am, a sense of self, a sense of Indian. Because being Indian is not something that you can learn from reading a book or watching a movie. It is instead a way of life, a living breathing entity unto itself. This was something that I did not realize until I left. I sometimes wonder what would have happened to me if I had not been raised on a large reservation. Who would I be if I had been raised in the city? Would I be confused like my father? Would I be confused like so many others, wondering, looking, searching? What would have become of me? Would I be searching for belonging, never knowing that what matters is *being*? Once you are comfortable with *being*, belonging is no longer an issue.

My children will lead a better life than I led, because I recognize what went wrong. I am now filling the gaps left by generations past. I have bits and pieces of information about how to raise Indian children in an Indian way. I now have to put that information together to create what I don't know, what I didn't learn from those around me. I am rebuilding a foundation. My children will have to fill the gaps left by me. My children's children will have to do the same. Sooner or later there will be no more gaps to fill.

If I do my job right, the cycle is broken, another cycle begun. I wish it were true for the rest of the stolen ones.

A Letter to My Grandmother

S. L. WILDE

Grandmother Edith, Nokomis:

Gone from this earth, you come to me in my dreams. This time, tossing restlessly, trying to call out to you, I am the one who cannot speak. Still the words, the questions, circle inside me. So I will write to you.

You nurtured me. You taught me to cook, to plant, to harvest— how to be. You gave me the love my mother couldn't seem to spare. You nursed me through a sickly childhood, poultices of leaf-wrapped, yellow herb warmly soaking sun into my congested chest. Most precious of all, after a lifetime of silently serving everyone while stilling your native tongue, you gave me the gift of your Anishnaabe voice. Throughout the day you seldom spoke, and when you did, it was in English. You sang only a wordless song while you worked. But as I fell into sleep beneath the weight and color of your quilts, your chamois-soft, lined brown hand would stroke my face, and your voice would soak into me like water into thirsty stone: *Kin indodewisiwin ododeminan Gaiashk, Ojisheia. Midwendijige.* "We are of the Gull Clan, Grandchild. Remember." Your words overflowed with pride and love but always were spoken in whispers. Why was this a secret?

As a child you were taken from your home. They robbed you of your name, your family, your culture, your context. They tried to steal your language and your pride. They "educated" you, then gave you away to be "adopted" by people who used you as a slave. Why did you use the name they gave you?

They taught you that what you were was wrong, dirty, shameful, bad—something you had to rise up and overcome with hard work, humiliation, and the will of the Lord. They used their God to silence you, to shame you. Why did you worship him?

You secretly taught me your past, your heritage, some of your Anishnaabe ways. But your daughters scolded you for working out in the sun in the garden without your hat—for letting yourself "get so brown." Why did you teach your children to be white?

You silently beaded my moccasins with flowers as your sons derided "that walking garbage" from the reservation. You accepted the sanctimonious condescension of my minister father with humility and deference, but when you spoke to me alone, your dark eyes flashed with anger and pride. The truths you taught me were a bright cord shrouded and woven through a thickness of denial, hate, and lies. It confused me. It confuses me still.

Your children grasped tight to white middle-class lives. But so many of your grandchildren turned their backs on their parents' hard-won way of life, living instead, despite sharp minds and strong talents, as white trash in an alcoholic haze. So many "didn't fit in." So many were just "too different." Did you finally see that the safety you had sought to give your children and your children's children wasn't really safety after all? Is that why you chose to speak to me? Can I be worthy of your choosing, worthy of this responsibility?

You imbued me with a sense of urgency, placed this unnamed task before me. Awake and dreaming I sift my way through clarity and confusion, self-doubt and surety. I set myself to learning the tongue you were forced to give up, to wrap myself around the syllables of my own Anishnaabe voice. . . . I would honor you, Grandmother. For all that you were, for the gift of your teachings, for myself and for my children's children, I seek the words to your song.

It Goes Something Like This

ERIC GANSWORTH

I have heard this story
before, she walks alone
her moccasins cracking east
coast sand kernels
along the whitewashed Atlantic
City boardwalk waiting
for the train that will take her
to a school she'd only heard of
that morning, discovering
strangers and a packed bag
with her parents as she came down
for breakfast, and suddenly the midway
music is cut by the more familiar
sounds of home, someone
singing a Tuscarora Social song.
He is dark and she
joins in the song
as they, two children, view the ocean
together for the first time.

They board the train and share
a seat the rest of the way
to Carlisle Indian School
and are married as
soon as they graduate.

Many voices have repeated
in the best oral tradition
this story of my grandparents
with great vividness
the beadwork design
in her moccasins
the song he sang
bending my doubting questions silent.
As I start to ask
why they hadn't known
each other on the reservation
or at least seen each other board or
why the New York
to Pennsylvania train stopped
at the New Jersey coastline
I realize they could have met
emptying headmaster chamber pots
or as voices in black
isolation chambers for speaking
a language still their only link
and I am satisfied with the version
I hear. Sometimes the story is
enough to bring me home.

Breeds and Outlaws

KIMBERLY ROPPOLO

I am Jefferson's idea realized;
I am not Indian.
I was the little "white" girl with
olive skin and hazel eyes who tanned easily.
I was the teenager who tried to mask
my round face and small, slanty eyes with makeup,
who wanted her skin to be white or brown, either one or the other,
who loved Mexican boys best,
because they looked most like her daddy.
I am the young woman asked occasionally
if she's Hispanic. It's hard to answer that as
I'm not Indian.

To me, Mississippi is a place of myth;
Oklahoma is a foreign land.
But I have learned more in my life
from Old Women than from anybody.
Even how to travel across Big Rivers.

When I was fourteen months old, my parents divorced, and I moved in
with my father's parents: Mammy and Pappy. They worked shifts, she at

the hospital, he at the oil refinery, so Mammy's sister Aunt Ruby moved in to take care of me. My Aunt Ruby bought me Indian toys, bells, dolls, beaded coin purses. The best was Minnihaha, a leftover black panther doll on which the toy company had put long braids and a red and white vinyl dress and called an Indian. Aunt Ruby made me a dress out of my uncle's discarded khakis, machine-embroidering it with moons, stars, the sun, and teepees. She painted my face with lipstick. She made me a tent out of a pink blanket and the dining room table. (I never played cowboys, just Indians.) She took me to visit the Alabama Coushatta people, and every time, we both had to fight an urge to dance too, sitting politely as spectators, paying money to watch a culture not far from her grandmother's. One time, I fell in love with the boy who did the Eagle Dance. I don't know who was more Indian, me or Minnihaha.

My Aunt Ruby was brown,
and she called me her little Indian sister.
I am not Indian.
She taught me how to pick and cook poke salad,
that dewberries and wild grapes were precious things,
that tobacco was good for bee stings,
and its smoke in a child's ear for an earache or stomachache.
When I was five, she taught me how to
make change and run a cash register.
And she put me in charge of the
entire front of the convenience store.
She taught me that I was strong, that I was capable,
that I could do anything I had a mind to.
Now she's in a nursing home,
curled to one side.
She's working on getting
her bones ready.
Making the job easy for someone.
She's forgotten it's 1998,
and Indians don't do that stuff anymore.

I was leaving Mammy's house the other day with my new baby on my hip, and as we stepped off the porch into the sunlight, she said, "Gee that baby's brown, must be all that Italian." (From my husband. I still think dark, long-haired men are better looking than anybody. Being Sicilian with a little bit of Cherokee sure makes a man easy on the eye.)

And I said, "You know, you're not so light yourself."

She responded, "I was the whitest one in my family." And she was. And she is. But she's still my Mammy, and she was my Mammy when no one else was there to be.

I said, "You know, looking at all those old pictures, I think Aunt Annabelle was the whitest."

"She was the darkest one of all." (Mammy is mad at Aunt Annabelle for not visiting. They're just getting old.)

When Mammy was growing up, children taunted her because of her brown skin, told her that her grandparents were "dirty Choctaws from Oklahoma." But she had been taught to hide the truth, so she couldn't answer, couldn't say that her people came from the Carolinas, from Virginia, to Georgia and Tennessee, and in 1839 to Mississippi. Arkansas and Texas followed. But when Grandpa Sam married Grandma Carrie, his family was mad because she was so dark. Because her name, Carolina Virginia McGarrity, reminded them who they were, too.

Besides that, Mammy says that Grandma Carrie's family had left Arkansas for their beliefs. Her daddy had believed all the cows were his, so he'd sold them.

My past is peopled by breeds and outlaws, traders and grandmas, and sometimes the women had to be all of those things at once.

Mammy grew up poor in a big, often fatherless family in the Depression. Her mother, Lena Fair Wright, wore her hair in twisted up braids and brewed beer in her kitchen to sell during Prohibition to have money to feed her kids. She made whiskey runs to Louisiana, putting the jars on the floorboards under blankets topped with several of her sleeping children. Mammy didn't want to be poor. And as far as she was concerned, she was white, which is what she would later fill in on all of the blanks of my life.

Mammy called to tell me Aunt Ruby is sick. But I knew she would call because the last time I visited Aunt Ruby, I rubbed her back and reminded her she was Indian. And I had a dream already about two months ago.

It was a beautiful dream. Aunt Ruby and I were in this log house that was part of a fort-like structure, and she could walk and talk again like she did when I was younger. Her hair was down, and the ends of it were green stalks with maize heads. But it was the European kind of maize, milo. She and I decided to make up a new corn ceremony. We felt like it was an okay thing to do. She said she would walk outside, and I would follow her. As we went, we picked up all the old corn lying about with the husks attached, but pulled back. It was Indian corn. I kept thinking to myself in the dream that I wanted to cut off the ends of her hair, the green parts, but I knew she wouldn't be okay with me cutting her hair. It is still very long and black for her age of 84. Anyway, we were supposed to throw all the old corn out before the newly harvested corn was brought in. It was clear that very many more people lived there, but I don't know where any of them were. We were alone as far as I can tell. But this wasn't a green-corn ceremony. It was a harvest.

I was surprised when I woke up the next morning that I hadn't gotten the call already.

> I'm digging up my grandmother's bones,
> to carry them in the house of my body
> where they rightfully belong,
> to hold them under my muscles and sinew
> like I did my children in my womb,
> to carry them at the same time like
> my Mother written on my soul.
> My mother, despite whatever she didn't give me,
> gave me more than roots.
> She gave me bones.

I feel like I'm straddling a fence, y'know. Only I ain't sittin' straight on the middle. On the left side of me's some deepdarkcool Mississippi woods. On the right side is a library, an interstate highway, and a house with running water, electricity, and a laptop computer sitting in the middle of the living room floor. I'm cocked to the left, my foot sinking in the red dirt and pine needles, a gray snake sliding by my little toe, looking at me. I can feel him brush past. No matter how hard I try, I can't pull my right leg over, 'cause there's this steel cord coming out of the ground, wrapped around my ankle.

I write as a crossblood and a woman, because that's who I am. I am the daughter of invaders who have been destroying themselves now for even longer than the five hundred years they have been chipping away at those they have invaded, but not conquered. I am the mother of those who will be free. I was born from my mother, from the Mississippi mud where I have laid down, too.

And I live to tell my story.

I have a set of tribal membership papers from a state-recognized tribe sitting on my file cabinet, a tribe that "real" Indians make fun of and call white, but a tribe that said they would accept me when my rightful tribe, the tribe of my mother's mothers, wouldn't because of the dates, the years since my people have been with my people. Even though back in time immemorial I would have been *Chata*. Or maybe I'll be *Tsalagi*. I've got more of that blood anyway, even if it's too old for Oklahoma. You'd think, knowing the stories about the times we're in, that folks would stop fighting about who's more Indian. That for things to change, we all got to be resurrected, that this Ghost Dance is one of the living. Besides, if we're going to "repatriate" artifacts, we ought to "rematriate" people.

I know this. If you act like you think you're white, white folks'll treat you that way . . . almost. If you have slightly brown skin and small eyes and high cheekbones and Creek lips, at the wrong moment, they'll see who you really are, and you'll know you can't get by with what a white woman can because you can't quite pass. (Not pure enough, not "clean" enough, where's my poise?) Even if they can't put their fingers on just what it is they can't take about you, they know, they smell you.

And I want to say to them, "Hey, I'm not Indian."

> There's a plan in these bits and pieces.
> I'm picking the decayed flesh
> out of my grandmothers' graves,
> off their bodies,
> trying to get to the bones—
> there's no one else to do it for them.
> I'm trying to see if I can climb them back,
> from shin to knee to lap to breast,
> my small tight fists kneading, needing,
> my nose rooting for the milk.
>
> Someday, I will be bones.

Wetumka

PHIL YOUNG AND ROBERT BENSEN

The lineage of *Ani-Yun-Wiya,* "The Real People," survived and was passed on through a fiery cord that did not burn up nor consume when we grasped it. Somehow my own confusion was a sign that the cord was not completely broken.

—Phil Young, "Cowboys and Indians #1" installation
  at TriBeCa Gallery, New York City, 1993

It gave Grandpa a start, heading back to the animals, to find this Creek fellow named Fish sitting like a stick on the porch rail, no good-day whatsoever, holding out his pipe for tobacco or a cup to cool his tongue. He gave my grandfather some language that he taught us kids—I can say *Inkshche kamanashka,* that's hello, how are you—corn is *sofki*—and we used to say to him, Grandpa, teach us some Indian. And he would. We'd say what is that? Creek, he'd say. And we'd say we thought we were Cherokee. We are, he'd say. Don't tell anybody, either.

> The mountain began as a seed in a mirage.
> They heard: a sigh longing to escape the mountain.

> Birds and the first dawn found them.
> Their shadows lay before them.

In each footprint
vines and tender shoots broke through.

One day he hitched the wagon and told my grandma that he was going to go into town to get us enrolled. A half hour after he'd left, he unhitched the horses and led them into the barn. He walked in the house hanging his head down. Sat at the table. Put his head down. One of the kids asked him, Well did, did you do it? He just shook his head. Later on he told one of them that he got afraid. The Klan was very active in that little town. Too, Grandpa was shy. Well, not that shy, he had thirteen kids, but I remember him wearing long underwear even in summer in the Oklahoma cotton fields. They say when he died the skin on his arms and up from his ankles was baby skin.

The mountain grew each day with their walking,
but by night it drifted down the white river of stars.

The girl said to her brother, her twin:
If you walk by day and I by night,
we will hold the mountain fast within our gaze.

He and my grandma had moved to the Creek Nation in 1904 from Arkansas and set up sharecropping a few miles out of town. Her brother killed a man but escaped and changed his name. His son, my cousin once removed—we were all once removed, you could say—always had to stand and be counted as an Indian for federal school aid. He'd stand, but he was clueless. His dad wouldn't talk about any family, any relations, almost any past at all. The man had changed his name from Ruddell and never told anyone, not even his son; especially not his son. They spelled it Riddell, but said it "Riddle." So it was. Once he solved it, he's been finding his people all over creation.

Now a cat prowling the lowest ridge watched him
wait for her to wake this final day.
He caught the wind playing with her apron of grass.
He fanned it back with his own hand,
then he left his house and entered hers.

One route goes back to the courthouse at Searcy, Arkansas. My grandpa's birth records burned in the courthouse fire at the turn of the century. So we're trying to go from Arkansas back to family names on those old Eastern Band census rolls. I recently found out where my great-grandmother's buried. At the Arkansas Historical Association I may find a newspaper obituary this summer that might say where she was born. That's one next step. It's an obsession bordering on the absurd, like trying to learn the language. By tape. There's no community, only necessity. I'd like enough language to express some things in it, to write it a bit more. When I hand out T-squares in 2-D design, I mark them with little Cherokee letters. The students will ask me, What's this? I'll say, It's *da,* it's *cla,* it's this or that. Sequoyah's wife threw his first syllabary in the fire: We don't need this. We speak English and Cherokee and we don't need this. We can write in English. That's enough.

> The cries from their lips crossed
> and the river began that flows both ways.
> Each bead of their sweat caught dust and salt
> and rose up as one of our mothers,
> rose up as one of our fathers,
> and they held their children, waiting
> until the river told them to cross over.

The first time we tried to enroll with the new federal Cherokee Nation of Oklahoma had to be the late 1880s, when a lawyer told my grandfather's grandmother that he needed forty dollars to process the enrollment. But she died, and the papers never came through or got lost or mice ate them. A lot was recorded in a letter to one of my aunts who died a couple of years ago. She was going to copy some information down out of an old family Bible and said that the person who had it was living up in Indiana. Indian-Uh. He was dead by then, but his son has the Bible in a trunk that was passed down with letters and land-grant claims for land in Indian Territory, that showed that my great-great grandma did get her kids' names down. The son said that his dad went over into Oklahoma with the land-grant officer who showed him his land. People were already living on it. He wasn't about to take the land from them. But the trunk had these documents and some correspondence from my great-great grandmother. The guy who had them, his second wife let their kids play in there in the attic. The kids left it open, and the mice chewed the paper to tiny shreds. A lot of history we'll never piece together.

> Past the still, deep middle of the river,
> where the water begins to slide the other way,
> the children changed into snakes and turtles,
> into lizards and frogs that bit their mothers on the arms.

Something else: a red gourd with the names of every first male child scratched in it at birth. The gourd was started by a Scottish great-great-great-grandfather who came through the Cumberland Gap into Arkansas. I found out Sunday, first time I talked to the guy who has it in Arkansas, that he's also got an old family album of tintypes. He thinks there's some of my great-grandmother and possibly her mother. Talk about cheekbones, this woman's got cheekbones from here to the top of her head. They had to have dropped off The Trail of Tears in Arkansas near the town now called Cherokee. We've got people in Kentucky and southern Missouri and Texas. This Texas bunch put up heavy resistance. A side of me wishes my ancestors had resisted, but even if they didn't, they didn't exactly comply. These people never got where they were supposed to go.

> The women shrieked and beat at their wounds,
> the children swam off laughing. The men and women
> were old when they reached the other side.
> It was late, yet they inclined to seek the ones in the river.
> They peered in, they saw what they had become.

The disconnection blows me all over the place, tying it up. This summer when I get around that eastern area of Arkansas, go to those grave sites, I wonder what's going to happen to me. In December they had an exhibit of cradleboards. They bundled their babies into them when it was cold and when they were on The Trail of Tears. Some of those cradleboards got to Oklahoma empty as the ones in the museum. I stood there and it blew me away. Because, I was thinking, somewhere back, one of my relatives carried one of me in one of them. Ten thousand died on the Trail. It's almost like I wanted to feel myself in one of those, that's what was going on.

> The story of their coming came to the children.
> Some looked behind them. Some looked before them.
> Some searched books, some the temper of their own bodies.
> Some made room in their houses.
> Some said they had never left.
> Some asked the earth for the memories it had hidden.
> Some hid in the memory of the earth.

I had them send me the Dawes Commission rolls. My great-grand-mother's name is there, and my grandpa's name is there, and the names of his brothers and sisters are all right there on the commission rolls, right? But they're the wrong people. The first set, they've got numbers that go over into different enrollment card numbers. Under the first number all the people in that family are listed, and their age, and so on. You can see Lula Alice, 84, and my grandpa's name, and these others that aren't relatives, see? But my grandpa wasn't one year old in 1904. There was one point where everybody thought, Man, we found it! We thought they were right where they were supposed to be. But that wasn't it. Not them. Not there.

> The old people recognized themselves in all these things,
> and said among themselves, "Everywhere we look,
> our children survive, and their desire.
> When seeds falter, we still water them.
> Like the river, we have never ceased.
> Like the wind, what can stop us?
> What would stop the wind becomes its voice.
> What would stop the river only shows its power."
> Then they gathered what they could and set out walking.

Cousins by the millions and aunts and uncles would gather in Wetumka at my Grandpa and Grandma's small wooden framed house, only one they owned since coming to Indian Territory in 1904. We'd find anything we could put a plate on, from ironing boards inside to upside-down washtubs outside. Among the knickknacks and funeral-home calendars and Folger cans waiting for the next delivery of Brown Mule drifted smells and flavors of fried chicken and poke, black-eyed peas and new potatoes covered with gravy thick as wallpaper paste, and seasoned with enough grease and salt and pepper to keep you going the whole day. When Grandma and Grandpa died, the hub of the wheel broke, and we scattered like fireflies trying to find their way home in the dark, some still in Oklahoma, some in California, and me here in upstate New York. We grandkids used to beg Grandpa to do a jig dance across their flowered, vinyl, living-room rug. His suspenders kept his baggy pants up past his belly button, but he'd stoop over and pull up the knees of his britches and get set to kick up a lick like he used to do when he was a little boy dancing on the tables in saloons in Arkansas, accompanied by his uncle's banjo-playing. Grandma would yell, "Oh, Will, cut out that foolishness." But the grandkids would prevail and would he ever begin to dance!

The Long Road Home

LAWRENCE SAMPSON

I remember my mother, beautiful as she was, with her black hair spilling down over me, pulling me into her lap, hugging me, and uttering a sentence I have never forgotten: "You're going to have to find a new mother."

I remember giggling, thinking as a child, being oblivious to those times when lives are suddenly, permanently altered. It was my sixth birthday. I've often wondered if any child truly comprehends the loss of a parent. Surely she was joking; she and my sister were my whole world. I knew and loved my father, but my parents were not married, so Dianne and Mom were my life. I often wonder what I would say if I could go back a grown man and talk to her at that precise moment. What would I say, knowing my mother was dying? The longing I have felt since that last happy moment with the woman who gave birth to me is indescribable. The words have not been invented to do so.

Within a few days, the Sampsons, recent acquaintances of my mother's, gathered my sister, me, and all our belongings together, and took us up to their home. We had visited before, and even stayed the night, so I felt safe there. A very unusual event happened during this time, for Houston, anyway. It snowed. I waited in the car while Dianne gathered our things, looking at our cat sitting at our front door, watching the snow fall.

Some weeks later, we went to see my mother at the hospital, when they told me she was sick. Many years later, I would learn about her illness and what had killed her. The sickness to which her death would be officially attributed medically was not what had killed her. According to one doctor who came to know her in her last days, her death was caused by a broken heart derived from thirty-one years of struggle. Her struggle was to find herself and who she was, and it resulted in an illness no medicine could cure. The peritonitis infection may have stopped her body from functioning, but that was sudden and quite unexpected, according to the doctors. The fact that she knew enough to tell me in advance about finding a mother is evidence enough that she knew of her fate, and that she was tired.

Many times in my life, I have known the feeling of sheer exhaustion, not only physical, but of a deeper, perhaps spiritual nature. At those times, I think I have an idea of how my mother must have felt, only many times worse.

For the next three months, I was hidden from my father by the Sampsons. I lived on a farm north of Houston, with what were to become my new grandparents, the Ellises. They were good people, and during these months, I enjoyed farm life. I remember picking corn, shucking it, and feeding the husks to the cows. It seems I was happy, or close enough to what I now interpret happy to be, living in the swirling hectic nature my life had become. It was here, on a typical spring day, that the Sampsons brought Dianne to see me. She wanted to talk to me, so we went walking. There, in the middle of a cow pasture, she told me my mother had died. There are moments in our lives when time seems to stand still. Every smell, every sound, every detail is vivid in our memories. This was one of those times for me. I know I did not fully understand death, but I had the unmistakable sense that I was spinning and losing my balance. As an adult, I now understand the concept of not having closure with an issue, of not accepting a fact you are unable to process intellectually or emotionally. Although I do not remember it, my sister has since told me of times when I would talk about Mom coming to get me. I know now I missed her terribly. On this day, Dianne went on to tell me why I was living here in this secluded place: to keep my father from finding me. He probably didn't even know my mother was dead yet, and the Sampsons wanted to adopt us. I felt like things that would affect me were going on, but without any say in them, I was powerless. What followed is now a blur of hearings in courthouses, meetings with psychologists, and other mind-numbing details. I was told, "Your father doesn't want your sister. Your father is a dirty Indian. Your mother didn't want you to live with your father; she wanted you to live with us. Your father is a bad man."

At some point during these endless meetings, my father was allowed to see me and my sister. I was afraid of him. He asked me about a tricycle he had bought me some years before, and although I remembered it, I told him I didn't. I told him I didn't remember anything about him. I wanted the meeting to be over, not realizing the impression the Sampsons had made on me already. Now, as a man with children, I cannot imagine the depth of pain this meeting must have caused my father. I found out later that he had made assertions of brainwashing against the Sampsons. When I look back at how they molded my feelings toward my father, whom in later years I would come to love so intensely, I am amazed at the ability of people to program others' thoughts, especially a child's. I can see how my father, as an Indian man in 1973—a time of heightened tension in America with Indian people, a time of Wounded Knee and forced sterilization of Indian women by the US government— could not win custody of his own child.

And so my life began with the Sampsons, a life I still have trouble understanding. With all the challenges a life of thirty-two years as an Indian can entail, I still identify this time with the Sampsons as the worst period of my life. It was less than a month after the adoption, I think, when I suffered the first beating. A pet turtle had been turned loose in the backyard, and although I had not done it, I was beaten until I admitted doing it. Admitting to things I didn't do in order to end beatings, or to avoid them altogether, would become a common occurrence in the Sampson household. At times these beatings were so severe I had to miss school in order to heal up, so no marks were visible. Epsom salts baths were fairly common as well. I was a convenient target for whatever abuse was forthcoming: verbal, physical, or mental. I can describe how virtually every common household item feels when it hits you, whether it be a phone receiver, a coffee table, or a can of food. I was forced to eat dog food. I remember being told repeatedly by my new "brother" how we were not related. I remember one of my new older "sisters" telling me that my mother was a whore. I was seven, I think.

The worst part of all this was that I was no longer close to the one remaining blood relation in my life. Dianne was loved and doted on by Mrs. Sampson, as she was in the same age group as the three Sampson children. I was several years younger. Although Dianne would later participate in my abuse, I have never been able to stop loving her, despite an underlying sense of betrayal. We remain somewhat close to this day.

I was chastised for the fact that it had cost ten thousand dollars to adopt me. And although it was a quite benign subject to me at the time, it was to become a significant memory later in life. For the next eight years, I experienced what I can now say only made me stronger. Being forced to work long hours in the family roofing business, missing up to eighty days of school a year to do this, was the norm. The beatings were regular events, especially the ones for "lying." When I first was told about my mother being a whore, I didn't know what that was. I was to learn rather quickly that I was different. Not living with my biological parents and having their memory actively tarnished and suppressed left me without a foundation of knowing who I was and where I came from. My past was actively being erased, yet I didn't belong in my current surroundings either. I didn't fit in. I was the proverbial black sheep. I have since heard John Trudell, the powerful Indian poet and activist, talk of our DNA and our cellular memory of who and what we are. I've heard him speak of not learning these things, but remembering, as First Nations people, who and what we are. I didn't fit in because I WAS different. I felt different. My having darker skin embarrassed the Sampsons, as frequently people would ask about my ethnicity. Living in Houston, with a large Hispanic population, I was encouraged to tell people I was Mexican, if I had to say anything at all. I learned "even that" was better than being Indian. The message was made very clear to me, everything about me was wrong, especially being Indian.

I was thirteen, I think, when my father made contact with the Sampsons and inquired about seeing me. During my adoption, he had been instructed never to contact me. The years without me in his life became too much, I guess, and the Creator saw to it that he contacted Mrs.

Sampson at the most opportune time. Surprisingly, Mrs. Sampson eventually acquiesced, as Mr. Sampson had died of cancer about a year before, and as I got older, and bigger, I think I was growing out of her control. Even though my father's visits gave her another control mechanism, I relished the weekends I was allowed to have with my father.

All the time I sat in my darkened bedroom licking my wounds from the latest round of beatings, I had known that my father was out there somewhere, and I would see him again. I had clung to this belief with a ferocity I didn't realize. I now know that the most immediate impact of our time together was my developing a positive self-image. He was intensely proud of his Cherokee heritage, despite what it had caused in his life. His mother lived just across the Tennessee state line from the Qualla boundary, the Eastern Band of Cherokee reservation, where I have relatives. She had been spit on as a child and ridiculed as a "dirty Indian," so the fact that she became guarded about her heritage is understandable. As a result, she had raised my father in a nontraditional manner but aware of the culture nonetheless. So he was extremely proud of who we were. When the subject of my treatment at the hands of the Sampsons came up, I told him it was mostly my fault. He asked me if I really believed that, and for the first time, I began to think about it. How could a child have been wrong in so many instances, and adults have been so innocent? Was I really that bad? As a result, I began to feel better about myself, and who I came from. I decided never again to accept the type of treatment I had grown used to. Mrs. Sampson attempted one last beating when I was fourteen, but I defended myself. I began to feel anger not during my solace, but in dealing with her. Even though she smashed a radio against my head, it didn't seem to faze me. In fact, I had decided she couldn't hurt me any more. Today, I have no contact with the Sampsons. At one point, we tried a sort of reconciliation, but I know now that isn't possible. It isn't about forgiving, but forgetting. And in truth, it seemed to me their effort was in word only; there was no substance behind those words or actions to back them up. I do not know what they could have possibly done, but that is their problem, not mine. Having children of my own now, I cannot fathom doing what they did to an innocent child.

My life with my father was like living in another universe. I now became the oldest, with a younger brother and sister. My father doted on us, a new experience for me. My younger siblings were actually quite spoiled, and I think I went through a sort of culture shock. My father did have a temper, though, and at times he was filled with rage, a rage that has been called cultural anger, for obvious reasons, including the fact that I had been stolen from him.

It is hard to put into words what he did for me. One thing was the establishment of a pride I had never known before: pride in myself and pride in my culture. He was an obvious source of information about my mother and my Delaware heritage. I learned how my mother, who was half Dutch-Amish, had been brought up in their typically regimented life, with strict discipline. Unable to conform to the rigid expectations, she had been kicked out of her house or had run away. In either case, she ended up on the streets: a half-Indian woman in the mid-fifties, living on the streets. She lived a quite difficult life, eventually dying at the age of thirty-one. She met my father when he was about twenty years old. A year later, I was born, and when I was nine days old, we all moved to Texas together, so Dad could get a better job than was available to Indians on and near the reservation. After my mother had passed on, the Sampsons had tried hurriedly to adopt me. My father told me about his frantic attempts to stop it, with frequent trips between Texas and Tennessee, gathering birth records, pictures, and such. He told me of attempts to deny his paternity with me, and how he had proven it, and of false signatures being submitted in adoption proceedings. He also told me about the evidence he had found detailing a ten-thousand-dollar payment to the adoption judge: the same ten thousand dollars I had been chastised for costing the Sampsons. As a teenager I began to see not only the Sampsons for what they really were, but also the disservice that had been performed by an unwitting judge and an adoption system that blindly decides what is best for people based on incorrect assumptions, racism, and corruption.

After high school and college, I joined the army and became a paratrooper stationed at Fort Bragg, North Carolina, just a few hours from my reservation. Funny how life works out. Now I was four hours from my reservation and within six hours of my entire family, as Dad had moved back home by now. During my time at Fort Bragg, I traveled back and forth to see my relations, learning more and more about them, our culture, and our history. I learned to speak my language. I got out of the service in 1993 and moved back to Houston to pursue a career in the private sector. I have grown out my hair, and I braid it. I am a Northern traditional dancer at powwows. Also, I have become active in several organizations, and have founded a few myself, that address needs in the Native community. The Native American Arts Council of Houston will expose modern Indian art forms, particularly music, and hopefully garner funds for a cultural center. The South East Texas chapter of the American Indian Movement will address a whole host of issues, including the mascot issue, grave repatriation, curriculum development, land rights, and civil rights. I frequently speak at churches, schools, teachers' groups, and other civic gatherings. I try to teach that being Indian is more about your culture, your language, and your history, than a race issue. It is a state of mind and a lifestyle that makes us who we are. We have so much to be proud of! My father passed on two years ago exactly, at the time I am writing this. But, just as when I was a child, I feel him watching over me. And, as when I was a child, I cannot wait to see him again.

When the Heron Speaks

BEVERLEY MCKIVER

At lunchtime Beverley walked down to the river. She liked the illusion that she was momentarily escaping the city. Most of the time, she walked alone. She sat on her customary bench and breathed in deeply, hands on her knees. With the bicycle path further up and this way restricted to pedestrians, only the occasional passerby would disturb her reverie.

She closed her eyes and sighed, the breeze washing over her face. It wouldn't be long until the path was deep with snow and harsh winds blew off the frozen waters. She opened her eyes to gaze across the river at the far shore, enjoying the hazy effect of the late summer rays.

A great blue heron soared above the middle of the river. She noted the S-curve of the neck and the spindly legs extending behind the bird as it flew. She acknowledged the bird with a mental salute. She had been seeing herons for most of her life. When she drove to work, on many mornings a heron would pass overhead, seemingly on the same schedule she was. Once, on a strange highway, one swooped across the road ahead of the car, startling her. She thought back to the misty mornings of her childhood on one of her adoptive father's interminable fishing trips. "Before the fish get up," he would say, as she dragged her unwilling body out of bed. One lengthy truck ride, one lake, one portage, and one creek later, a heron would rise up out of the mist, flapping slowly, leading the way in front of the canoe. Ungainly birds, she thought. But beautiful.

They had not fared well from the aftermath of the ice storm that had swathed the northeastern part of the continent with a thick coating of ice. She gave a prayer of thanks for the gentle lady at the Wild Bird Care Center who oversaw the recovery of several injured fledglings after a colony of nests had tumbled from the damaged trees. A year earlier, herons had been in the local news when a couple of inexperienced birds had lingered too long and been found half frozen. Every year stragglers were loath to leave their northern homes. Thawed out at the care center, the insatiable birds had gobbled down an alarming amount of fish, quickly draining the small center's budget. She had sent in a check then and reminded herself to send in another one. She chuckled to herself. They were always getting into scrapes, but it seemed as if there was no shortage of herons. Survivors they were.

A colony of nests was a short walk down an abandoned road close to her house. The city had not yet crept out this way, and it was unlikely that this seemingly useless tract of land would be developed. The road was even truncated in spots by beaver engineers and deep channels filled with brown, still water. In winter, the road was a busy highway for the snowmobilers, but the land rested during the summer months. Any temporary bridges erected by enterprising adventurers would be quickly dismantled by the vigilant beavers.

In the early spring before the leaves were on the trees and the air was still too crisp for mosquitoes, she regularly took binoculars down the trail so she could spy on the birds. They had been back in the north country for a couple of weeks and she greeted their return with quiet joy. The heronry was barely visible through the trees. The large nests, looking like Dr. Seuss creations, were assembled with large sticks and brush near the tops of the taller trees. The swampy terrain prevented her from getting too close, but she wouldn't have gone any nearer; herons were skittish birds who liked their privacy. They were known to abandon their nests when disturbed. She contented herself with watching their pterodactyl shapes gliding from nest to pond and back up again. She liked a scientist's notion that birds might be relics of the dinosaur age, that they had survived a global cataclysm and endured in another form.

One evening, the swamp was quiet. The sky was still bright to the west but around her the shadows grew longer. The air became damp and heavy as night settled in. Above her, Canada geese flew in formation back to their nightly quarters. The amphibian choir was reaching a crescendo. Her two dogs, whom she had brought along for company, were growing impatient. She had turned to go when the silence was pierced by a hoarse, guttural croak high above her. She and both dogs looked up, unable to identify the sound, unlike that of a crow or raven. To her surprise, a heron winged its way overhead. That voice was arresting. She had heard somewhere that whenever the heron speaks, the other birds stop to listen. The croaks continued at regular intervals, fading into the distance as the bird disappeared from view. She went home elated. It was as though the heron had called to her.

Recalling that evening, she leaned back, tipped her face to the sun and brought the sound to mind. Even as she did so, that distinctive cry split the silence, the air around her was buffeted by strong wings and a heron descended in front of her. She dared not breathe. For a long time she and the heron regarded each other.

"Go home," the bird intoned. She began to tremble. "What?" she whispered. The bird turned its beak toward the west for what seemed like an eternity. She followed its gaze upstream but found no answer there. Turning back to her, the bird spoke again. "You must," it said and launched itself westward. She watched the bird until it was a speck in the distance, until it vanished in the glare of the noonday sun.

She sat stunned for a moment, her thoughts churning. She wondered if she had dozed off and imagined the episode, but her palpitating heart convinced her that she had experienced something wondrous.

Forty, overweight, in no shape to run back to the office, she went as quickly as her short legs would allow. The herons spoke when there was danger. Was someone close to her in trouble? She squeezed into the elevator with the returning workers. When she reached her desk, she glanced at her phone. No flashing light. That was good. She picked up the receiver and dialed her husband's office. "Call me," she barked when voice messaging kicked in. Glancing at her computer monitor, she was alarmed to see a heron cruising its way lazily across the screen. She opened the settings menu. There it was: Heron.bmp. She glared at

Graham, working at a nearby desk. "Is this your idea of a joke?" she growled at him. He opened his eyes wide at her tone and loped over. "That screen saver's been around for ages," he said, looking puzzled. She looked again. Ten happy little macaronis danced the macarena. She reopened the settings menu. The heron selection had disappeared. Knowing she couldn't explain what she had seen without appearing a bit loony, she waved him away impatiently, glaring at his retreating back.

Trying to swallow the lump of panic in her throat, she picked up the phone again and dialed her daughter's school. She identified herself to the office assistant and asked to speak to her daughter. "Please hold while I page the classroom," the assistant replied. When her daughter came on the line, Beverley asked if she had her key, and was everything okay? "Of course I do, Mom. It's time for gym, can I go now?" she replied.

Beverley blew her a kiss, sighed, and hung up. She hastened around the corner of her desk, banged her knee, and cursed under her breath. She approached her supervisor's desk.

"I've been called home," she stated flatly, quelling a hysterical giggle. The woman looked surprised.

"An emergency?" the supervisor asked, concerned.

"No, just some business I have to attend to," she replied. "A little bird told me," she thought to herself, suppressing a snicker.

"All right. You've been working lots of overtime lately. Take whatever time you need," the woman granted.

A talking bird, a heron vision—it was all a bit much. Perhaps she had been working too much overtime. The drive home was uneventful. She scanned the sky for her winged mentor. Nothing. Once she reached the house, there was nothing to do but wait and think. An hour ticked by. She thought about what the bird had said. "You must go home."

Where was home? Home was the life she had made for herself. It was the life and house that she shared with her husband and daughter.

It was also her past. A thousand miles to the west lay the home that she had left when she was nineteen. She dialed her parents' house. Her mother answered brightly and expressed surprise at hearing from her in the middle of the day. Not wanting to alarm her, Beverley said only that she had taken the day off and felt like chatting. As they chattered together, it became apparent that there was nothing out of the ordinary.

Satisfied, she bid her mother good-bye and hung up. Everything seemed to be normal on all fronts.

Except one. She wandered over to the hutch and picked up the picture. Her normally placid world had been shaken with the arrival of the picture. A couple of months earlier, her mother had mentioned that Frances had been asking about her. She and Frances had been at the same foster home.

Frances had stayed, adopted by the foster family, while she herself had been adopted by a childless couple. Frances was a kind girl and they had gone to the same high school, but being in different years, they had moved in different circles. She had not seen Frances since high school. Her mother went on to say that Frances had a picture for her. "It's a picture of you just before you left their family. She found it when she was sorting through her mother's belongings. Her mother's gone into a nursing home."

About a week later she received a letter from her parents. When she opened the envelope the picture fell out. She examined it closely. The little girl in the photograph was not a happy camper. She was seated on a small stool in the middle of a field of endless grass, scowling at the camera. She wore a cotton dress and had tucked one leg beneath her. Her head was too large for her small body, just like Beverley's own daughter's had been. Her straight, black hair was cut short in bowl fashion. On her face was an expression of anger and defiance. The little girl's eyebrows were drawn together, creating a line down the middle of her forehead. She reached up and traced the line on her own forehead. So, age had not put it there.

On the back was penciled July 1963. She knew nothing about the little girl who had existed before that date. She had no recollection of the person the girl faced behind the camera.

While she was looking at the picture, her daughter roared into the room, slamming into her mother for a hug. She peered at the picture her mother was holding. "Who's that, Mom?" the girl asked curiously.

"It's me when I was five," Beverley replied.

"You don't look very happy." Her daughter laughed. Beverley looked down at her daughter's face, so like the one in the picture, but so very different. Her daughter's face was exuberant, with dancing eyes. Her child faced every challenge head on. The child in the picture was fearful and wary. She hugged her daughter as fiercely as she wanted to hug the little girl in the photo.

Over the next few days, the little girl stayed in her thoughts. Her face floated before her, demanding answers. Seated stubbornly on her stool, the child quietly waited. She couldn't shake the feeling that the little girl wanted something from her. This was ridiculous. She knew what had happened to the little girl, how the story had gone.

The nice judge asked her if she wanted to stay with her new parents. With five-year-old wisdom, she shrugged. What choice did she have? Her new mother asked her if she wanted to keep her own name or get a nice, new one. She thought about all the pretty names she could have, but her present name was the only thing she owned in the world. She would keep her name, she announced.

Twenty-five years later, in the days approaching her daughter's birth, she had discovered in a baby name book that her own name meant "beaver meadow." Their fashionable pelts had almost gotten them eradicated from this country and had brought irreversible changes for the original inhabitants of Turtle Island. Herons too had been victims of fashion: their plumes were prized adornments of ladies' hats. Now both creatures were returning. The beavers were deemed to be a nuisance and a threat to property values. In the name of progress, the war resumed against the symbols of a nation. She knew whose side she was on; the beaver had created a home for her beloved herons. She was thankful that she had kept her name.

Growing up, she was a brown face in a white world, a crow in a flock of seagulls. She endured the *Woowoo!* taunts from the other kids and being called *Pocahontas* and *Tonto*. She was told that her mother had given birth to her in a jail. Jailbird. The good Christian folk pointed to the broken people staggering down Main Street, Canada; "There are your relatives."

Mortified, she wanted nothing to do with those people. As an awkward teenager, she put talcum powder on her face to lighten her skin and did her best to blend in. Never giving her adoptive parents any trouble, she left the nest when she was able to fend for herself. She educated herself enough to earn her keep and got on with the business of living.

Years later, she signed up for a summer course at the local campus. The first course to leap out of the catalog at her was entitled "The Native Peoples of Canada." People were always reminding her she was an Indian, she might as well learn something about them. She read about how their communities had endured catastrophe after catastrophe and had been assaulted with disease, warfare and ecological disaster. She marveled that she even existed. She went to her first powwow. Surrounded by all those black-haired, brown people, for the first time in her life she didn't stand out in the crowd. She spoke to no one and didn't dance in the circle. She was all too aware of the labels given to Indians like her. Red on the outside, white on the inside. "What else could I be?" she thought with resignation.

By most standards, she was happy. Stable marriage, healthy child, good job, nice home. What did the little girl want from her? Wasn't it enough to know that she had survived, had made it to adulthood relatively unscathed? The child persisted, her mute eyes questioning: Why did this happen? Does anyone miss me? Is there anyone else like me? Who am I?

She took the picture to a camera store and asked to have several copies made. The clerk took the picture from her, looked at it, and asked, "Is this you?"

"Yes," she replied without smiling. The young man looked at the picture again, unable to pinpoint why it made him feel uneasy.

He swallowed. It was on the tip of his tongue to say something like, "Cute kid," but he looked up at her. "Don't," her eyes told him, "it isn't true." He put the picture into an envelope.

"Should be ready in a week," he said.

She wasn't sure what she was going to do with the pictures. She thought of the faces of children that graced bulletin boards in grocery stores with the caption, "Have you seen this child?" She realized guiltily that most of the time she walked by without a glance. This child, however, demanded recognition from her.

She thought about the other brown-skinned children scattered across North America. They had disappeared like drops of water into an ever-widening pond. Nowadays, there were even trendy names for these kids. North of the border they were called "Sixties Scoop," which sounded like a new flavor of ice cream. Australia had the "Stolen Generation." In the States, the names were more poetic, like "Lost Birds." She was a member of a social phenomenon. Reams of paper had been produced about their plight, yet no one seemed to be able to adequately explain how it had all happened or what was to be done now, if anything.

She thought of the Pied Piper story in which the piper danced away with all the village children, never to be seen again. She couldn't remember the reactions of the people in the story, but she remembered her horror at the children's disappearance. Why had the piper taken the children? Had the villagers failed to give the piper what he wanted? She wondered if her generation had been missed from the many communities they had been taken from. Was it possible that such a wide-scale disappearance could go unnoticed?

She filled out the requisite forms for the agency responsible for her adoption. She got the information from her father, who was not surprised when she informed him that she would like to search for her birth relatives. "I always knew you would," he said calmly. "I'll help you in whatever way I can." The agency sent her more forms for the provincial adoption registry and told her there was a seven-year waiting list for that service. They told her it would be at least a year and a half before they could provide her with any information from her file. She was warned that the information contained in such a file might be sketchy or nonexistent. The counselor asked her if she knew anything about herself that might narrow the search. "I'm an Indian," she replied. The counselor suggested that she contact the tribal family services agency in her area of birth. She pestered the tribal agency until at last she spoke on the phone to a youthful-sounding woman who said she would "ask around."

Now she sat on the couch looking at the picture of her younger self. She had done as much as she could, and the possibility of anyone trying to reach her seemed remote. Thirty-five years had rolled by, and no one seemed to have the slightest interest in her whereabouts.

She regarded the dark little girl and realized that her own skin had faded. Twenty years of office lights had given her the pale skin that she had coveted as a teenager. Maybe this wasn't an improvement after all. Her hair, however, was returning to its natural coarse straightness and remained raven black, something that her office mates envied. After many years of battling with perms and short do's in an attempt to have mainstream hair, she wanted to see what her real hair looked like. She recalled the hairdresser of her childhood who had used rubber gloves when washing her hair. After a couple of visits, Estelle refused to cut her hair anymore, claiming that it dulled her scissors. Beverley stuck out her tongue at the memory of the hapless hairdresser and banished her back to the vault. "Take that, Farrah," she snorted. "Maybe you should get better scissors."

The phone jangled through her musings, and Beverley roused herself from the couch. When she answered the phone, a woman asked for a name that she realized with a jolt was her own. Never in her memory had she heard her first name and her birth surname pronounced together. The effect was much more profound than when she had left her maiden name behind and had to become accustomed to her new married name. Heart pounding, she answered, "Yes."

"I work in the band office," the woman said. "When I got the fax from the tribal agency, I talked to the people here and then phoned right away. You should talk to my dad. He knows who your family is."

She leaned weakly against the doorframe, her eyes flooding. Through her tears she looked toward the heron suncatcher in the window. "*Meegwech*," she whispered. "Thank you."

Memory Lane Is the Next Street Over

JOYCE CARLETTA MANDRAKE

She sits comfortably in the armchair. A calico dress reaches her ankles, leaving only the toes of new sneakers showing. Her eyes are shining lights in a face framed by a halo of wavy salt and pepper hair held loosely in a soft bun by ebony combs. She appeared quietly in the room. She is an old woman with a purpose in mind. I have seen her shadow within myself. I call her "Grandmother."

The day is beginning to warm as the sun floods the room with light and warmth. Outside, birds twitter in their joy of the day. The atmosphere is relaxing, perfect for chatting with Grandmother about days gone by. I am happy that she is here. Grandmother is a healer for my mind and soul. She is from my future time, although she pretends not to remember who I am. It is her way of healing.

"Tell me about your parents, your early memories or anything you would like to share," she says, her voice soothing.

"You know that I am adopted?" I ask, pretending she doesn't know. I sit upon a small couch filled with pillows and a marmalade cat. The cat has claimed my lap and purrs in her slumber.

"Yes. Tell me about your birth."

"When I was born, my adopted mom watched the process through the window of the delivery room. I did not breathe at first nor did I cry. The doctor took me by the heels and held me up. He dipped my body into cold water with no effect. He dipped me into hot water as well in his effort to jump-start me, spanking my bottom after he did each dipping. He did this several times before I cried out and began to breathe. My poor mother."

"Which one?"

"My adopted mother. She wanted a baby very badly. All three of her natural children had been miscarriages or stillborn. The stillborn children lay at rest in their tiny wooden boxes in the town's cemetery. White and purple lilacs stood in chipped mason jars on Memorial Day. The grass was always freshly mowed on that day."

"What of your father?" Grandmother plumps up a pillow behind her back.

"My adopted father wanted children as much as my mother. He wanted his wife to be happy; he loved her very deeply. He told me when I was older that he knew that I was coming to live with them. He knew my soul. He said he was told about me before I came."

"He was religious, then?" The old woman's dress rustles as she leans forward to reach her tea and a fresh cookie.

"No, my father was a mystic and a theological scientist. He was extremely well read and he had a burning curiosity about life and God's role in daily living. We did not, however, attend church. I was taken to many churches to see how other people worshipped. I went into bars with my father to see the depths of the sadness that is sometimes there. I never started to drink and I still don't drink. I think that the sadness of those people in the bars haunts me. The major lesson I think I learned from the bar visits and the church wanderings was respect for other peoples' values. The choices may not be what I might choose, but everyone's path is different.

"When I say that my father was a mystic, it is because he saw things with an inner vision. For example, when I was a small child, I would play with an imaginary friend. My father saw this friend. I don't remember this friend, just a feeling of warmth and joy.

"I believe that he prayed a great deal and meditated daily. Once he interrupted his meditation, saying that we were to let the people coming to the door in. He told us who it was and what they were wearing even though his eyes were closed and he was away from the windows. Some people might not believe he could do this, but I believed with the faith of a child. I believe in him even now."

Grandmother reaches for another cookie and smiles her encouragement. "What of your adopted mother? What did you learn from her?"

"Unconditional love, a warm lap, a great deal of patience and tolerance with children. And how to cook. And responsibility. When I was in seventh grade, my mother developed multiple sclerosis. I was the oldest of three children. My father was unable to be home to care for her, because he worked and owned a small gas station and service shop in the valley where we lived. I learned to cook from my mother while she was in her hospital bed. The bed was in the living room. I would go from the bed to the kitchen until I got supper finished. Whenever my father was home, he would cook and bake for his family. It was a hard and painful time for me. I was on the edge of adolescence, and it seemed like my mother was deserting me. To me, her sickness meant no more birthdays, Thanksgivings, and Christmases. Selfish, yes; lonely, absolutely. I was placed in the role of caretaker, cook, and housekeeper when my father was out of the home. I would go to my eighth grade class once a week for assignments and to turn in homework. Thank God that I was bright and self learning."

"You sound a little angry." The old woman's eyes are dark and filled with mist.

"Yes, I am angry. I am a forty-three-year-old woman who is still angry with her mother for dying and leaving her alone. Let me stop for a minute." I had been clenching my hands and stroking the cat on my lap, who protests with a loud meow, as I pull her fur. "I could at this minute bawl my eyes out. That is how hurt and angry I feel. All I can think about is no more birthdays, no more holidays and yes, I would have liked to share my son, her grandson, with her.

"I am very thankful for my father. He was always there for us. His pain must have been great. He lost his wife and his business, and had three children to raise. His wonderful presence filled our home with love. Birthdays still came, Thanksgivings and Christmases were different but happy.

"After all, my father was a great cook. I remember one Thanksgiving in particular. We went to my friend's house. It was up at the head of the valley at the base of the mountains. My friend and I were fifteen. She was full of excitement to cook the dinner, but she tried to stuff the turkey with a whole chicken. Enter my father to the rescue. Her poor old dad did not have a clue, because my friend's mom had been the one to cook all the meals. We were all motherless children, but I was the lucky one, for I had my dad."

"How was it being raised by whites? Did you have an opportunity to be with other Indians?" she asks. There are memories in Grandmother's eyes, but my memories are the ones being shared on this day.

"My parents loved me, their families and friends loved me. Other children made me feel different with the ugly words and hateful things they would say. Cuts, bruises—I got a lot of those just falling from a bicycle or out of the hay loft, or my favorite, down and through the tree. I have scars from a great many unforgiving tree branches. It is amazing how soft and beautiful trees look from the ground, but quite a different matter when you are plummeting through the gently waving branches.

"But I remember worse hurts from other sources. I guess that I am lucky: a wrongly placed kick or blow could have killed me. You might wonder where my father's God was at those moments. I believe that the loving presence of God was there keeping my spirit alive despite the pounding fists, the ripping hands. My wounds healed, a broken bicycle was repaired. My father soothed and healed with his words of wisdom and understanding. He would tell me to envision love and peace oozing from my body and to forgive those full of hurt and anger. I did it.

"Remember the girl with the Thanksgiving dinner, the one who tried to stuff the chicken in the turkey? She had been a torment to me for many years, until one day she pinned me to the wall in gym class. I was in tears from pinched arms and a bleeding lip. Other white girls came to my rescue, only to call the fat girl wicked, vile things. Yes, my tormentor was a very fat, ugly person. The other girls picked on her and teased, 'Fatty, fatty, ugly fat pig.'

"To my surprise and to the bewilderment of all around, I told them to stop the name-calling. Silence was very loud in the locker room at that moment. Girls began drifting from the room. I stared at the fat girl, and she stared at me very quietly with a puzzled look on her face. She handed me a wet paper towel and left the room. I was alone.

"Something else happened. I saw a great light in the room and I felt a loving presence. I felt safe. I have never told anyone that before."

"Why are you talking about it now?" The old woman's question is a soft whisper.

"Perhaps I feel safe now. I am not afraid of what other people might say. My father often mentioned such things. I have always been very private with my feelings and beliefs. For example, I have wondered about my natural mother. I talk to her in my head. I wonder who she is, if she is alive, if I have brothers and sisters? The list is endless. I don't know anything about my natural father. My mother is a different matter. I still wonder if she's out there."

Grandmother smiles, "What do you see when you see other people of your native background?"

"I see possible members of my immediate family, especially if they are of my tribe. I don't ask. It would be an invasion of their privacy, but I always wonder and whisper in my heart: Are we family?

"I had an opportunity to experience the subtle humor of my Indian friends in high school. It was a different school in a different town. It was great! I was excited to see faces like mine. When I went to college, my friends from high school were close by on the reservation. I went to my first powwow in college. My father had never taken me to any while I was growing up. We lived hundreds of miles from the reservation. My father worked all the time with people depending on him to repair farm machinery. We had animals to care for, eggs to be gathered, a cow to be milked, a garden to be watered and harvested.

"I believe that the thought of my heritage never really occurred to him. He taught all his children respect for the land and all life on the land. Since we lived close to the mountains, five miles away, he would take his family fishing in the cold running streams. We would have a picnic with all the wonderful things that my mother could pack in baskets. She would prepare the fire and relax reading on a blanket. My father would take us up the mountain exploring. We would slide down the mountain on large pieces of slate. Our pants would be in ruins and my mother would throw up her hands in dismay quite often.

"My father enjoyed hearing people call him 'the old Indian who owns the service station.' My father claimed to be Paiute. I asked an aunt if it was true, but she said it was true only if my father was born on the wrong side of the woodpile. There were twelve in my father's family. Every child was the product of one mother and father. No one else claimed to be Paiute. It wasn't that they were worried about being part Indian, it was probably simply not true.

"My father was dark because of the sun. He was a farmer when he was home. He would plow and irrigate the fields. He like to watch things grow. To my father, growing plants were a sign of the Creator at work. He was closest to God in his fields and garden.

"I am not dark skinned. My friends on the reservation would tease me, 'Ah, you are too white, you need more sun.' Fortunately, I did not burn but tanned quite nicely. We would spend all day and night at a powwow.

"I don't remember much about my first powwow. I remember elders playing stick games, my friends telling me that I was too white, and the races. The footraces were for money. Because I was a fast runner, I ran in the races for spending money. We would spend the money on carnival rides and food. My friends and I stuffed ourselves on fry bread, corn on the cob, and whatever else an eighteen-year-old could find to eat.

"I went to several powwows after that, but I was alone. My friends had moved. I would gaze with longing at the dancers, always afraid to dance because I did not know the steps. My dear sweet husband encourages me to try and has offered to dance with me.

"Grandmother, you have told me of the great love that dwells in the hearts of the Indian people. But I am still more comfortable talking and listening to spirits than talking to our people.

"When I was in college, I joined the Indian club and helped in setting up teepees in the middle of campus. We had drummers and singers come for a mini-powwow. The drums beating, the throats of singers flooding the air—the feelings that came to me then are stirred whenever I hear the drummers and singers now. Joy! Simply joy! The music was in my heart, and there it will beat forever.

"I remember the sweat lodge. My visions started in the sweat lodge. Balls of light, a great wolf. Wolf is walking down a forest trail. The forest brothers stand tall on both sides. I am following gray wolf with the balls of light dancing around us. Suddenly I stop. I cannot go further. Wolf stops. He says to me, 'When you are ready, you will follow.' He disappears.

"My fear has stopped me. It is my fear that stops me from the circle dance, the friendship dance. It was fear that chased me in a dream. I was in a lodge with many doors with a black bear following me. I ran in terror, in and out the doors, up stairs, always trying to get away. When I stopped for a moment to catch my breath, the bear stopped too. He stood up and looked me directly in the eyes and asked, 'Why are you running? Why are you afraid? I will come back when you are not afraid.'"

Grandmother looks carefully at me and smiles gently, "Were there any dreams or visions that did not frighten you?"

"Yes. I dreamed of a great lodge with three doors in the center. I entered through the left door. The room was filled with a beautiful light. I was dressed in white buckskins. A woman dressed in white buckskins stood in the center of the lodge. She was very glad to see me. There was a fire roaring in a pit. I stood by the woman and we began to pray with our arms uplifted. From the fire came the feathered brothers and sisters flying four times in a circle around us and then up through a large opening in the ceiling. We continued to pray, and the creatures of land emerged from the fire: bear, cougar, wolf, deer, and all of the four-footed animals came out of the fire. They circled four times and left through the ceiling. That was a good dream for me.

"There was another one. I ran and hunted with cougar. I was cougar, chasing down a great stag for our young to feed on. Padding quietly through the forest, frost forming on my whiskers. The cold air, the sound of a bird rustling in the brush, the running and leaping upon the stag were all very real to me.

"I was alone to interpret my visions and dreams. I had no elders to guide me. However, changing into cougar did not bother me. Why should it? I had metamorphosed into an eagle or hawk many times in my dreams. Flying and gliding in the air. What freedom!

"One summer evening as I sat working on a basket, I looked out the window and saw an Indian warrior striding from the East to the West. He was dressed in buckskins, and his face was painted in colors of the rainbow. He was taller than the mountains. There was a sweat lodge that night that I did not attend because it was my moon time. I have always wondered about the vision. But then, I went to the window and raised my hands into the air and prayed.

"I had many good times in the sweat lodge. I enjoyed the prayers even if I did not understand the language. I believe that my heart and soul knew the meaning on a deeper level. I felt at home.

"Once I was asked to come help a family with their troubles. A man who I knew from the Indian club asked me to help with a healing. Why he chose me to come and help, I don't know. He did not know me very well. There was a family who had lost the mother. They were very sad and became frightened when they started to see her walking the fields by their home. We took the husband into the lodge for healing. The medicine man who had brought me said prayers. He talked to the man and said prayers over him in Shoshone. He performed his healing on the man. After he finished, he asked me to help the man.

"Memories of how my father helped his children came to my mind, and I placed the man's head to the South. I cleansed him with an eagle feather. I asked him to hold the feather close to his heart. I acknowledged the presence of the Great Spirit. I began the healing. I let the energy of spirit flow through me. My hands traveled up the man's body from his feet to his head. My hands were held several inches from his body. I sent peace and contentment sailing through the man until I reached past his head. I announced, 'It is done.'

"When we drove back to campus, the medicine man told me he was able to see sparks flying off my fingers during the healing. We were successful. The man and his family never saw the spirit of the dead wife and mother walking in the fields again."

Grandmother moves forward in her chair to pull the marmalade cat into her arms. The cat settles, purring with contentment. She studies my face thoughtfully, "Is there something else you wanted to say?"

I cannot look at Grandmother. I study my hands instead. There is a long silence before I speak again. I remember that I am safe. She is the salve for my soul, helping the memories to return.

"I remember another sweat lodge time with this man. It was several months later. There were five people in the lodge. It was toward the end of the ceremony, during the fourth round. I was sitting upright as I always did. It was dark in the lodge with only the hot rocks glowing in the pit. I was deep in thought and prayer. I felt a probing on my genitals by someone's fingers. I did not move. I kept myself sitting upright. I did not know what to do. The fingers went away. After we had left the lodge, this man told me that he thought that I was very powerful. I knew that this man had touched me in the sacredness of the lodge uninvited. A great deal of trust went out of my heart that day. My heart is beating fast and I am uncomfortable in the telling of what happened. Perhaps that is why I need to say it. I was violated. I am angry. All of this by someone who was a healer and a medicine man.

"A great deal of trust has crept back with the goodness of my husband and many dear friends. I know that I am loved and protected by my Creator. I feel this in my prayers. I am loved.

"Being adopted, Grandmother, was not a rejection from my birth mother; it was a gift! It was a wondrous opportunity to reach closer to the Creator.

"For I was given to the right family, at the right time. And all the lessons I have learned have made me stronger. I believe that without the sorrow, I would not know the joy that is in my life. My adopted mother dying and the cruelties of youth brought even more strongly to me the unlimited and continual love of my father for his children.

"My greatest lesson has been learning unconditional love. I pray daily to let Divine Unconditional Love fill my being, so that I can let it shine from my heart into the world. I remember you, Grandmother. You are the angel in the night who protects me. You are my highest self. Grandmother, you are a reminder of the great love that is mine and that is for everyone. Thank you for returning time and time again in my life in your various forms."

The old woman smiles. "I am you, Granddaughter. I am your future when all fear is gone." Grandmother in her calico dress stands up with the marmalade cat in her arms. She brushes a few cookie crumbs from the front of her dress and the top of the cat. I hug and kiss the old woman in my mind as she begins to fade away in the warm afternoon of memories. The marmalade cat is dissolving with her. She smiles. Her halo of hair shimmers in a sun's ray.

Lost Tribe

ALAN MICHELSON

Mom had said, *You're adopted,* and was reading to me from the book: *Dogs want to take care of their puppies, cats want to take care of their kittens, and the lady and man who made you wanted to take care of you.*

I wanted us to be reading *Peter Pan* again, not this boring adoption book with the sorry-looking family. They looked weirdly flattened in the pictures, *run over.* Whoever colored them made the kid's skin a lot darker than his parents, so they didn't even match. And they didn't even have any adventures, unless you called having a birthday party one.

I didn't know about this *lady and man who made you* stuff. It made you sound like Frankenstein, like something brought to life by mad scientists. Finally I had to come out and ask Mom, Did I grow in your belly?

No, she said after a fairly long pause when I thought I was in trouble. You didn't.

You were born in Buffalo, both she and Dad had said, but maybe they meant *in* a buffalo and I was part beast! Half boy, half *bison* and soon I'd be getting *shaggy.*

Was it a *lady's* belly? I asked hopefully.

Of course! said Mom.

Another . . . *mother's?*

Yes, Mom said.

Did Dad make me with her?

He did not! Mom said. Your other—she made you with someone else.

Another father?

Yes.

Where are they?

We don't know.

How come?

There are privacy laws protecting everybody involved in an adoption.

From what?

Mom had to think that over a little. From getting all mixed up, she finally said.

Aren't they ever going to visit us? I asked.

Mom said that they couldn't, that they were young and in school and that's why they had given me up. She had already told me how she and Dad had *tried* to have a child of their own. Was there a trick to it? I wondered. *We went to doctors,* Mom said once, staring into space.

Sometimes in my room I thought about it all. How, in a way, I was someone else and me at the same time. Like Superman. He's Clark Kent some of the time but only because he has to fool everyone. Fooling everyone is part of being super. When you're super, you need a secret identity. Being like the Man of Steel in some way made me feel a lot better. Buffalo was my *Planet Krypton.* To save me from its *doom,* my parents, brilliant young students, launched me into space in a tiny rocket zooming toward Earth. Where a kindly bespectacled couple like Mom and Dad could raise me as one of their own.

Leave it alone, it's *dead!* said my cousin Andy, about the little bundle of skin at our feet. It had a roundish, pink body covered with a dirty gray stubble and patches of greasy, matted stuff. I had almost stepped right on it in my thongs. Now I was bent over inspecting it, my first dead animal. Dead anything, not counting *father,* of course. But no one let me see Dad dead.

What do you think it is? I asked Andy. It had something headlike half-buried in the grass and a pair of trailing feet or claws.

I'm not sure, he said. It could be a bird. I think that little flap may be a wing.

Then where are its feathers?

It's a baby bird, stupid. Their feathers take a while to come in, Andy said.

The shriveled, matted mess on its wings had been getting ready to sprout into feathers! It reminded me of the egg Mom once cracked open that had something growing in the yolk, something struggling to be a chicken.

I'm getting a stick, I said.

What do you think you're going to do with that? Andy asked in his bossiest, older-cousin tone.

Holding it like a sword (I tried thinking of *Zorro*), I prodded the bird. Gently, in case there was still a spark of life left in him. In case it was not *too late* like with Dad. I touched his little red feet but they were curled up and limp. Then I touched it on the wing, which made it rock spookily from side to side, like a dead bird *puppet*.

Gimme that! said Andy, trying to grab the stick away.

It's *my stick,* I yelled, yanking it out of his grip.

Okay, okay, he said.—*Baby!*

I wasn't done with the bird. I wanted to see its face and needed the stick for it. I wanted a better look at death, and no one was going to stop me. Repositioning the stick under the wing, I resolved to flip it over on its back.

Somehow, when I did this, its body flipped but not its head. The tiny neck was twisted around like a corkscrew.

Oooooh, *maggots!* Andy bellowed. The bird belly was crawling with maggots and ants.

One of the windows of the beach house opened and Andy's mother's voice blared out of it, *What are you boys doing?*

Alan's poking a dead baby bird with a stick, Andy said.

A what? shrieked my aunt. She had both palms under the window, trying to force it open wider.

A dead baby bird, Andy repeated.

Get away from it, she screamed. It's *filthy with germs!*

She lifted the screen and leaned her red face out the window. Open-mouthed, all set to deliver one of her awful verbal spankings, she suddenly broke off. Looking annoyed, she retracted her head from the window like an angry turtle. Someone inside was talking to her! Pieces of conversation, *dead bird, machen die kinder,* floated down to us, carried by excited voices.

My last chance with the bird. Risking *germs* I grabbed the little head with bare fingers and turned it over, face-up. It was pitiful-looking, like a tiny ostrich with two black eyes. The top of its head was covered with the same sort of fuzz that Dad's was toward the end.

After a few years of widowhood with Grandma and me, Mom started dating.

I'm going out for the evening next Saturday, she would suddenly announce, and sure enough, a week later a strange car would pull up in front of the house and the date guy would get out. I hated most of them on sight. Mom, dolled up in a nice dress, perfumed to the hilt and made up in her Ingrid Bergman face, would let the jerk into our house!

Usually she made a point of introducing me to him. This is *Sol,* she would say, and I'd have to shake Sol's big, outstretched hand and inhale his cloud of aftershave. By the time they left for the date, the living room reeked, and once Grandma even opened a window.

I'd be asleep when she got home, but the next morning there would be a souvenir left somewhere. A miniature paper umbrella, a huge matchbook with a name like *Lombardo's* on it above a picture of the Roman Colosseum, or maybe just an unused lobster bib or a couple of packets of those moist towelettes. Mom liked nightlife but could never pass up a free *anything.*

She discouraged all of her suitors, however, finding romance-killing defects in every one of them. *He's not much of a dancer, you know,* or *He lives with his mother.*

But Harvey won Mom over. It took him a year of dates, long-distance phone calls, love letters, and jewelry. Mom liked his eyes—her favorite ocean blue—and his beaming smile. No one could resist it, not even Grandma, startled from her permanent state of worry. I liked his croaky voice, deep and tobacco-charred. His handiness with the tools that choked the trunk of his Buick. In his husky, Vitalis-scented presence, Mom bloomed. Grandma took the most convincing.

He's *not* divorced—I told you he's a widower!

So vhat heppened to deh vife?

Cancer was what happened to her, a different kind than Dad's. When

I felt sad on his behalf, sad that Mom was living it up with Harvey, I concentrated on some of Dad's dying words to Mom: *I want Alan to have a father one day.* Maybe Harvey's wife had said something like that to him before she died. About their kids, who were losing their mother.

Loss left you *deserving*. *Deserving* of a father, a wife, a husband, a mother. That was part of it, that we *deserved* each other. Each other and a fresh start.

Didn't we?

Once Mom and Harvey were engaged the word *future* got tacked onto everything. Harvey's daughter became my *future sister Rhonda*. Mom was her and her brother's *future stepmother*. Go tell your future brother we're eating.

Hey, our *future lunch* is ready.

The future lasted until their wedding day.

After we moved into the new house together, the trouble started. We were a much better future family than a new one. A lot of the friction was between the new brothers, the *Two Alans*.

That's how we were known.

In the beginning Harvey tried calling us *Alan Number One* and *Alan Number Two,* but neither of us wanted to be the second Alan. Also, it sounded too much like you had to go to the bathroom, like you were *Alan Pee* or *Alan Crap.*

Then my aunt, Andy's mom, made a suggestion. Her suggestions had a way of becoming *iron laws.* Why not call *our Alan* AJ? she proposed.

AJ was a nickname branded on me when I was a little tyke. I had just ignored it at the time and tried to get everyone to call me *Chip* instead. But no one cares about the name you want and they wanted to call me AJ.

BJ, Alan immediately said.

It's AJ, I said.

BJ, he repeated. You know what *BJ* stands for?

I don't know, what?

He made his standard, bitter, "mask of comedy" grin and chuckled. C'mon, guess, he said.

Big Jerk? I said. Breakfast Juice?

"Breakfast Juice" made him double over laughing.

You really are a little child, aren't you? he said. We were only a year apart in age, but childhood was a complete waste of time to Alan. It just prevented him from getting laid and making money, which is all he wanted to do. For that reason alone he despised it and anyone, like me, who actually enjoyed it occasionally.

Luckily, after the first year we went to separate schools. Alan stayed at the Shittick, with its screwed-down desks and dark-varnished gloom. I transferred to the Greensward, the kind of low-slung, modern, yellow-brick elementary schools that you knew they had in *Denmark* but were rare in Boston.

The Greensward. Where Newness was King. Green blackboards, Formica desk tops, vinyl floor tiles, recessed lighting, *intercoms*. Blond wood cabinets full of neatly stacked boxes of paper, thumbtacks, pink erasers, crayons, glue, chalk, metal compasses, rubber bands.

Presiding over it all was our teacher, Mrs. Nard. From the moment she first swept into the classroom, we knew we were in for a strange couple of years. She was one of those immense people forced to inhabit a tiny body, who spill over in every direction. Once on *Afternoon Showcase* there was a movie about a batty silent picture queen who lived in a spooky mansion with her butler. Mrs. Nard reminded me of her a lot.

She taught mainly by *exaggeration* and by turning everything into a *show.*

She called the school the *campus,* the coatroom the *vestibule.* If you could draw, you were the *class artist,* dance and you were *our choreographer.* We weren't so much in school as on stage, in constant rehearsal for one of her productions. For our French lesson we had to perform a number from *South Pacific* in front of the entire school. Nard's Nerds, they dubbed us.

They weren't completely wrong. There were some awful nerds in the class, hard-core teacher's pets groomed from nursery school. The kind who *suggested* homework and looked forward to square dancing. Who wore ugly shoes and had weird neck rashes. Left unchecked, they would have made Nard's class even doofier than it already was.

That's where *Command Force Network* came in. Vance and I started it when we were sitting beside each other in the back corner, before Nard made me move my desk smack into nerd territory near the board.

Where I was forced to make eye contact with her all the time, like the nerds, who loved it. I was cut off from the Command.

You're behind their lines, Vance said, *in their sector. The true test of any spy.*

How were we to stay in touch?

There's a way, said Vance. *Give me a week.*

A week later he handed me a little bag at recess. It felt like candy inside, but it wasn't. It was capsules. What're these?

Open one and see, said Vance, facing off into the distance.

I pulled one open and a tiny, rolled-up piece of paper fell out. Unrolled, it was a message printed in my friend's precise script. *Note capsules* was the way we communicated after that, handing them off en route to the blackboard, stashing them in places Vance called drop sites. Vowing to swallow one if caught, Vance single-handedly saved the Command from Nard's effort to destroy it.

His genius was obvious from his first home project for Nard. The subject was geography, and Nard was characteristically vague and loopy about the assignment. Most of us traced maps out of old *National Geographics.* One kid brought in a bullfighter poster from Spain, which Nard loved. Vance came in with a heavy-looking box.

And what do you have for us, Stephen, Nard said. *Show* the class.

Vance cleared his throat and opened the box. Inside was a scale model of *Mount Vesuvius* made out of plaster and painted. It looked better than the tunnel mountain in my cousin's model railroad, the one that cost a fortune in the hobby store.

How absolutely *marvelous!* said Nard. Where on earth did you get it?

I made it, Vance said in a low voice. Then, louder, *I designed it to emit smoke but I'll need to light a match. Do I have your permission, Mrs. Nard?*

I think she would have let him light one of the nerds on fire at that moment. She told him he could use a lighted match *if he was careful.*

Vance did something and smoke started coming out of the volcano crater. Lightly at first, like a cigarette, but then it really started pouring out. Nard went white. Vesuvius looked about to blow! The fire evacuation made us miss arithmetic, which of course Nard was trying to get us to call *math.*

And then there was the science project. Some of the nerds went to town—caged mice, Tesla coils, the whole bit—but Vance just brought in a single manila envelope and plunked it down on the table. What's *that?* the nerds all said in chorus.

Pictures, said Vance.

Pictures! said the nerds. What kind of a science project is that? The *art* project was last month.

Vance's pictures turned out to be close-up photographs of the moon's surface he had taken through his telescope. *Lunar photographs* on black and white glossy paper, crystal clear, like NASA. He even printed them himself in his home darkroom. How did Vance do it?

It's just a matter of good optics, he said. *German lenses are the best in the world. Both my instruments were made in Germany.*

Vance was German on one side. *I come from a long line of German engineers,* he once told me. He had a grandfather from the Black Forest who had written and illustrated a famous book about trolls.

How about you? Vance said.

Oh, *Russian,* I said.

Russians are a *formidable people,* Vance said approvingly.

What did I know? Maybe one of Grandma or Grandpa's ancestors had *not* been a scared Jew with a beard and a hat, had not been *a Torah scholar* in a muddy little village somewhere that no one ever heard of, that even Grandma was ashamed of. *We came from Pupik.*

What country was that in?

You vanna exact address?

I just want to know what nationality we are, if we are *Russian* Jews or *Polish* Jews or *Lithuanian—*

You vanna know ayif ve were goyim? Vhat kine a goyim ve were?

What happened to us Grandma? In the Bible we're a great people—

The Chosen.

Okay, the Chosen. We had Joseph and Moses and David. Kings and armies with chariots that won battles. We had the Ark and the Temple. How did we end up tailors in Poland?

Sha!

A long line of German engineers. Vance was proud of his ancestors even though they were *Krauts* and lost the war. Even though they had loved *Hitler* and gone *Nazi.* He had model *Messerschmidts* hanging in his room!

You just wanted to be proud of what you were. I was proud of the biblical Jews, but how long ago was *that?*

In the warning dream, we killed him on the beach. The Two Alans locked in combat, this time over a loaded gun. It went off and hit him square in the chest, in the heart, no chance. Our anguish when he fell, clutching himself.

Harvey's face with the same sunburn, the same grimace when they carried him down the front steps in the gurney. Wrapped, in the style of his beloved *schvitzbord,* in a crisp, white sheet up to the armpits. *Heart Attack. DOA.*

An hour before the ambulance, Mom's taut, stricken face answered the door. That, too, seemed strangely familiar at the time. *He came home early with chest pains. I thought you were the doctor. Where's your key?*

Harvey was upstairs in bed. I mumbled something just as the phone on the night table rang. Infernally loudly. Rang twice before he nodded for me to get it.

Mom! It's the doctor!

My yell made him wince. *I'm killing him again,* I thought.

On my way out I closed the door of their bedroom behind me. Wrong again, he wanted it left open. The last time I opened it had been on the night of my dream, frantic to see if he was still alive. Only his deep, oceanic snoring had convinced me that he was.

I was confident in the car, the only one. Listen, lightning didn't strike twice in the same spot, did it? Dad's death was protecting Harvey. Nobody could lose two fathers in a row, the odds were too strongly against it. The odds, the *odds.*

Not long after the funeral I tried getting Mom to give up one of her secrets. Like most of our showdowns, this one was an outdoor event.

She glowered at me across a patch of the burnt, yellow crabgrass that passed for lawn at my aunt's. A chalky, crusted dog turd lay midway between us like a marker of some kind.

Why do you *suddenly* need to know? Mom was asking. *Suddenly* was an accusation in our gravity-bound family, who would have been happier on Jupiter, where they could be *completely immobile* and not have to cope with *velocity*. Mom and her sisters were as sensitive as horses to anything sudden, and my unexpected question, *What was my real mother's name?* had really spooked her.

I'm just curious, I said, now that I'm a bit older. I had *now that I'm bar mitzvahed* ready as a backup.

Did anyone *approach* you, a *stranger?* Mom asked, glancing around. *Did they put you up to this?*

No, no. No one *approached.* I told you, I'm just *curious.*

Are you telling me the truth?

Mom had a touch of Jewish deafness at times. Where *they just can't hear you.*

Hey, can we please get back to *my* question for a second? About a certain *name?*

I don't know the name, Mom finally said. Her eyes said, *I know, but forget it, buster.*

Now it was my turn to play detective. *Wasn't her name on any of the adoption papers you had to sign?* Mom looked a lot like Barbara Stanwyck when she was lying.

Dad handled all that, she said, I was too emotional. I didn't want to know any names at the time. I was like the ostrich who buried its head in the sand.

Where it's remained ever since.

This side of adoption was the worst. This *ostrich side* it had. What was such a big deal about a name?

Mom could be thinking I'd ditch her for the Real Mom, I thought. Who ditched me. The whole thing was getting pitiful.

Against the backdrop of my aunt's ailing shrubbery, Mom looked seriously drawn. Hiding her head in the sand hadn't spared it much, I thought, from whatever grayed hair, carved wrinkles, and injected eyes with bitterness and hurt.

Mom's grief.

Facing away toward the woods across the street, I closed my eyes. The lot wasn't very big, just one in a chain of wooded lots that snaked through the neighborhood and ended a mile away in a pine grove. They were where Andy and I used to go exploring, and they were riddled with our secret hideouts. Our favorite was a deep pit left over from an uprooted tree.

Out of some corresponding crater in my brain, something was trying to surface. A word. A name. One that started with a "G." Hard "G." "GR." GRRR—

Suddenly, in the Martian firmament of my closed eyelids, a disturbance. It was like a meteor shower of green particles, vivid against the red. GRRReen. *Green!*

Her last name was Green, I said. *Carol Green.*

Mom's jaw literally dropped. *How did you know?* changed pretty quickly to *Someone must have told you.*

And who would that have been, I wondered. Maybe, like my buddy Superman, I was developing *powers.* Or maybe it was just a lucky guess. What was my Magic Eight Ball's standard advice?

Ask again.

Alan, Gert was saying, *Alan.*

Gert was Mom's cousin from Buffalo. We were sitting at one of the tables at a family wedding, under the stifling canvas tent set up in somebody's gigantic yard. The rest of Table Three were gone, either gorging on seconds or fox-trotting on the grass. Occasionally a woman dancer's high heel would spike itself into the ground and stake her to the spot for a moment, breaking the couple's rhythm. I didn't get the point of summer parties if you still had to wear a suit and tie. And tread around on spongy grass in shiny shoes like some mafioso who wore dress shoes *everywhere.*

I had just come from the bar with fresh cocktails. A year of college in New York City had been my introduction to a lot of things, among them, Scotch, although I hated drinking it out of the silly wine goblets that the bartenders fobbed off on you at these things. Gert was sipping out of hers with one hand. The other was clutching mine.

Oh, Alan! she said after gulping it down. Alan, Alan.

Gert was the nearest I had to a godmother. She had been at the hospital with Mom and Dad when they first came to see me. There was the story that I had pooped in her hand once when she was holding me. The same hand, probably, that was still squeezing mine.

Alan, Gert said, *it's good to see you, Alan.*

Like Mom, she wore eyeglasses. From certain angles there was even a resemblance, which added to my suspicions, at times, that it was she who had given birth to me. That she, and not the Jewish nurse, was my long lost Other Mom. But I didn't look like Mom, so their resemblance was really irrelevant. Now Gert's glasses were streaked with tears. What was it about me and crying women?

Alan, she said, dabbing her eyes with a paper napkin. Printed in gold on it were *Gloria and Keith* and the date. Alan, honey. Alan.

Gert. Tell me what you know.

Gert, I said.

Alan, she said. Alan.

I have a few questions I'd like to ask you.

Oy, *questions*, Alan, she said, fanning herself with a cloth napkin. What type of questions, Alan? Wait, I think I can guess.

About my background, I said. The band was playing "Alley Cat."

I knew it, said Gert. Alan, I knew it.

I was wondering if I have my facts straight, I said.

Facts, Alan? Alan, what *facts?*

I told her my story of the Jewish doctor and nurse. How they struck up a hospital romance that had led to me. A story that Mom would neither confirm nor deny. Gert was shaking her head.

No, Alan, no, she said. *Alan, no.*

A waiter came by and poured coffee. Which neither of us touched. Both of us swallowed more Cutty Sark instead.

Gert was now gently patting my hand. Maybe she sensed my attachment to the story. My need for it to have been true.

How do you know? I said.

I *worked* there, Gert said. Alan, I worked there and would have known them if your story were right.

There were no young Jewish doctors or nurses at the hospital?

Of course there were. But none, Alan, who had a child together, believe me. *Alan, believe me.*

I took a long drink from my water glass and when I had drained it, I suddenly felt tipsy. The dancers spinning around in the *hora* twenty feet away were making me queasy, too. Clarinets pierced my eardrums.

Do you know who they were? I asked Gert. *My parents?*

Her eyes flooded with a fresh batch of tears.

Alan, she said. *Alan, honey, I don't.*

There was no warning dream for Mom. But plenty of notice. Nearly five years from the time she found the lump. Fucking cancer.

At the end Mom was so serene. Were George and Harvey waiting for her in heaven? How would they arrange it? I wondered.

The last day there were too many people in her room. Do you want me to stagger the visits? I asked her. No, she wagged her head. Her voice was all but gone. My beautiful Mom. With her gypsy bandanna on her peach fuzz head. I tried rubbing her feet, which she always loved, but they were numb.

You're a peach, were her last words to me.

She died on a holiday. Independence Day.

My acceptance to art college arrived in the next day's mail. Maybe Mrs. Nard's *class artist* had belonged there all along. Columbia and New York hadn't really worked out. The art school was adjacent to the museum on one of Olmstead's parks. *Museum School.* Just the name of the place gave me a lift. I loved Boston for this, for the mausoleums, cool, and dark, where it housed its treasures. And for the statue of the Indian on the front lawn of the museum.

I fell for a classmate in Litho. Together we fell for painting. And Bach (Carty with her fiddle, me with our old spinet). And for Wolfie, our maestro, who could trace *his* teachers back to Mozart.

He's looking like a *Spaniard* today, don't you think? Wolfie said. Come in, Michael, and let us see you.

Michael was what Carty called me. Wolfie's full name was Wolfe Wolfinsohn, and he thought mine was Michael Michelson. It was too late to set him straight. And not that easy. Plus, I had had it with *Alan* for a while. It felt like my *slave name,* one that belonged to the son Mom and Dad hadn't been able to have. Belonged to one of the three dead infants I had been drafted to replace.

I think 'tis the Basque beret, observed Wolfie from his wing chair. And possibly his coloring. Show us your profile.

He had a weird way of putting you on display. *Show me your hands!* he once commanded my surprised best friend, who raised them so briskly that Wolfie might have been pointing a gun at him.

I stepped in front of the French doors, the brightest spot in the shady room. Right next to the hulking, humiliating Steinway, behind which hung the charcoal portrait of Wolfie in his prime. In leonine profile, Strad tucked under his cleft chin, he looked almost *unfairly* dashing.

Tell me, while you're over there, if you see *Picasso* coming up the drive? said Wolfie. We're expecting him and his four wives for tea, you see.

Wolfie's string quartet had once been top of the line. Famous composers had dedicated works to them, written pieces in their honor. He had played chamber music with Einstein in Princeton. If I hadn't been certain that Picasso was dead, I might have been taken in.

Let's have a look at you, Michael, he said, making a show of finding and donning his eyeglasses. What sort of overcoat is that, have you joined the *Resistance?* How long before we drive the dogs into the sea?

Not long, I said.

Marvelous! he said. Now, back to the more pressing question of your *physiognomy.* Could there be some hot, Sephardic blood in your veins, mixed in with the Ashkenazic? Shall we begin addressing you as *Miguel?*

Uh, sure, I said. What difference did it make what I was called? Wolfie's Miguel was just as plausible as Carty's Michael or Mom and Dad's Alan. *You look international,* my Japanese calligraphy teacher Mr. Aso had said once, during a similar exchange.

Japanese calligrapher. Russian-Jewish violinist. Somehow the label reduced and expanded you in the same breath, linked you to people and places supposed to have left traces in your blood. Mysterious capacities, like Wolfie's for the fiddle, and vulnerabilities, in his case, to the Parkinson's that robbed him of most of his gift. Maybe the time had finally come to find out if I had any innate capacities besides losing parents and to see what additional vulnerabilities I had to look forward to.

Wait a second, I've got Gertie on the line, said my cousin Zach. Zach always had the latest in phone technology. He was plugging me into a three-way call.

There was a click and then a silence. After fifteen or twenty seconds I thought I heard breathing on the other end. Hello? I said.

Alan? said the familiar voice. Is that you, Alan?

Yes, Gert.

Alan, Gert said. Alan, Alan. Honey, it's long distance, I'll get right to the point. Zach tells me you're still curious about your background.

I am, I said.

Are you, Alan? said Gert. Alan, are you? Because I have to know. I have to *know,* Alan.

I said I am, Gert. I said it, and I meant it.

Alan, I may be able to help you, she said, sniffling. I have a girlfriend, Alan, who worked for the doctor who delivered you. She may know how to contact your birth mother.

Really?

Alan, really, she said with a choked sob. *Really.*

Please don't cry, Gert. There's no need.

I made her a *promise,* Alan. Miriam, your mother. She made me swear never to tell you anything! Alan, she made me swear!

She's gone now, Gert, I said. Nothing can hurt her anymore.

God, did I really say that? It was part soap opera, part Dickens.

After trying to reassure Gert that helping me couldn't justifiably hurt anyone else, we hung up. She promised to keep me posted on her progress. But hadn't she also promised Mom something?

About a week later she phoned. I asked her if her friend had turned up anything.

Alan, said Gert. Are you ready for this, Alan?

Ready for what?

Is there anyone there with you, honey? Carly?

Carty? She's in the other room playing the violin.

Sit down, Alan, said Gert. Alan, sit down.

I'm sitting, Gert, I lied. What did you find out?

I don't know how to tell you this, Alan, she said.

Maybe she *was* my mother, after all. Why else would she be so worked up? She seemed to be hyperventilating.

Oh my God, Alan, she's Indian! said Gert. She's Indian, Alan!

What are you talking about?

Your mother! She's an *Indian,* Alan, she said. Do you understand what I'm saying to you?

You mean American Indian?

Yes. Alan, yes!

What tribe? I asked.

Tribe, Alan? Gosh, honey, I forgot to ask. They're from Canada originally, I think.

And what about my father, I thought. Was he a *Yak?*

I was a *Jewish Indian.* Maybe that explained the hawk nose and Hawaiian deep tan in summer. The love of nature. And of *finery.* And the conspicuous lack of chest hair. Jews have hair *on their hair.*

I remembered a long afternoon Andy and I spent in the woods.

Trying to learn to walk *like an Indian*. We read about it in a book. That the Indian walked toe first, toe-heel, instead of heel-toe like the white man. Which is how he could silently steal through the forest. That was being silently stolen from him. Anyway, toe-first walking was tiring, and made you look like you were *prancing*. We went back to our Jewish walking, which was take four steps and complain. Which was walking to the *car*.

Wasn't there a theory that the Indians were really Jews? The Ten Lost Tribes of Israel? God knows, they were as popular with the Christians. But I found it hard to believe that the Jews could have been so *good with their hands*. Or spread out so far over two continents. If the Indians had been the Lost Tribes, they would have all crowded onto Manhattan, arguing.

Over the next few months I got more reports from Gert. Alan, *I spoke to her on the phone, Alan,* and then, *I met her for lunch.* Gert told me that Carol was divorced and worked as a hairdresser. That she was very glad that I wanted to get back in touch after all these years. And wanted my address so that she could send me a letter.

Over the years I had composed my own letter to her.

Dear Birth Mom,

I think I may be your former egg. Loved the nine months in your womb, miss the gurgling. Sorry we lost touch.

Yours?

Alan

Eventually, a letter did arrive from her. *How are you? I am find,* it began. She wanted me to know how hard she had prayed that she would hear from me one day. How she had never stopped thinking about me and praying for me. How sorry she was for having to give me up. Her handwriting was regular and even, out of a penmanship book. She had underlined certain words and used several exclamation points for emphasis. Her note paper had little daisies on it.

She had included a picture of herself. I wiped my eyes so that my first look at her wouldn't be blurry. It was a Polaroid someone had snapped of her in a bathroom. She was gorgeous! In her tank top and cutoffs she looked way too young to have been my mother. *Young student* had been Mom's only description of her. And somehow it was still accurate. Her thick black hair was piled on top of her head in complicated ringlets. Joy in her smile.

It took me the better part of a year to respond.

The museum was in a park. After the long ride from Boston, eight hours on the road, we found it on the map and drove right to it. The opera wasn't until evening, leaving time for a detour into town. Being in Buffalo again felt strange. Being in a Greek temple filled with art didn't.

In the gallery with the huge Clifford Stills I resumed my deliberations. Should I look up Carol or not? I couldn't decide. We still had not had any direct contact. Although she had made it clear that on her side the channels were open. What was the blockage on my side? Jagged feelings, dark and subterranean as the shapes in the paintings lining the walls. In the car, Carty had listened quietly to the same boring soliloquies she had been hearing for months. *You'll figure it out, Mike,* was all she'd say.

Where did we go after the museum? To an address across town I had gotten out of the phone book. We parked in front of the little house, Carol watching. At one point, a woman pulled up in a station wagon and unloaded endless bags of groceries onto the porch. Assisted by strawberry blonde children, who looked just like her.

The Phillip Glass opera about Gandhi was soothing as a lullaby. *Satyagraha,* its name, came from the Sanskrit *satya,* truth, and *graha,* persistence. My sister Rhonda played an Afrikaner woman who saves Gandhi from a mob. The voices and instruments serenaded the surrounding trees, whose mossy tops were silhouetted against the blue night sky. It was a park we were in, but cornfields once. Indian country. Their farms had stretched to the landing and lined this side of the river for miles. Not far beyond the stage, the Niagara swept past on its way to the falls.

I phoned her the next morning. *Carol, this is Alan.* She gave me directions to her house, which was only a few blocks from the museum. Porch, doorbell, stairs. At the top of the staircase, a petite, pretty woman in navy blue and white. With really big hair. My Other Mother. Her older sister Dee, my aunt. *You're both wearing white pants,* someone said.

We sat together on the love seat. Her eyes, almond-shaped and

Polynesian-looking, were already tearing up. *I didn't want to give you up. I was fifteen.* Her sister brought us drinks. Carty settled into a big, pink velour chair. For the next half hour Carol poured out her story. An older sister, a hangout, Joe's, *jazz,* cigarettes, dancing. A manly Italian boy who set his sights on her. Despite the fact that she was underage. *He used to come to the house. He ate dinner with us every Sunday.*

Terrified, she kept the pregnancy secret as long as she could. The family doctor confirmed it at six months, when she had just begun to show. He advised her mother, who cleaned for him, to consider putting the baby up for a adoption. *She's a child herself. You'd have to raise it.* When informed, the Italian boyfriend showed up at the house with his brother and plunked some bills down on the kitchen table. *Take care of it.* Her irate ironworker father threw them out.

Gert told the doctor about her cousins in Massachusetts who were looking for an infant to adopt. *Some nice Jewish people,* he had told Carol's mother. No one told Carol anything. She mistook her first contractions for a stomachache. The dog woke everyone up. Carol gave birth to me in the hospital. Papers were signed. They didn't let her see me.

I told your father you were going to be here. My what? *I said to him, Guess who's back in our lives?* She wanted me to call him. I had a few things I wanted to call him.

I was ushered into the kitchen. Why was I calling him again? Carol dialed the number and handed me the phone. After several rings, a gruff *Hello who's this?* Opposite me, hanging on the wall, were a gigantic wooden fork and spoon. *I think I'm your son,* I said. *Wha?* said the voice.

While we waited for him to drive over, we looked at family photos. A boxful. Snapshots of Carol's daughters, parents, brother, and sisters. Smiling people who looked like me. *Family.* Margo, her younger sister, stopped by briefly with her daughter and son. There were old photographs from the reserve, Six Nations of the Grand River, Canada. Where her parents, *my grandparents,* Elmer and Eleanor, had been born and raised on farms. There were dark, mostly handsome people, riding in buggies. Standing at the edge of cornfields in straw boaters and suspenders, high-necked blouses and long skirts. Smoking cigarettes in front of log houses.

He's here, said the sister at the window. I slipped out onto the porch in time to see my father climb out of his Cadillac. He was brown, deeply tanned, wearing brown shirt, pants, and shoes. Even his coat was brown. Hadn't I worn an all-brown outfit the previous Thanksgiving?

You look more like their side, he said, imitating my crossed arms. He was right. With his wispy hair, big schnozz, full mustache, and paunch, he looked *Mediterranean.* He also looked uncomfortable as hell. Of course, everyone chose that exact moment to disappear. So he and I were left alone in the hallway to size each other up.

Y' wanna measure? he snapped, grabbing his crotch. *Figure out the batting order?*

He seemed like he could have easily fathered the other Alan.

No thanks, I said. I didn't want to trace my parentage back *quite* that far. What was next, arm wrestling?

Someone got us inside and seated next to each other on the love seat. *Mom* brought us cold drinks. Sy eventually relaxed and launched into his story. He was a city building inspector, who had started out as a plasterer. He had been the youngest in a big, Sicilian family. *They never would have let me marry an Indian. They were upset I married an Italian girl who wasn't Sicilian.* Their first stop, as immigrants, had been New Orleans, where they had made a lot of the wrought-iron grillwork. *We came from a long line of Sicilian blacksmiths.*

He died seven years later, on New Year's. Heart attack. I never saw or spoke to him again after that weird afternoon. It was different with Carol. Slowly, over the years, we mended broken bonds. *Born Indian, raised white,* was what the Ojibway poet said after listening to my story. Carol and I saw each other a couple of weeks ago up at Six Nations, where I was officially restored to the band roll last summer. Their nickname for themselves up there is scones, the name of their special, delicious bread. *Is he the Jewish scone we've been hearing about?* someone asked. *And does he always walk like that?*

The Connection

PATRICIA AQIIMUK PAUL

It was to be a journey home, a journey of fulfillment and connection, and it became all that. The journey to my ancestral villages in northwest Alaska, to meet relative after relative, brought the connection I sought as a Native woman, as an Inupiaq. Even though many other Natives were adopted out of their families and communities, our experiences are unique. We each need to tell our stories.

I have been telling my story since I was sixteen. It was tortuous to recount it over and over to one stranger after another in the hopes that someone could make the connection I sought. However, the one who helped most wasn't a stranger, but a sister-in-law who told me that she knew of my "real" mother. How shocking that my own adoptive family knew my parents' names and, even though I had inquired, no one would tell me.

With the name of my birth mother—Elizabeth Hensley—I started searching. I inquired among my coworkers and as luck would have it, the family name, Hensley, was well known. A coworker suggested I contact a state legislator named Willie Hensley and ask about my mother. The resemblance between my younger brother, Jim, and the campaign photo of this state legislator was uncanny. I placed a long distance call to

Juneau. Willie Hensley indeed knew my mother and knew she had children. Willie had been adopted by his aunt, Priscilla (Garfield) Hensley, who was my great-grandmother. Willie had been raised alongside my mother in our traditional sod home. There are still remnants of this sod home in the tundra along the Noatak River. Willie later introduced me to a younger half-brother, Gary Grove, and eventually to my birth father, Merrell Gwynn Harris, Sr. I am one of the lucky ones to find the connection, and I continue to make that connection with my family and community.

My brother, James Daniel Witkowski, and I had been adopted and raised together. He was a year younger than I, and I remember babying him and looking after his requests. Tragically, his life ended at twenty-three years of age, when an infection settled in a leaky valve of his enlarged heart. He had led a very rough life as a homeless person on the streets of Seattle, suffering at the hands of the other homeless who fought him ferociously. He was tremendously tall, towering over me, and his weight fluctuated greatly. I recall his high school shyness and his pumping gas and working on the construction of the Alaskan pipeline. He always made good money when he worked. I left Alaska in search of adventure and Jim stayed behind. There have been times since Jim's death when I have struggled; I tell myself over and over that I need to succeed for the two of us, for Jim and me. His early death is one of the injustices that our family has experienced.

We are just a few of the children who were raised away from our families and away from our immediate culture. I have come to understand the reasons that Native children are adopted out of their culture. Wanting Native populations to be assimilated into the melting pot, the US government instituted mechanisms based on this policy. But they have since learned that Native people are healthier members of society when we practice our cultural ways. The Indian Child Welfare Act protects our children from being adopted out, helping us to preserve our culture.

My connection with who I am as a Native woman has been strengthened by marrying into a traditional Indian family. My husband of twelve years, Kevin Paul, comes from a very large and tightly knit family who practices all of their cultural ways. He understands why I traveled over two thousand miles away from him, our children, and our home in the Swinomish Tribal Community of La Conner, Washington, to my mother's village of Kotzebue, Alaska. I was seeking to discover what happened in my early life and what happened in my family's life. I don't have all the memories of a complete childhood, but I have heard my family history. Family knowledge is important culturally and this makes it doubly important to me, because I want to know not only all my relatives but also everything about my culture. From traveling to the villages of my Inupiaq people, I learned that I have a big family and that subsistence is integral. We live off the land and from the waters as we have for centuries. Seal oil, *oogruk* (walrus), caribou, blackberries, blueberries, cranberries and salmonberries, whitefish and sheefish were equally part of my diet in Alaska.

I spent over twenty years trying to locate my older sister and finally had success when I wrote to the editor of *The Council,* an Alaskan Native newspaper whose circulation included Natives in all fifty states. My sister's Yupik foster brother, Tommy, who had a subscription, saw the letter. I had included my telephone number and Tommy called me. He knew Mary had a brother and sister. After he verified who I was, he said to wait by the phone and that my sister, Mary, would call me within a short time. I was cooking dinner and paced the kitchen floor waiting for her call. She arranged for Southwest Airlines to fly me for our reunion, and Channel 5 in Little Rock, Arkansas, filmed our reunion and interviewed us for the evening news! Here was my older sister, with a southern accent, happily married to Lynn Kellar, with two grown sons, Mark and Mitchell, living in Springfield, Arkansas.

What we have been able to piece together about my birth family revolves very much around my birth mother, Elizabeth. She left me a legacy partially recorded in photographs, which I inherited through both of my grandmothers. "You know your mother was a wild woman, don't you?" one of her childhood friends, Ray Snyder, asked me in the Inupiaq village of Kobuk. I do. I know she was an alcoholic her entire adult life. I know she spoke Inupiaq and made fun of anyone else who tried to speak it. She had a deep, sarcastic sense of humor. Her first child was born out of wedlock in 1949, and later she married a military man who was to be my father and father to my brother. I know from talking with my birth father that he was very mean and abusive toward my mother because of the child born out of wedlock. My father saved his correspondence with the Territory of Alaska in which he signed away ever seeing his children. He saw the situation as impossible. He could not afford to send for us children and he was not given any other option. He said that he was told that he would be able to see us kids again, despite this correspondence. He asked his mother, my grandmother Pearl Harris, for money so he could send for us, but she said she didn't have any money.

I know the details of how our mother lost custody of us three children. She went on a drinking binge in Fairbanks and ended up in the city jail. She told me that they brought the papers into her cell and told her that she had to sign them to give up her children. (I learned my mother's side of the story within a short time of reconnecting with her when I was eighteen years old.) She had abandoned us, leaving us alone for days while she went out partying. My sister tells me that Mom left us a carton of milk in the fridge and a candy bar with instructions for her to cut the candy bar into three portions for our meals. My sister was seven. Our baby brother was crying in his crib. After being alone for three or four days, we were outside in a fenced yard. A neighbor noticed and inquired about us. We were placed in a foster home, then in a Catholic orphanage in Fairbanks in July 1956. A month later, my brother and I were adopted by Roman Edward Witkowski and his first wife, Barbara (Burkett) Witkowski. My sister was in and out of foster homes for a few years until she was adopted and then moved to Arkansas.

My birth certificate lists me as being white with white parents. I grew up in a mixed racial neighborhood of whites, Athabaskan Indians, and Eskimos out by the airport in Fairbanks, Alaska. Every year of my elementary education, I would bring an enrollment form home from school to my parents for their signature, and they would have a little discussion over the category of my race and their relationship to me. It wasn't an issue that I was a slender, brown-skinned daughter to them, because they claimed that I was their daughter and nothing less. This gave me a sense of closeness to them, but also a sense that something in my life was amiss.

I was fortunate that my stepmother Dorothy always encouraged me to spend time with Alaskan Native women and families. I would babysit for Native families, and when I made friends with other Native children, their mothers always took an interest in me. Their mothers were friendly and talkative and treated me in a gentle way, which let me feel comfortable around Native people.

I yearn to know our language. Once I learn an Inupiaq word, I can pronounce it fairly accurately—an ability that my own daughter does not have, because she is not around fluent speakers of the language. However, in our home we speak words from several Native languages: Colville, Swinomish, Athabaskan, and Inupiaq.

As a child I learned that Eskimos and Indians didn't get along, that we warred against each other. I learned that Indians are thieves, that Eskimos are the friendliest people in the world, and that Eskimos must never marry Indians because they will never get along. I grew up with these perceptions of what Natives were, without quite realizing that I, myself, was living the experience of a Native.

When I married into an Indian tribe, I discovered that the experiences I lived through as a Native woman were no different from those of other Native women. In becoming reconnected with Native Americans and our cultures, I found much to drive me to work hard toward my goals, which culminated in a juris doctorate degree. With it, I have traveled extensively to speak on indigenous issues. During Christmas break in my third year of law studies, I went to Guatemala to work with Mayan women, taking along my eight-year-old daughter, Katherine. We traveled freely in the plateau region around Lake Atitlán. I spoke about cultural preservation to indigenous women in this developing country. These women wanted an education for their children and to protect their culture. They had already been encouraged to westernize their dress. They did not appreciate the pressures to quit wearing their *huipiles,* which are beautifully embroidered blouses designating their Pueblo or village.

The following year, I visited Sweden after presenting a paper at an international conference in Tampere, Finland. In Sweden I learned of women struggling to keep their cultural identity in the face of oppressive military regimes, women who had fled their homeland in Turkey to live freely as Kurdistans. These oppressions are very similar to what Native women have experienced in North America, including the boarding schools that our parents were forced or talked into attending. No wonder most of us don't know our languages, when our earlier generations were punished for speaking them. These pressures continue today with

Native American prisoners being denied privileges when they refuse to cut their hair. Governing authorities continue to define the scope of our cultural behavior by designating how many of a particular wild species we can capture, kill, and eat. The recent gray whale controversy with the Makah Tribe in Washington State is a prime example. Whales are an integral part of my Inupiaq culture. I ate plenty of Beluga and black whale meat when living in Kotzebue, Alaska, where I worked for two months in 1999 for the NANA Regional Corporation, my tribal entity.

What makes my story unique, perhaps, is the adoption of my son. He is the child of my cousin within my birth family, Paula Hensley. My path of seeking justice includes taking into my heart and home an infant child. Joseph Qualauruq was born in my mother's village of Kotzebue in 1983. He is a feisty, spirited individual who revels in a challenge. In accordance with Alaska State law, both of Joseph's birth parents signed away their parental rights in the state judicial system, although the adoption is an open one. We finalized the adoption in Muckleshoot Tribal Court in Washington. Paula and I exchange photos of our children and families even though we are thousands of miles apart. She currently lives in Nome, Alaska, with her children: Isaac, Priscilla, Alexander, and Louis. I have her oldest child.

Raising the children of extended family is a very common practice among Native peoples. Recently in Alaska, I was a guest in Native homes in seven villages in our region. I discovered children as young as four years of age who had been adopted by parents in their forties, fifties, and sixties. It is my wish now to adopt other Inupiaq babies and raise them with my husband, Kevin.

Pushing up the Sky

TERRY TREVOR

"I want to cancel my appointment," I told the woman at the front desk. "Instead of birth control counseling I need a pregnancy test."

The doctor at the Free Clinic rubbed his beard. "If you don't have any money you'll have to apply for welfare." He scribbled an address on a piece of paper and handed it to me.

"Number thirty-two," the social worker called out. I was number fifty-six. My shorts were soaked with sweat and my bare legs stuck to the orange plastic chair. The room was filled with women and crying babies. I thought of my mother at age fifteen, pregnant with me. Finally my name was called. I was led into a small cubicle. The social worker lit a cigarette, and smoke poured from her nose like a dragon.

"Are you giving the baby up for adoption?" she asked. The question unnerved me. She eyeballed me up and down and hissed, "You've written down that you're Indian—if it was going to be a white baby it would be easier to find a family to adopt it." I clenched my jaw to stay calm. Brown haired and green eyed, most strangers didn't place me as Indian, but the baby I hadn't meant to create was more Indian than white; the father of my child-to-be was a full blood.

This was my first glimpse at the way biology and culture collided in adoption. The social worker looked at my stunned face and shook her head. It was 1972, I was a nineteen-year-old, unmarried college student, and pregnancy had caught me unprepared to become someone's mother. Before I had to make a decision, however, I miscarried. At least I did not have to surrender my child to another.

Twelve winters later, in 1984, I sat in the lobby of Holt International Adoption Services. The room was decorated in pastel wall paper, with a nubby textured sofa. This time I was married and on the receiving end of adoption; within the next twenty-four hours my husband and I were due to become the parents of a one-year-old Korean boy we named Jay. Since I'm Native American, naturally we first looked into an American Indian adoption. However, the Indian Child Welfare Act of 1978 (ICWA) requires efforts be made to place American Indian children with birth relatives, then with tribal members, and then with families from other tribes. To apply with the Native American Adoption Exchange I needed to provide an enrollment number or certificate of degree of Indian blood. While the ICWA was needed to reduce the movement of Indian children into non-native families, the requirement of enrollment is like having a pedigree and, ironically, another barrier Native Americans have to face. The only proof I need is my grandfather's word, but the law leaves me not being Indian enough to adopt an American Indian child.

We decided to explore the international options. It was important for us to be able to generate a heartfelt connection to the culture, customs and people of the country we chose to adopt from. But we were limited to those countries which allowed for adoption in the United States, and of those we could have chosen, South Korea stood out as one with which we felt we could make such a connection.

Usually infertility prompts couples to pursue adoption, but I have never walked the infertility treadmill. When my husband and I decided we wanted to become parents, I gave birth to our daughter Vanessa in 1981. The pregnancy was completely normal, yet when we decided to add more children to our family we chose adoption. There were lots of children needing parents and we wanted more kids. We were positive we wanted to adopt, not to serve a social cause, but simply to raise another child.

Three years later we adopted a second Korean child, a girl, ten-year-old Kyeong Sook. At the time our son Jay was four and our daughter

Vanessa was six. Korean children had been adopted into our Native American–Caucasian family, and common sense told me it was necessary for all three of our Korean and mixed blood Indian children to put down roots in both Korean and Native American communities. In my mind the best way to blend my adopted children into our Native American family was to continue to help them maintain a connection to their Korean identity.

My basic philosophy holds tight: culture and heritage are important, not just for Native American children, but for all children. Since two of my kids were of Korean descent it made me an "in-law" in the Korean way. As their mother I believed I was responsible for leading them to people who could teach them something of Korean ways and beliefs. I knew my kids needed to grow up feeling at home in the Korean-American community.

The first change I made was to begin attending an all-Korean church. We are not an every-Sunday-church-going family. Many Sunday mornings found us in the Lord's mountain house or camping on his beach front property. Still the Korean church made a huge effort to include us. There was no time to wonder if we would be accepted. Pastor Lee and the other church members extended their kindness to our family time after time. Even though it was clear the Korean community welcomed us, I felt uncomfortable joining a previously all-Korean group. I found I had the same feelings of being different that my kids talked about feeling in an all-Caucasian setting. At least most of the Korean women were as short as I am and my high-cheeked face felt right at home, but I'm a light skinned mixed blood, and everyone there was one-hundred-percent Korean with black-brown eyes and very dark hair. Their appearance, strangely enough, took me back to my childhood family, to my full blood great grandparents and the full blood cousins I so little resemble.

Soon I discovered the element of Korean culture I loved best—the tradition of neighborhood families gathering. Korean community connectiveness is not something that happened to us with one social event or one project. It was gained through years of Korean community picnics, late night conversations over bowls of *naengmyon* noodles. While our children explored the constantly evolving question of what it means to be Korean American, I worked to build lasting relationships and to let my new friends know that my interest in doing so was genuine. Perhaps some in the Korean community oppose Korean adoption, but most welcome the kids and their families with open arms. Since non-Koreans do not romanticize Korean culture as non-Natives romanticize Native American culture, few Koreans have experienced the attempt by non-Asians to join into the Asian community.

Adoption of Korean children into American families began in significant numbers after the Korean war ended in 1953. The war left thousands of children either orphaned or abandoned. Back then adoptive parents were told by social workers to take their babies home and forget he or she was adopted. Families pioneering in the early years of international adoption believed that the children were American now and had to be Americanized as soon as possible. But particularly in Korean adoption, physical and other differences within the family brought sweeping changes and unique issues. Unfortunately many adoptive parents cut everything Korean out of their children's lives.

Such a practice prevailed in 1984 when we adopted our son from Korea, but I believed in embracing an adopted child's ethnic heritage. My opinions were sharp, like a new tooth making its way through the gum. I was too ethnic for some in the adoption community and not ethnic enough for those who opposed transracial adoption. I was fearful of generating hostility. My fear had a basis. I had run into hostility after I'd written an article suggesting that Caucasian adoptive parents embrace an adopted child's ethnic culture.

I learned to let criticism roll off my back, especially as one Korean friend introduced me to another, and as a result of their commitment to sharing their traditions with our family for the past ten years, we have come to know Korean culture. Now every winter the Korean Lunar New Year called *Sol* takes place at our house and my kitchen is piled high with boxes. Like Native Americans, Koreans have a tradition of giving gifts. *Duk-kuk,* the special Korean soup made with rice cake, simmers on my stove, and the familiar click of sticks from the game *yut* drifts from my living room. Usually we invited more people than can comfortably fit inside our house. If the winter weather was graceful, the overflow spilled out into the backyard.

"This year couldn't we do with a smaller party," I asked my children.

My son Jay gasped, "We like the big party."

"Didn't you know it's our favorite holiday?" My younger daughter Vanessa confided. "I was hoping it would be okay if I invited three friends this year instead of only one."

Our Korean Lunar New Year celebration is part family reunion, part cultural revival. Guests remove their shoes at the front door, as is proper. Strains from the folk song "*Arirang*" float from our cassette player and there are tremendous doings in the kitchen to make hot spicy foods for happiness. After everyone has eaten at least two plates full of food, a folk guitar is pulled out and we sing. The familiar melody has me humming along while the group sings the lyrics in Korean. The evening leaves me contented and at peace. The expressions on my kid's faces shows me how tradition touches their hearts, the place where they are still one-hundred-percent Korean.

"Being adopted was a big transition for me," Kyeong Sook explains. "Now I understand the importance of becoming Americanized, and I know I can do it without letting go of my connection and need for Korean culture in my life."

"Sometimes when I smell rice cooking and everybody is singing in Korean I can almost remember being a baby in Korea. It's not a regular memory I can think about as long as I want. It's much quicker than that," Jay admitted. With a typical teenage manner he dismissed my attempt to peel back the layers, to question how he felt about Korean community involvement in our lives. A palpable energy hovered in Jay's now husky adolescent voice, "It just makes me happy, Mom, that's all."

There it was. A feeling that had been planted deep inside him many years ago had taken root and was sprouting. It didn't matter if he couldn't tell me in words; the memories were circling his heart.

Korean community gatherings provide our family with some of the deepest sharing I've ever known. Like a slender golden thread Korean culture weaves into my heart. I remember the words my great grand-mother said to me when I was ten: "Child, we're Indians and our lives are like quilts. The Indian people have been scattered into odds and bits and we're determined to remake our whole cloth."

Loving my children as I do, with ferocity and purpose, I want to gather bits and pieces of Korean culture, braid it into our lives, and help them maintain a connection to their heritage. In my growing up family there was a lot of denial of our Indian ancestry. At times I felt part of me was missing and the part of my heritage denied became more important than the part that was clearly defined. I needed to feel a stronger connection to my own origins in order to glimpse why some adoptive parents might choose not to embrace their adopted children's ethnic culture. In adoption an underlying concern emerges that biological families never have to face: our children's history is not the same as ours. Because two of my kids had been adopted without a well documented paper trail, I seldom spoke about my own well documented family heritage. My silence made my kids uncomfortable. When I opened the subject up, they relaxed and began to understand it was all right to express their feelings about not knowing who their birth relatives were.

Adoption perceptions are changing quickly. One of the few things you can be sure about in adoption is that there will always be change. In most instances same-race, same-culture placements offer children the best opportunity for a genuine connection to their own heritage, yet I also believe a person of any race and culture who is willing to make a cultural commitment can be a good parent to a child of another race. It is important to assess whether the potential adoptive family understands the need to provide ties to the child's culture of birth. Defining the extent of those ties is an opportunity that families need to embrace deliberately. While adoptive families of Korean born kids are widely claiming Korean identity for their children, few are moving into or putting roots down in the Korean community. But there is a growing understanding that transracially adopted children have a dual identity and there is more responsibility than ever before to incorporate an adopted child's birth culture into the family fabric.

In the summer of 1998, when my son Jay was fourteen, we spent two weeks in Korea. It was his first time back. My son journeyed to the orphanage where he lived until he was a year old. He spent an afternoon caring for babies who were awaiting adoption. We stayed with a Korean family who spoke no English. The day we arrived, thirty seconds into our visit, the neighbors began to arrive, all with children in tow. Round-faced women, apron-bound, carried pots of the sweet, ice-cold rice drink *shikye* and platters of *pindaettok*—mung bean pancakes garnished with green leaves of chrysanthemums and red pepper slices.

An air conditioner hummed in the corner of the room. Outside it was 105, not counting the waves of heat from the pavement. Inside the house cool air blasted around me. The group sprawled on the floor, everybody sat cross-legged and loose-limbed. No matter that all conversation was taking place in Korean; it needed no translation, I could feel the power of togetherness. I could see back to my own childhood. In my mind I was again in the kitchen of my great-grandmother's house, gathered with deep-eyed uncles and aunties with their high cheeked faces. My son begin to answer the question, "What would it be like to grow up in Korea?" He walked as if his feet grew up from the ground. I could tell he felt a connection to the land that formed him, carved the high bones in his face.

When we returned home in August it was clear Jay had gone full circle. Then in November we discovered that our son had an inoperable brain stem tumor. His voice grew raspy, it became difficult for him to swallow or breathe, and pneumonia set in. Three months later Jay died, at home, in our arms, at the age of fifteen. The pastor of our Korean community church gave a eulogy at our son's memorial service. A friend sang "Amazing Grace" in Korean. Elders said prayers in the Korean language. In the huge sadness of losing my child, I felt the true joy of sharing in a rich heritage that belonged to him and to all of us as integrated and accepted members of the Korean community. It was a perfect ending for a boy who started out in Korea.

Three Dragonfly Dream Songs

ANNALEE LUCIA BENSEN

Any Dragonflies I Want to Be

There was an old woman with no hair
and a drum. I was in the movie
and I was a dragonfly while you were at work.
You came back and saw me,
and you went in the movie. I was
a dragonfly and in the movie.
That's the name. Dragonfly. My name.
I can change to any dragonflies I want to be.
They call me Annalee, but my name
is Annalee Dragonfly. That's why I had wings
and nobody could reach me when I was downtown.

It was a man had the drum. An old man
with long hair, hair as long as mine.
He caught me and put me *on* the drum.
He had some lotion on his hands.
Then he put me on his head and I went down his back.
He could roll his tongue like this: [rolls tongue].

That was a nice story. Bravo! Bravo!
Could you draw me as a dragonfly right on the paper?
Of course you can make me as a dragonfly.
Dragonflies have hands too.

(age 4)

Blue Dragonfly

I was a blue dragonfly and the lady caught me
and put me in a blue dragonfly house.
It had a face carved on the door with feelers on it.
And when the lady invited me out to play
I got in some water and then she gave me a hot dog.
It was yummy. Really delicious.
Then she let me in her other house of dragonflies to visit them.
Then I gave her a big hug and a nice kiss.
She said, "Come in. I'm going to show you my village."
It's the same one where we've been.

I was the blue dragonfly, not the red one.
And a girl picked me up and I got a chance
to look around the different places.
And I saw a little house—even the oceans—
and I got in the house,
and I remembered about my family.

There were holes in the little house.
I gave her a little hug and flew in her hair
and made myself a little house with her hair.
She had tie shoes. I tied her shoelaces
and I scooched in one of the parts and tied a knot in it
and it was all finished.
She had a blue shirt. And green pants.
And she gave me a toy heart.
Then I gave her a big toy heart.

(age 5)

The Corn Spirit

One day I flew out to Pine Lake with my friend spider on my back.
An Indian man sat in the middle of the lake and shucked corn.
The corn he shucked flew up in the air, and when there was enough of it,
it all flew over to a house somewhere I couldn't see, but over and over
he shucked corn and it gathered and flew to another house.
I asked him what he was doing.
He said he was shucking corn for poor people.
He said that after the person ate all the corn, in its place would be food,
all kinds of food, and every time someone ate a fruit or something,
the same thing would grow back.
Breakfast and lunch and dinner would be there
the next day and the next and forever.
Then he shucked two pieces of corn for us. We ate the corn
but when I looked back to say thanks, he was gone.
He was a spirit, and he was gone.
And then we flew home, thankful.

(age 11)

Notes

Introduction

1. A 1996 study concerning the ICWA's effectiveness, by Ann E. MacEachron, Nora S. Gustavsson, Suzanne Cross, and Allison Lewis, found that state adoption rates of Indian children decreased by ninety-three percent and foster care placements by thirty-one percent, based on limited data from between 1975 and 1988. They found the discrepancy between Indian and non-Indian adoption rates considerably reduced. The scant data did not show improvements in the Indian/non-Indian discrepancy in foster care placements, placements in Indian foster homes, or removal of Indian children to substitute care for vague grounds such as "neglect" and "social deprivation" (454–58). On the other hand, testimony at the 1988 US Senate hearing on ICWA amendments concluded that "progress has been made," but "the Act has not reduced the flow of Indian children into substitute care. In fact, the number in care has increased by roughly 25 percent since the early 1980s" (230–31). The study from which that conclusion was drawn found widespread inconsistencies in compliance with ICWA procedures, unfamiliarity with or resistance to the ICWA, and lack of respect for tribal courts and other authorities. Further, Plantz and coauthors report that while tribal child welfare programs are providing commendable service in following good casework standards and "achieving family based permanency," these programs must compete annually for limited Title II funds, and are often funded one year but not the next. The result is uneven staffing, high caseloads, frequent referral to public or other services, and impairment of much needed child protection, day care, early warning and crisis intervention programs, family therapy, legal services, and child advocacy. Other studies have found ICWA effectiveness limited

by faulty implementation, a lack of recognition within state codes and jurisdiction, federal underfunding of implementation and evaluation studies, and social agencies' lack of awareness of the policies and procedures required in Indian casework (Hollinger 471, MacEachron et al 459, Matheson 232). Within the operation of the law, conflicts and ambiguities hamper fulfillment of its intent. In a case review, Barbara Ann Atwood found enforcement constrained by the issues originating in "tribal sovereignty, federal preemption, and state interests" (1067–73). In her thorough study of state and federal court actions, B. J. Jones wrote that the objective of consistent application of the ICWA (an intent of Congress as stated by the US Supreme Court) has been "illusory" and "a farce." Jones recommended federal court supervision of state court decisions primarily to regulate the expansion of the "existing Indian family exception" (which permits courts to determine who is a "real" Indian child) and the use of the "best interest of the child" standard to deny transfers of Indian child custody cases from state to tribal courts.

2. Canada apologized in the *Statement of Reconciliation* for damage caused by the residential school system, but not for that of the Sixties Scoop: "I was very confused and hurt by the apology and actions around the residential school issue—they left out the foster kids," said Charles Wagamese, a former social worker (qtd. in Porter). Apprehension reportedly continues, and the highly publicized 1999 case of "Buddy," the Cree grandfather who lost custody of his grandson against the adoptive claims of a Connecticut couple, have renewed concerns (Kruzenga). Eric Robinson, member of the Manitoba Legislative Assembly, said, "We are now faced with a second generation sixties scoop. There have been more than 3,000 Aboriginal kids shipped out of province and out of the country" (qtd. in Hertlein 15). This very complex case has thrown into relief cultural biases inherent in the "best interests of the child" test, which, according to Viola Thomas, President of the British Columbia United Native Nations, does not "incorporate our traditions and customs" or "extended family roles and the community" into custody decisions (qtd. in Hertlein 14). Indeed, since the case of *Racine v. Woods* (1983), the Supreme Court of Canada has adhered to the theory that "cultural background and heritage diminish in the best-interests test as time passes and bonding strengthens within the adoptive family" (Stokoe 364–66).

Part 2. Boarding and Residential Schools

1. A vast body of literature is available on US and Canadian Native American boarding, residential, and day schools, as well as public education, in autobiographies, histories, and other studies. For an excellent survey of different approaches to studying American Indian education, see Coleman on pre-Reorganization schooling, Barker's article and Adams's book on the boarding school period, Lomawaima on the history of a single school (Chilocco Indian School), Child's study of boarding-school children's letters, and Garrod and Larimore's anthology by college graduates. For Canadian/First

Nations studies, see Canada's *Report of the Royal Commission on Aboriginal Peoples,* volume 1, chapter 10, "Residential Schools," and Miller's excellent article on documentation of school history. See also Canada's apology in *Statement of Reconciliation.*

While positive accounts of schooling exist, their scarcity emphasizes the far more prevalent grievances for which the Dominion of Canada apologized in 1998. For an autobiography that presents a more favorable view of boarding schools, see Emma Minde (Cree), who wrote that her education reinforced traditional Cree values in a time of cultural disintegration (45–55). See also Dorothy R. Parker's study of the Phoenix Indian School's second half-century for a portrait of a successful school and the unfortunate impact of federal reforms from the 1930s on.

Works Cited

Adams, David Wallace. *Education for Extinction: American Indians and the Boarding School Experience, 1875–1928.* Lawrence: UP of Kansas, 1995.

Atwood, Barbara Ann. "Fighting over Indian Children: The Uses and Abuses of Jurisdictional Ambiguity." UCLA *Law Review* 36 (1989): 1051–1108.

Barker, Debra K.S. "Kill the Indian, Save the Child: Cultural Genocide and the Boarding School." *American Indian Studies: An Interdisciplinary Approach to Contemporary Issues.* Ed. Dane Morrison. New York: Peter Lang, 1997. 47–68.

Bell, Genevieve. *Telling Stories out of School: Remembering the Carlisle Indian Industrial School, 1879–1918.* Diss. Stanford U, 1998.

Bensen, Robert. "Creatures of the Whirlwind: The Appropriation of American Indian Children and Louise Erdrich's 'American Horse.'" *Cimarron Review* 121 (October 1997): 173–88.

Berkhofer, Robert F., Jr. *Salvation and the Savage: An Analysis of Protestant Missions and American Indian Response, 1787–1862.* Lexington: U of Kentucky P, 1965.

——. *The White Man's Indian: Images of the American Indian from Columbus to the Present.* New York: Vintage, 1979.

Bird, Gloria. "Breaking the Silence: Writing as Witness." Ortiz 25–48.

Canada. *Backgrounder: Gathering Strength—Canada's Aboriginal Action Plan: A Progress Report—Year One.* Indian and Northern Affairs Canada (INAC). 11 June 1999 ⟨http://www.inac.gc.ca/news/jan99/98.123bk.html.⟩

——. *Report of the Royal Commission on Aboriginal Peoples (RCAP).* Royal Commission on Aboriginal Peoples. 5 vols. Ottawa, Ont.: Canada Communication Group, 1996. May 1999 ⟨http://www.inac.gc.ca/rcap/report/note.html.⟩

——. *Statement of Reconciliation.* 1998. Indian and Northern Affairs Canada (INAC). 3 June 1999 〈http://www.inac.gc.ca/strength/declar.html.〉

——. House of Commons. Special Committee on Child Care. *Sharing the Responsibility.* Ottawa, Ont.: Queen's Printer for Canada, March 1987.

Carroll, Andrew, ed. *Letters of a Nation: A Collection of Extraordinary American Letters.* New York: Kodansha Intl., 1997.

Child, Brenda J. *Boarding School Season: American Indian Families, 1900–1940.* Lincoln: U of Nebraska P, 1998.

Coleman, Michael. *American Indian Children at School, 1850–1930.* Jackson: UP of Mississippi, 1993.

Cushing, Frank Hamilton. "The Origin of the Dragonfly and of the Corn Priests, or Guardians of the Seed." *Zuni Breadstuff.* Indian Notes and Monographs 8. New York: Museum of the American Indian, Heye Foundation, 1920. 55–124.

Davin, Nicholas Flood. "Report on Industrial Schools for Indians and Half-Breeds." *Papers of Sir John A. MacDonald* 91 (March 1879) 35428–45.

Fernandez, Lydia. "Canada Federal Government Tries to Reconcile Its History of Abuses." *Native Americas* 15.1 (1998): 4–5.

Fletcher, Alice C. *Indian Education and Civilization.* US Bureau of Education Special Report, 1888. Millwood, NY: Kraus Reprint, 1973.

Franklin, Benjamin. *The Works of Benjamin Franklin.* Ed. John Bigelow. 12 vols. New York: Putnam, 1904.

Garrod, Andrew, and Colleen Larimore, eds. *First Person, First Peoples: Native American College Graduates Tell Their Life Stories.* Ithaca: Cornell UP, 1997.

Getty, Ian A. L., and Antoine S. Lussier. *As Long as the Sun Shines and Water Flows: A Reader in Canadian Native Studies.* Vancouver: U of British Columbia P, 1983.

Grinde, Donald A., Jr. "Thomas Jefferson's Dualistic Perceptions of Native Americans." *Thomas Jefferson and the Education of a Citizen.* Ed. James Gilreath. Washington, DC: Library of Congress, 1999: 183–208.

Hall, David J. "Clifford Sifton and Canadian Indian Administration, 1896–1905." Getty and Lussier 120–44.

Hanke, Lewis. *Aristotle and the American Indians.* Bloomington, IN: Indiana UP, 1959.

Harjo, Joy, and Gloria Bird. Introduction. *Reinventing the Enemy's Language: Contemporary Native Women's Writing of North America.* Ed. Harjo et al. New York: Norton, 1997.

Hawthorn, H. B., et al. *A Survey of the Contemporary Indians of Canada.* Vol. 1. Ottawa, Ont.: Canada Department of Indian Affairs and Northern Development, 1966.

Heinerman, John, and Anson Shupe. *The Mormon Corporate Empire.* Boston: Beacon, 1985.

Hertlein, Luke. "Where Are Our Children Going?" *Aboriginal Voices* 6.3 (1999): 14–15.

Hollinger, Joan Heifetz. "Beyond the Best Interests of the Tribe: The Indian Child

Welfare Act and the Adoption of Indian Children." *University of Detroit Law Review* 66 (1989): 451–501.

Institute for Government Research. *The Problem of Indian Administration* (The Meriam Report). Baltimore: Johns Hopkins UP, 1928.

Iverson, Peter. *We Are Still Here: American Indians in the Twentieth Century.* Wheeling, IL: Harlan Davidson, 1998.

Johansen, Bruce E. "Reprise/Forced Sterilizations." *Native Americas* 15.4 (1998): 44–47.

Jones, B. J. "The Indian Child Welfare Act: In Search of a Federal Forum to Vindicate the Rights of Indian Tribes and Children against the Vagaries of State Courts." *Pathways.* March 2000 ⟨http://www.nicwa.org/pathways⟩

Johnston, Patrick. *Native Children and the Child Welfare System.* Toronto: Canadian Council on Social Development and James Lorimer, 1983.

Karttunen, Frances E. *Between Worlds: Interpreters, Guides, and Survivors.* New Brunswick, NJ: Rutgers UP, 1994.

Kimelman, Edwin C. Review Committee on Indian and Métis Adoptions and Placements. *No Quiet Place: Final Report to the Honourable Muriel Smith, Minister of Community Services.* Winnipeg: Manitoba Community Services, 1985.

Kruzenga, Len. "Grandfather Forced to Give up Child to U.S. Couple." *Windspeaker* [Edmonton, Alberta] 16.12 (1999): 1.

Lifton, Betty Jean. *Journey of the Adopted Self: A Quest for Wholeness.* New York: Basic-Books, 1994.

Lomawaima, K. Tsianina. *They Called It Prairie Light: The Story of Chilocco Indian School.* Lincoln: U of Nebraska P, 1994.

MacEachron, Ann E., et al. "The Effectiveness of the Indian Child Welfare Act of 1978." *Social Science Review* 70.3 (1996): 451–63.

Mannes, Marc. "Factors and Events Leading to the Passage of the Indian Child Welfare Act." *Child Welfare* 74.1 (1995): 264ff. May 1999 ⟨http://proquest.umi.com.⟩

Matheson, Lou. "The Politics of the Indian Child Welfare Act." *Social Work* 41.2 (1996): 232ff. May 1999 ⟨http://www.umi.com.⟩

McKenzie, Brad and Pete Hudson. "Native Children, Child Welfare, and the Colonization of Native People." *The Challenge of Child Welfare.* Ed. Kenneth L. Levitt and Brian Wharf. Vancouver: U of British Columbia P, 1985: 125–41.

McKenzie, Helen. *Native Child Care in Canada.* Background Paper 284E. Ottawa, Ont.: Library of Parliament, 1991.

Miller, J. R. "Reading Photographs, Reading Voices: Documenting the History of Native Residential Schools." *Reading Beyond Words: Contexts for Native History.* Ed. Jennifer S. H. Brown and Elizabeth Vibert. Peterborough, Ont.: Broadview P, 1996.

Minde, Emma. *Kwayask ê-kî-pê-kisinowâpahtihicik/Their Example Showed Me the Way: A Cree Woman's Life Shaped by Two Cultures.* Ed. and trans. Fred Ahenakew and H. C. Wolfart. Edmonton: U of Alberta P, 1997.

Morse, Bradford. "Native Indian and Métis Children in Canada and Victims of the Child Welfare System." *Race Relations and Cultural Differences: Educational and Inter-personal Differences*. Ed. Gajendra K. Verma and Christopher Bagley. London: Croon Helm; New York: St. Martin's, 1984.

National Indian Brotherhood, Assembly of First Nations. *Report of the National Inquiry into First Nations Child Care*. Summerstown, Ont.: National Indian Brotherhood, 1989.

Native Council of Canada. *Native Child Care: "The Circle of Care."* Ottawa, Ont.: Native Council of Canada, 1990.

Norgren, Jill. *The Cherokee Cases: The Confrontation of Law and Politics*. New York: McGraw-Hill, 1996.

Ortiz, Simon J. *Speaking for the Generations: Native Writers on Writing*. Tucson: U of Arizona P, 1998.

Parker, Dorothy R. *Phoenix Indian School: The Second Half-Century*. Tucson: U of Arizona P, 1996.

Plantz, Margaret C., Ruth Hubell, Barbara J. Barrett, and Antonia Dobrec. "Indian Child Welfare: A Status Report." *Children Today*. US Department of Health and Human Services. No. 9EZ084A. Jan./Feb. 1989: 4–29.

Porter, Jody. "Seeking the Lost: Returning Home." *Wawatay News* [Sioux Lookout, Ont.] (20 May 1999): 1.

Priest, Loring Benson. *Uncle Sam's Stepchildren: The Reformation of United States Indian Policy, 1865–1887*. 1942. New York: Octagon, 1972.

Prucha, Francis Paul. *The Great Father: The United States Government and the American Indians*. 2 vols. Lincoln: U of Nebraska P, 1984.

Rogin, Michael Paul. *Fathers and Children: Andrew Jackson and the Subjugation of the American Indian*. New York: Knopf, 1975.

Silko, Leslie Marmon. Introduction. *Native American Literature*. Ed. Ken Lopez. Hadley, MA: Ken Lopez, 1994. N. pag.

Stokoe, Vicki. "Native Children in White Homes: Is This Appropriate Adoption Procedure?" *Family and Conciliation Courts Review*. 32.3 (1994): 346–78.

Tobias, John L. "Protection, Civilization, Assimilation: An Outline History of Canada's Indian Policy." Getty and Lussier 39–55.

Todorov, Tzvetan. *The Conquest of America: The Question of the Other*. Trans. Richard Howard. New York: Harper & Row, 1984.

United States. Cong. Senate. *Indian Child Welfare Act: Hearing before the Select Committee on Indian Affairs*. 100th Cong., 2nd sess. on S. 1976. May 11, 1988. Washington: GPO, 1988.

——. ——. *Indian Child Welfare Act of 1977: Hearing Before the United States Senate Select Committee on Indian Affairs*. 95th Cong., 1st sess. on S. 1214. August 4, 1977. Washington: GPO, 1977.

———. ———. *Indian Child Welfare Program: Hearings before the Subcommittee on Indian Affairs, U. S. Senate.* 93rd Cong., 2nd sess. on Problems That American Indian Families Face in Raising Their Children and How These Problems Are Affected by Federal Action or Inaction. April 8–9, 1974. Washington: GPO, 1975.

Vaughan, Alden T. "'Expulsion of the Savages': English Policy and the Virginia Massacre of 1622." *William and Mary Quarterly.* 3rd ser. 35.1 (1978): 57–84. May 1999 ⟨http://www.jstor.org.⟩

Vizenor, Gerald. "The Ruins of Representation: Shadow Survivance and the Literature of Dominance." *An Other Tongue: Nation and Ethnicity in the Linguistic Borderlands.* Ed. Alfred Arteaga. Durham, NC: Duke UP, 1994. 139–68.

Source Acknowledgments

Lee Maracle, "Black Robes," from *I Am Woman* by Lee Maracle. Copyright © 1996 by Press Gang Publishers. Reprinted by permission of Press Gang Publishers, Vancouver, BC.

Delia Oshogay, "Oshkikwe's Baby," from *Wisconsin Chippewa Myths and Tales* by Victor Barnouw. Copyright © 1977 by U of Wisconsin P. Reprinted by permission of the U of Wisconsin P.

Mary TallMountain's poems are reprinted from *The Light on the Tent Wall* by Mary TallMountain with the permission of Catherine Costell, literary trustee, the TallMountain Estate, P.O. Box 423115, San Francisco CA 94142.

Luci Tapahonso, "The Snakeman," from *Sáanii Dahataał/The Women Are Singing: Poems and Stories* by Luci Tapahonso. Copyright © 1993 by Luci Tapahonso. Reprinted by permission of the U of Arizona P.

Terry Trevor's "Pushing up the Sky" includes material previously published in "Dancing the Rice," published by *Friends of Korea* 4.4 (November 1998), and in "Filling a Niche," *Chosen Child* (February 2000). Reprinted with permission.

Phil Young and Robert Bensen, "Wetumka," from *Akwe:kon (Native Americas)* vol. 10 no. 3:26–29. Copyright © 1993 by Cornell U. Reprinted with permission.

Severt Young Bear and R. D. Theisz, "To Say 'Child,'" from *Standing in the Light: A Lakota Way of Seeing* by Severt Young Bear and R. D. Theisz. U of Nebraska P, 1994. Reprinted with permission.

Zitkala-Ša, "The Toad and the Boy," from *Old Indian Legends* by Zitkala-Ša. U of Nebraska P, 1985. Reprinted with permission.

Contributors

SHERMAN ALEXIE (Spokane/Coeur d'Alene) has won numerous awards, including a 1994 Lila Wallace–*Reader's Digest* Writers' Award and a citation for the PEN/Hemingway Award for the Best First Book of Fiction. His fiction includes *Reservation Blues, The Business of Fancydancing,* and *The Lone Ranger and Tonto Fistfight in Heaven,* and his poetry includes *Old Shirts & New Skins, First Indian on the Moon,* and *The Summer of Black Widows.* His film *Smoke Signals* won the Sundance Film Festival Award in 1998.

BLACK BEAR (Blackfeet) is a doctoral candidate in sociology at the University of New Mexico, where he has taught in the Native American Studies program. He also taught social psychology and philosophy at the Institute of American Indian Arts (1995–1999). He has conducted workshops on crisis intervention, alcohol and substance abuse, and suicide prevention from Maine to New Mexico, and has published research in *The International Journal of the Addictions.* He teaches ceramics at Morehead State University, Morehead, Kentucky.

ANNALEE LUCIA BENSEN (Mohegan/Cherokee) is in primary school and an accomplished dancer, artist, and swimmer.

MARIETTA BRADY (Navajo) is a young writer and visual artist from Rock Point, Arizona, and a recent graduate of Fort Lewis College in Durango, Colorado, specializing in Southwest Studies.

MARIANNA BURGESS (1853–1931) taught at the Pawnee School, where her father was an agent, before being hired by Captain Pratt at Carlisle during the first year of operations. She was in charge of printing the school's publications, including the weekly newspaper *The Indian Helper*. Burgess worked at Carlisle from 1880 to 1904, when the school closed (Bell 105–07).

MARY ULMER CHILTOSKEY (Cherokee) is the author of several books on Cherokee plant use, cooking, and the history of Cherokee fairs and festivals.

PETER CUCH (Ute) grew up on the Uintah and Ouray (Northern Ute) reservation in northeastern Utah. He currently lives on the Squaxin Island reservation in Kamilche, Washington, with his wife and two children.

ERIC GANSWORTH (Onondaga), Assistant Professor of English at Niagara County Community College, was born and raised in western New York, on the Tuscarora reservation. His first novel, *Indian Summers*, was published in 1998 (Michigan State UP). He is currently completing a poetry collection and a second novel.

JOY HARJO (Muskogee) has won numerous awards for her poetry, the most recent volume being *The Woman Who Fell from the Sky* (Norton 1994). Many have heard her perform her poetry and play jazz saxophone with her band Poetic Justice. She and Gloria Bird are the principal editors of *Reinventing the Enemy's Language* (Norton, 1997), an anthology of Native North American women's writing.

GORDON D. HENRY, JR. (White Earth Chippewa) has his doctorate degree from the University of North Dakota and is currently teaching at Michigan State University.

E. PAULINE JOHNSON (Mohawk; 1861–1913) is renowned as one of Canada's greatest woman writers. For seventeen years she was in demand as a performer of her work on stage throughout North America and Europe. Her poems were collected in *The White Wampum* (1895) and her stories in *The Moccasin Maker* (1913).

MILTON LEE (Cheyenne River Sioux) and Jamie Lee are the owners of Lee Productions and Oyate Records, which is devoted to producing

Native radio documentaries and music programs. They are currently working on a Native music series called Oyate Ta Olowan, which is to be broadcast on Public Radio International and the American Indian Radio On Satellite network.

JOYCE CARLETTA MANDRAKE (White Earth Chippewa) was born in Salmon, Idaho, in 1954. She performs as a stage actor and singer and lives on the central Oregon coast with her husband, son, and small gray cat.

LEE MARACLE (Stoh:lo Nation of Canada) is a partner in the Native Futures Group, where she integrates traditional indigenous teachings with European education to create processes of healing for Native peoples. She teaches traditional health seminars and works to reclaim culture, sociology, law, and government through language, creative writing, and counseling. Maracle is the author of *Bobbi Lee: Indian Rebel, I Am Woman, Ravensong,* and *Sojourners and Sundogs.*

BEVERLEY MCKIVER (Ojibway), originally from northwestern Ontario, lives near Ottawa, Ontario, Canada with her husband and daughter. She is a database administrator for the Canadian Broadcasting Corporation. Her favorite activities include music, gardening, and walking.

ALAN MICHELSON (Mohawk) is an artist living in New York City. He has exhibited his paintings and created public installations in the Whitney Museum, the American Indian Community House, the New Museum of Contemporary Art, the Swiss Institute, and the Lower Manhattan Cultural Center, as well as in Madrid and London. He has been the recipient of fellowships from the Mid-Atlantic Arts Foundation and from the National Endowment for the Arts.

DELIA OSHOGAY (Chippewa) told "Oshkikwe's Baby" at Court Oreilles in 1942, and the story was published in an anthropological study. As with nearly all "collected" Native art, whether it is material or oral literature, information about the artist is scarce, because it was of scant interest to collectors and scientists.

PATRICIA AQIIMUK PAUL, JD, (Inupiaq) values greatly the opportunity to express a few words on her family history and connecting with her people and culture. She travels extensively lecturing and speaking on indigenous issues including traditional ways of resolving disputes, global feminism, and cultural preservation. Ms. Paul lives with her husband, Kevin Paul, and their two children, Joseph and Katherine, in the Swinomish tribal community of La Conner, Washington.

KIMBERLY MUSIA ROPPOLO (Cherokee/Choctaw/Creek) is a doctoral student at Baylor University, specializing in Native American literature. She teaches at McLennan Community College. She is a member of the WordCraft Circle of Native Writers and Storytellers, the Western Literature Association, the American Indian Philosophy Association, and the Association for the Study of American Indian Literature. She lives in Hewitt, Texas, with her husband and three children.

LAWRENCE SAMPSON (Delaware/Eastern Band Cherokee) writes, "Many of us have indeed had a long road home. The efforts to separate me from my culture only insured my absolute immersion and participation in it. I am involved in Indian social and political causes in the Houston area. We must keep our cultures alive—our traditions, languages, and ceremonies. Our struggle is not sacrifice lost, but natural energy, properly used."

MICHELE DEAN STOCK (Seneca) directs the Seneca-Iroquois National Museum. Her essays appear in the anthology *Iroquois Voices, Iroquois Visions* (Bright Hill P, 1996). She is a traditional beadworker and singer, with her recordings of Seneca-Iroquois social dance songs available on *Songs My Elders Taught Me* (Oyate Records 1997). She was writer/actor/producer of the eight-part video series *Keeper of the Western Door* and appeared in *How the West Was Lost*. She speaks on Iroquois culture for schools and universities, museums, and community organizations.

MARY TALLMOUNTAIN (Athabaskan; 1918–1994) was born in Nulato, Alaska. Adopted by a non-Native couple after her mother became terminally ill, TallMountain wrote as a way of reuniting with her family and people and claiming her heritage. Her poems are collected in *The Light on the Tent Wall* (UCLA P, 1990), *A Quick Brush of Wings* (Freedom Voices, 1991), and *Listen to the Night* (Freedom Voices, 1995).

LUCI TAPAHONSO (Navajo) is the author of *Blue Horses Rush In: Stories and Poems* (U of Arizona P, 1997) and *Sáanii Dahataał/The Women Are Singing: Poems and Stories* (U of Arizona P, 1993), as well as three other books of poems.

Terry Trevor writes, "I am a forty-six-year-old Cherokee/Delaware/Seneca Indian woman, a writer and an adoptive parent of Korean-born children, involved in promoting greater awareness and appreciation of the value of Korean heritage and community in the United States." She is the coordinator for the Friends of Korea Family Exchange Program. She is also board secretary for Korean-American, Adoptee, Adoptive Family Network and is a member of the WordCraft Circle of Native Writers and Storytellers. She lives in Santa Barbara, California.

Lela Northcross Wakely (Potawatomi/Kickapoo) is a member of the WordCraft Circle of Native Writers and Storytellers and has had work published in several journals, including *The Moccasin Telegraph* (now *Native Writers and Storytellers*). She has served as a volunteer court-appointed child advocate for Cedar Lodge in Oklahoma and now works as a children's home health nurse. She and her husband live in Chandler, Oklahoma.

S. L. Wilde is a Canadian writer and painter and a woman of Anishnaabe-Celtic heritage. The gifts of her Ojibway grandmother continue to bring her inspiration, purpose, comfort, and connectedness.

Virginia Woolfclan is the pseudonym of a multi-talented artist.

Phil Young (Cherokee/Scots-Irish) was born in Henryetta, Oklahoma in 1947. Exhibits and installations include "Phil Young: Traces of Identity" (Kohler Arts Center, Kohler, WI, 1995), "We Are Many, We Are One" (traveling 1997–1999), "Red River Crossings: Response to Peter Rindisbacher (1806–1834)" (Swiss Institute, New York City, 1996), "Decolonizing the Mind" (Center of Contemporary Arts, Seattle, 1992), "The Fifth Biennial Native American Fine Art Invitational" (Heard Museum, Phoenix, AZ, 1991). He curated "For the Seventh Generation: Countering the Quincentennial" (Columbus, NY 1992). He was awarded a Joan Mitchell Foundation Grant in Painting and Sculpture. He is a Professor of Art at Hartwick College in Oneonta, New York.

Zitkala-Ša (Gertrude Bonnin; Yankton Sioux; 1876–1938), in *Old Indian Legends* (1902), was one of the earliest Indian writers to record tribal oral stories. She described her first eight years on the Yankton Sioux reservation in "Impressions of an Indian Childhood." In that work, with others in *The American Indian Stories* (1921)—including "The School Days of an Indian Girl" and "An Indian Teacher among Indians" about teaching at Carlisle—she contrasts her traditional upbringing with that which she had witnessed at government-run schools. Those contrasts comprise an extensive critique of federal Indian policy.

About the Editor

Robert Bensen is Director of Writing and Professor of English at Hartwick College, Oneonta, New York, where he chairs the Department of English and Theatre Arts. He teaches courses in creative writing; American Indian, Caribbean, and British literature; and a seminar on American Indian law and literature. He is the editor of *One People's Grief: Recent West Indian Literature* and literary coeditor (with Maurice Kenny) of *Iroquois Voices, Iroquois Visions*. He has published critical essays exploring the conflict of cultures in the works of many American Indian and West Indian authors, including Louise Erdrich, Leslie Marmon Silko, Derek Walcott, Earl Lovelace, and Jean Rhys. Bensen is a poet as well and was awarded the Robert Penn Warren Award for Poetry in 1993 and a prestigious National Endowment for the Arts poetry fellowship in 1996. His poems have appeared in the United States, Caribbean, and Great Britain, in such journals as *Paris Review, Partisan Review, Ploughshares, Caribbean Writer, Poetry Wales, Slow Dancer, Tamaqua,* and *Akwe:kon.* He is an invited non-Native member of the WordCraft Circle of Native Writers and Storytellers. His wife, Mary Lynn, is Associate Reference Librarian at SUNY–Oneonta. They and their daughter Annalee live in Oneonta, New York.